"The concepts of going north t~~...~~ ...~~...~~ ...~~...~~ ...~~...~~ ...~~...~~ ~~the god~~ of self in the frustrations of life have equipped me to live more fully and passionately for God. In applying these simple principles, I've drawn closer to God and transformed everyday relationships. The principles are biblical, practical, and have revolutionized the way I view my life and circumstances." —**Shelly Beach**, Christy Award winner

"Socrates said, 'The unexamined life is not worth living.' Achieving critical self-awareness about how we manage our world and how we relate to others is not accidental. Neither is it comfortable. It cost Socrates his life. It reduced Paul's circle of friends. When others point it out, we deny it; when we see it, we endeavor to bury it and go our self-deceived merry way. When we press it in our relationships, we encounter misunderstanding and increased tension. Is it really worth it? The Heims will press you to decide. Read at your own risk . . . you will be glad you did." —**Dr. Gary T. Meadors**, Professor of Greek and New Testament, Grand Rapids Theological Seminary

"In *True North*, counselors Gary and Lisa Heim do more than point us in the right direction; they invite us to join them in their own spiritual journey. I found the chance to walk with them through the kind of issues we all struggle with both insightful and personally renewing." —**Martin DeHaan**, President, RBC Ministries

"Longings, lies, and strategies vs. truth, hope, and love. Gary and Lisa Heim invite us to take a practical and honest look at our longings, the lies we tell ourselves when those longings are thwarted, and the harmful coping strategies we develop in response. It is so easy to go south instead of north, to grumble about our disappointments and grasp at imitation life. *True North* isn't about changing your circumstances or the people around you. It's about a proper orientation to God while living with other sinners in a cursed world; it's about understanding what happens in your heart, finding strength in God, and loving well. Bring an honest heart and mind to your reading of this book (and maybe a small group too) and you find good shepherding here." —**Dr. Brian Webster**, Associate Professor of Old Testament Studies, Dallas Theological Seminary

"Orientation is a strategic component of any enterprise . . . whether you're climbing Mt. Everest, flying through a blinding storm, or just trying to get through another day. Gary and Lisa have done all of us a huge favor in both calling us and enabling us to know how to orient our lives toward survival and success. *True North* charts a clear and compelling life trajectory and gives us something solid to cling to when the downturns in life confuse our emotions and disorient our instincts." —**Dr. Joe Stowell**, President, Cornerstone University, Grand Rapids, Michigan

FOREWORD BY DR. LARRY CRABB

TRUE NORTH

CHOOSING GOD IN THE
FRUSTRATIONS OF LIFE

GARY HEIM & LISA HEIM

Kregel
Publications

True North
© 2011 by Gary Heim and Lisa Heim

Published by Kregel Publications, a division of Kregel, Inc., P.O. Box 2607, Grand Rapids, MI 49501.

In the majority of anecdotal stories, names and identifying details have been changed. The remainder are used with permission.

The author and publisher are not engaged in rendering medical or psychological services, and this book is not intended as a guide to diagnose or treat medical or psychological problems. If medical, psychological, or other expert assistance is required by the reader, please seek the services of your own physician or certified counselor.

Library of Congress Cataloging-in-Publication Data
Heim, Gary.
    True north : choosing God in the frustrations of life / Gary Heim and Lisa Heim.
       p. cm.
    Includes bibliographical references.
    1. Christian life—Baptist authors. 2. Struggle—Religious aspects—Christianity. I. Heim, Lisa. II. Title.

BV4501.3.H438   2011   248.8'6—dc22   2011013181

978-0-8254-2751-0

Printed in the United States of America
11 12 13 14 15 / 5 4 3 2 1

To Brandon and Kailie.
Parenting you has been our joy.
May you always choose God in the
frustrations of your lives.

CONTENTS

Foreword **9**
Acknowledgments **12**

Part One: You Are Here
1   Life Is Difficult   **15**
2   Will You Go North or South?   **25**
3   Groaning: God's passionate pursuit of your heart   **37**

Part Two: Going South
4   Grumbling: The first sign you're headed south   **61**
5   Grasping: Your attempts to gain control   **81**

Part Three: Going North
6   Grace: The power to turn north   **109**
7   A Great Gift: The new identity we need   **138**
8   Gratitude: The response to God's love   **157**
9   Giving: The fruit of a grateful heart   **175**

Part Four: You-Turn
10   Getting It   **197**
11   Growing It   **215**
12   Giving It Away: Mentoring others   **238**

Notes **249**

FOREWORD

DR. LARRY CRABB

No one disputes that our culture is changing. Many applaud. A few are troubled, particularly by the steady drift toward wrongly believing that truth is unknowable, that politically correct moral relativism is moral, that new definitions of marriage are necessary and healthy, and that excitement-driven religion markets well and must therefore be of God.

Some of the troubled few stand against what troubles them. Some don't. Failing to stand against something you claim to oppose is a short distance away from welcoming it, or at least to smiling tolerantly at it. Christians who don't stand against God-dishonoring changes in culture tend to gradually accommodate their theology to the other side in order to avoid conflict.

The result, visible across America, is a church that proclaims a popular Jesus more committed to social activism than to soul conversion, a mobilizing Messiah who prefers building programs that meet felt needs to building communities that relate in a way made possible by the Messiah's death and resurrection.

Those who are especially troubled by the movement of religious culture toward repairing our fractured world with only a nod toward worshipping a crucified Savior—I am among them—must see what troubles us as an opportunity to seize and not merely a misfortune to mourn. Our crucified Savior and risen Lord has told us how he wants us to seize the God-ordained opportunity that lies before us and stand against what is wrong. Speaking to his Father shortly before he was killed, Jesus prayed, "May they"—referring to his followers in the ages to come—"experience such perfect unity that the world will know that you sent me and that you love them as much as you love me" (John 17:23 NLT).

After four decades of ministry that has centered on bringing biblical truth into our personal and relational lives, it seems unarguable to me that the most important and powerful response that Christians can make to our culture is to get along with each other in radical ways that only Good Friday and Easter Sunday make possible. Hebrews tells us that we can "share in his holiness," that we are called to "work at living a holy life" (Heb. 12:10, 14 NLT).

To live holy lives together (to slightly revise a phrase from Dietrich Bonhoeffer), to live in *relational holiness,* requires that we first concern ourselves with *personal holiness,* that we pay attention to what's happening in ourselves as we relate to others.

The first step in becoming an answer to our Lord's prayer is, I suggest, to recognize and confess, without excuse or defense, our *relational unholiness.* How do we relate in ways that reflect our self-centeredness? The second step involves a look inside to see the cesspool of our *personal unholiness,* all the hurts and wounds and fears that "justify" our unholy ways of relating.

The third step requires a practical theology rooted in the gospel of Jesus Christ that shines light on the narrow road that leads to *personal holiness,* to a Spirit-led way of thinking and desiring that empowers us to live in *relational holiness,* a self-denying, God-honoring, Christ-revealing, Spirit-enabled way of relating that every human being was created to enjoy.

We must be clear. That kind of unity is supernatural. It goes miles beyond, infinite miles beyond, the kind of sociable and missional togetherness that too often we mistake for Christian community. Peter tells us that we actually participate in the divine nature (see 2 Peter 1:4) and are therefore equipped to relate like Jesus, to be committed to the glory of God and the well-being of others at any cost to ourselves. At *any* cost to ourselves.

The most urgent call of God to Christians today is to be spiritually formed, to grow in personal and relational holiness. I'm convinced that many Christians want to respond to that call but don't know what it means or how to proceed.

True North, the book you're now holding, provides a clear, theologically sound, and practically accessible road map that shows the way to a personally and relationally holy life in the middle of a fractured world. Gary and Lisa are long-term close friends whose journey together toward holiness I deeply respect.

Drawing from personal experiences in marriage, parenting, pastoring, and counseling, they speak candidly about difficult experiences with which all of us can relate. More importantly, they depend on well-thought-through biblical theology that offers the living water every thirsty soul is dying to drink, as they gently tear off the sociable masks we hide behind and uncover the relationship-killing poison that energizes so much of how we engage with ourselves and others. And then, when we feel properly humbled and helpless, they throw us the lifeline. They hold the rope steadily and draw us toward the North Star that can be seen most clearly when the night is darkest, just before dawn.

Practical, readable, engaging, and accessible, *True North* deserves a wide reading. I'm a chart addict, and the charts sprinkled throughout are worth the price of the book. I envision Sunday school classes and small groups reflecting on this book and discovering the path to the personal and relational holiness that we were created to enjoy, that Christ died to provide.

I long for Christians to seize the opportunity that a decaying culture provides the church, to model an alternative way of living and loving that will make the world sit up and take notice. There's no firmer foundation for evangelism. There's no better way to delight the Trinity. I believe God is pleased with this book and will use it in many lives. And maybe he'll use it to build a community that stands against culture by displaying a better way.

ACKNOWLEDGMENTS

We would like to thank:

Louie Konopka for his godly leadership of Blythefield Hills Church for the past thirty years, and for his sermon series on Romans, which became the impetus for this book.

The people of Blythefield Hills Church who have courageously shared their stories to help us all learn what it means to live north.

Steve Welch and Don Pearson who believed in this paradigm long before it was a book.

Shelly Beach and Ann Byle, seasoned writers who have edited our manuscript and encouraged and coached us along the way.

Dan and Colleen Lokers, Ron and Becky Underwood, Tim Hoyt, Tim Jackson, Kurt Dillinger, Chris and Katrina DeMan, and Carrie Muller whose friendship, feedback, and support have strengthened us through our journey of writing *True North*.

Aubrey High for going the extra ten miles in securing permissions for quotes and putting our manuscript in the proper format to submit to Kregel Publications.

Steve Barclift, Dawn Anderson, Cat Hoort, and everyone else at Kregel Publications who have been so kind and helpful in the process of publishing.

Tim Beals, our agent, whose guidance and expertise has helped us get this far.

Drs. Larry Crabb and Dan Allender, whose teaching, friendship, and mentoring have been foundational to our lives and ministry.

PART ONE

YOU ARE HERE

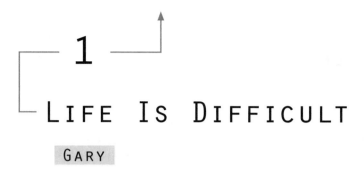

1

LIFE IS DIFFICULT

GARY

"In this world you will have trouble."
John 16:33

Flat tires, flooded basements, cranky kids, wounding words, the loss of a job, a broken body, a painful marriage—"trouble" comes in all shapes and sizes. But here's the gut punch that really knocks the wind out of us: trouble comes when we don't expect it, when we're unprepared.

Bob and I were close friends. We sat in the back row of Mrs. Horsewell's third-grade class. I wasn't a good student. Cs, Ds, and an F or two always showed up on my report card. Bob knew it, and I feared others would too.

One day Bob's mom went shopping and took us along. As we all waited in the checkout lane of a local department store, I, for reasons I couldn't explain at the time, tried to impress Bob's mom. I planned my words and spoke up. "I'm coming to realize how important it is to learn to read well," I said with a reflective tone. "Learning to read well is the doorway to learning all other subjects." Something inside me swelled with excitement as I watched Bob's mom come alive.

"Gary," she said, "that's insightful!" I savored the moment of my significance. It lasted for about five seconds.

Then Bob spoke up. "Yeah, Gary, you *sound* real smart here, but when it comes to school, you're pretty dumb." My moment of glory turned to shame. The secret of my incompetence was exposed. My shame turned to anger, and

15

my anger to rage. I closed up and withdrew into a bitter, shame-filled silence.

The next morning I was waiting for Bob behind school. He had no idea what was coming. Releasing the rage that smoldered in me, I knocked him down and beat him up.

Yep, in this life you'll have trouble, and trouble comes when you're unprepared—when you least expect it. It was true for me that day, and it was true for Bob the next morning. Things seem to be running according to schedule, and then, out of nowhere, you get humiliated, beat up, rejected. Someone speeds by and throws you an obscene gesture, your car gets broadsided in the intersection, your computer freezes up minutes before the report's due, or your teenager grows more defensive and withdrawn despite all your efforts to help.

M. Scott Peck began *The Road Less Traveled* with three words: "Life is difficult."[1] How profound.

Just yesterday I was talking with a young, divorced lady who fights loneliness and depression as she tries to take care of two young children and learn a new and frustrating job. She, like most of us, resonates with the truth—life is difficult. And she, like most of us, struggles with knowing how to choose God in all the chaos of her life.

The old sage, seasoned with wisdom by the refining sorrows of life, wrote in Ecclesiastes, "What is twisted cannot be straightened; what is lacking cannot be counted" (Eccl. 1:15). Trouble and difficulty weave their way through the common events of our daily lives. Life rarely works the way we want it to. Give it time, and something or someone has a way of frustrating our plans. How did the apostle Paul put it in Romans 8:22–23? In this life we groan.

THE PROBLEM: FRUSTRATIONS IN CHOOSING THE GOOD

But here's the problem. While everyone struggles in this fallen world, few people have learned how to struggle well. That is, groaning usually causes us to grumble. That day at the department store, Bob frustrated my plans. Without knowing it, I wanted to impress his mom because deep in my eight-year-old heart I believed I was just a stupid little kid who would never be respected by anybody who was anybody. Still, in my loneliness I longed for someone to affirm me and tell me I was worth noticing.

But what emotions do we feel when the "Bobs" of our life, in one way or another, thwart our plans? When frustrating circumstances or difficult people block our path to getting the love and respect we want, most of us will admit to feeling anger. Just like my anger drove me to beat up my friend, these emotions usually drive us to react with behaviors that are anything but helpful. We speak harsh and attacking words, or we choose to emotionally withdraw from people who let us down. We gossip and spread dissension throughout the body of Christ, or we manipulate to get our way. What's more, we easily justify our feelings and behaviors. We go to friends we know will side with us and support our attitudes, and we poison them against the people who hurt us. When trouble comes, we quickly react in harmful and self-serving ways that come from our fallen natures rather than from the Holy Spirit. Instead of growing in gratitude for who God is and all he has done for us, we grow negative and become faultfinders.

> We are too quick to resent and feel what we suffer from
> others, but fail to consider how much others suffer from us.
> Whoever considers his own defects fully and honestly will find
> no reason to judge others harshly.
>
> THOMAS À KEMPIS

Studies show that our society has grown increasingly frustrated, angry, and negative. Moreover, research has found that we talk to ourselves at the speed of thirteen hundred words a minute and 77 percent of our self-talk is negative.

A parish priest who had listened to confessions for fifty years was asked what he had learned about mankind. He said two things. First, people are more unhappy than one thinks, and second, there is no such thing as a grown-up person.[2]

How many Christians do you know who are so centered on Christ that when faced with offense and frustration they respond in ways that draw you to God? It's rare, but not impossible. Jean Vanier is an example:

> I remember my visit to a top security prison in Kingston, Ontario.
> I told the prisoners about the men and women we have welcomed in
>   l'Arche
> —their pain, their sense of failure and rejection, their depression,

sometimes even their self-mutilation. . . .
I knew that I was in fact telling them their own story,
the story of their lives, their experience of rejection, grief, insecurity,
      and failure.
At the end of my talk one of the inmates got up and screamed at me:
"You," he said, "you've had an easy life!
You do not understand what we are living!
When I was four years old, I saw my mother raped
      right in front of me!
When I was seven, I was sold by my father for sex.
When I was thirteen the 'men in blue' (the police) came to get me.
If anyone else comes into this prison to talk about love
I will kick his bloody head in!"

I listened to him but did not know what to say or do.
It was as if he had me against a wall.
I prayed
and then I said: "It's true what you say. I have had an easy life!
It's true, I do not know what you have lived.
But what I do know is
      that everything you have just said is important.
People outside the prison often judge you
      without knowing your pain . . .

Will you allow me to tell people outside
      what you have just told me today?"
He replied, "Yes". . .

When the question time was over
I went up to this man and I shook his hand.
I asked him his name . . . I was inspired to ask him whether he was
      married
and when he said "Yes" I asked him to tell me about his wife.
This man who had been so violent
who had seemed to have such hatred in him,

broke down in tears.
He told me about his wife, who was in Montreal,
    in a wheelchair.
He had not seen her for two years!
I was in front of a wounded, vulnerable little child,
weeping, crying out for love and tenderness . . .

In the midst of all the violence and corruption of the world
God invites us today to create new places of belonging,
places of sharing, of peace and kindness,
places where no-one needs to defend himself or herself;
places where each one is loved and accepted with one's own fragility,
    abilities and disabilities.[3]

Too often, however, when frustrations or offenses come, we react just like people who don't even believe in Jesus. We verbally attack or emotionally withdraw from those who hurt or annoy us. It's important to understand what's at stake when we live this way.

THE STAKES: WORSHIP, WALK, AND WITNESS

First, what's at stake is *worship*. I love to experience the soul-stirring joy of connecting with God during a worship service. God loves it when his children delight in him. But Jesus said if we bring our gift to the altar and there remember someone has something against us, we should leave that place of worship and do all we can to be reconciled to that person (Matt. 5:23–24). True worship translates into loving one another.

Second, what's at stake is our *walk*. In his Sermon on the Mount, Jesus told us that it's easy to be friendly to friendly people. The worst of sinners do that. But the real litmus test for how close we walk with God is seen by how we respond to difficult and frustrating people (Matt. 5:43–48).

Last of all, what's at stake is our *witness*. Imagine your dearest loved one is about to die and he wants to share his deepest dreams for you. That's what Jesus did in the Upper Room on the night he was betrayed. Before his disciples, he poured out his dream for them, and for us who believe, as he prayed to his Father:

"I am praying not only for these disciples but also for all who will ever believe in me through their message. I pray that they will all be one, just as you and I are one—as you are in me, Father, and I am in you. And may they be in us *so that the world will believe you sent me.* . . . *May they experience such perfect unity that the world will know that you sent me.*" (John 17:20–21, 23 NLT, emphasis added)

God's trust in us is staggering. Jesus is saying that, based on the quality of our patience, kindness, and love for our spouse, children, coworkers, friends, and enemies, the world has the right to judge if Christianity is true. How we love each other is the evidence to an unbelieving world that Jesus Christ is the Son of God.

Learning to live for God through all the daily troubles and difficulties of life isn't something we can take or leave. Our worship, walk, and witness depend upon how we handle the daily chaos of trouble and hardship. This is where the rubber meets the road in living out our Christianity. Whether our groaning comes from tragic circumstances like losing our job or from frustrating people who constantly annoy us, it's possible to have an inner security in Christ that enables us to experience the joy of responding with gentle and healing words. Jesus invites us to live for him by learning to "live a life of love" (Eph. 5:1–2).

But life can be so difficult and discouraging. Relationships often don't work the way we long for them to. People wound and fail us, and we wound and fail others. It's so tempting to lose heart and live for something—anything—other than wholehearted devotion to God. Lisa and I know because we've been there.

Lisa and I have a good and growing marriage. We're experiencing love and laughter in ways we didn't decades ago. But it's a different kind of love than it was on our wedding day. We've significantly disappointed one another's original expectations of what marriage would be like. In the face of those failures, pain, and loss, we've struggled to learn how to love. Our experience is normal. No one learns to really love others without a struggle to turn from self-centeredness. And as we share our stories with you, you'll see how God has used our problems and failures to help us grow—in our personal lives, in our marriage, in our parenting, and in our ministries—as we've wept, laughed, prayed, and thought deeply about our lives in the context of the truths we share in this book.

Because of the depth of our own self-centeredness, we've found that nothing in life is harder and more confusing than learning how to love. But nothing is more important. Jesus said the Bible can be boiled down to one sentence: love God with all your heart and love others as yourself (Matt. 22:37–40). Life is all about life-giving, soul-stirring relationships. This is what we were created for. And we've found that in our groaning and confusion to love well, we've needed a lot of help in discerning which way to turn. Therefore, this way of thinking about the Christian life has become like a spiritual road map for our journey. This map is not a formula for spiritual growth. Instead, it provides a tangible aid to help us discern whether we're turning to God or away from him when we face the troubles and frustrations of everyday life.

These truths have been shaped and tested in our lives. For more than twenty-five years, Lisa and I have spent thousands of hours discipling and counseling individuals and married couples with problems such as loneliness, depression, anxiety, anger, parenting, and marital conflicts. As root issues come to light, we walk those people through this way of thinking and responding to life. As they start to understand what's happening inside them when they react to the groaning of life, they too can see what it means to intentionally turn to God and find his help. They turn to God, not just to make life work, but to become the kind of person who knows God intimately and who can reflect his good heart to others, despite the circumstances.

Jesus said, "In this world you will have trouble." But he didn't stop there. He continued, "But take heart! I have overcome the world" (John 16:33). I'm so glad to say, it is possible to truly change from the inside out; not perfectly, but substantially. Real change is a lifelong process. It doesn't come easily, and it never comes by just trying harder. First and foremost, it comes by learning how to grow our heart's affections for Jesus Christ and learning to make him the center and treasure of our lives.

THE CHOICE: NORTH OR SOUTH? GOD OR GODS?

It's all about the affections of our heart. Jesus said, "Where your treasure is, there your heart will be also" (Matt. 6:21), and he instructed, "Love the Lord your God with all your heart" (Matt. 22:37). Every day, all day, God gives us the freedom to choose who or what we'll give our hearts to. We call it going

north or south. We either turn north to God for the security, love, and significance we long for as we face the chaos of this broken world, or we go south to
the false gods of this world. When we go south, we live with ourselves at the
center of our lives. We relate to God and people as objects of self-gratification.
When we approach relationships this way, we'll fear the significant people in
our lives who might disappoint our expectations. We'll resent them when they
fail us, and we'll love them only when they come through for us. But that's no
big deal. The worst of sinners do that.

When we put ourselves at the center, life becomes a confusing, dark, and
chaotic world of anger, worry, and envy. Those kinds of emotions are signals
that tell us we're forsaking God and going south by putting ourselves at the
center of our universe. We try to get control over the chaos of life. We work
to protect our fearful hearts. We're trying to be our own god. Yet for all our
efforts to be in control, the result is greater chaos and hurt. We damage our
families, friendships, marriages, and God's reputation.

But it can be different when we choose to live north by turning toward God
and allowing him to be the blazing center of our lives. John Piper explains:

> I have a picture in my mind of the majesty of Christ like the sun at the
> center of the solar system of your life. The massive sun, 333,000 times
> the mass of the earth, holds all the planets in orbit. . . . So it is with
> the supremacy of Christ in your life. All the planets of your life—your
> sexuality and desires, your commitments and beliefs, your aspirations
> and dreams, your attitudes and convictions, your habits and disci-
> plines, your solitude and relationships, your labor and leisure, your
> thinking and feeling—all the planets of your life are held in orbit by
> the greatness and gravity and blazing brightness of the supremacy of
> Jesus Christ at the center of your life. If he ceases to be the bright,
> blazing, satisfying beauty at the center of your life, the planets will fly
> into confusion, a hundred things will be out of control, and sooner or
> later they will crash into destruction.[4]

Yes, when all the "planets of your life" revolve around the blazing center
of Jesus Christ, everything finds its proper orbit. Only in him do we find
rest (Ps. 62:1). When Christ alone is the center of our lives, when he has the

affections of our hearts, then—and only then—we become established. We become grateful, giving children of God amidst the chaos and groaning of this broken and fallen world. We live purposefully by seeking to reveal the greatness and goodness of God by how we give to others—even when they fail to meet our expectations. But, as Piper suggests, when we take the Son from the center of our lives, when we put *anything* else in his place—our marriage, our kids, sex, sports, work, hobbies, ministry—we become double-minded. Our passions begin to spin out of control. We succumb to worry. Lust, pressure, and conflict characterize our lives.

> Thou hast made us for Thyself and our hearts are restless
> till they rest in Thee.
>
> AUGUSTINE, *Confessions*

Will we choose God? Or will we depend on people, things, and circumstances to go our way? The great battle is for our hearts. We either go north to God or south to gods. There is no in-between.

Therefore, we passionately write this book with one purpose—to stir and stoke the fire of your heart's affections for Jesus Christ. And in so doing, it's our earnest prayer that you'll find a deepened resolve in your heart to cherish your wife and to respect your husband, to be patient with your children, to be loyal to your friends, and to serve your church and everyone you meet, so they too will *want* to make the glory and beauty of our spectacular, incomprehensible God the blazing center of their lives.

QUESTIONS FOR SELF-EXAMINATION AND DISCUSSION

1. "Life is difficult." In what ways have you found this to be true? How do those difficulties impact your relationship with God and others?
2. Studies show that 77 percent of our self-talk is negative. What common themes run through your mind when your self-talk is negative?
3. The author said our worship, walk, and witness depend on how well we handle daily trouble and difficulty. In what ways do your troubles and difficulties both negatively and positively affect your worship, walk, and witness?
4. According to John 17:20–21, 23, based on the quality of our patience, kindness, and love for our spouse, children, coworker, friends, and enemies, the world has the right to judge if Christianity is true. What does that say to you personally? What would people conclude about Christianity based on the quality of your patience, kindness, and love for your spouse? Children? Friends? Coworkers? Enemies?
5. Would you say Jesus Christ is the Blazing Center of the solar system of your life? If not, who or what holds that place? In what ways do the "planets of your life" spin out of control when something other than Jesus is at the center of your life?

2

WILL YOU GO NORTH OR SOUTH?

GARY

My soul finds rest in God alone.
Psalm 62:1

Tired, cold, and soaking wet, we kept hiking through the winding trails of West Virginia wilderness. I was leading eight junior high students on their first backpacking trip. The rain kept falling. Hope kept us moving; the church bus, just two hours away, would take us to base camp where dry clothes, a hot meal, and steaming showers waited.

Somewhere along the trail, Ellie, our senior high leader, came to me with a question. "Should we be going north or south?" she asked.

"North," I said confidently, not noticing the concern in her voice.

Pointing to her compass, she said, "We're going south."

Her words took my breath away. Nightfall wasn't far off. I panicked at the thought of being lost in the wilderness. The shame of failure flooded my soul. Condemning words haunted me: *I'm such a pathetic leader.* Fighting back the noise of shame and self-contempt, I tried to pray and think of what to do.

"Paul," I said to one of the students, "run ahead for a hundred yards and see if the trail makes a turn north. Look for any trail marker. Look for anything. Go!"

Desperately I waited for good news. Minutes later Paul came running back. "The trail keeps going straight. I didn't see any trail marker."

This can't be happening! I said to myself, trying hard to conceal my inner struggles. *We've been hiking for nearly seven hours. We followed the map. We've been so careful! How could we be lost?*

I stood in the rain with eight wet, cold, exhausted junior high students. They stared at me, waiting for my decision. Which way should we go? In the tension-filled silence, a student named Biz spoke from the group. "Why don't we pray?"

Throughout our trip, I'd been teaching the kids a life lesson: when you're in trouble, humble yourself and pray. I called it turning north to God instead of going south into unbelief, anger, and worry. Now my words were coming back to me. When you're in trouble, humble yourself and pray.

But doubts rushed through my mind. *What good can prayer do? How can God possibly show us which way to go in the middle of the wilderness? There are no trail markers. We haven't seen a person for two days. How can God make the way clear? It seems impossible.*

Ignoring my doubts, I clung to the truth that God can help us, even when it seems impossible. I thanked Biz for her faith and said, "That's a good idea. Let's get in a circle and pray." Holding hands in the middle of the trail, we asked our heavenly Father for help. One by one we offered our prayers of faith and hope.

"Dear God, we need help. We're lost and don't know what to do."

"Please help Mr. Heim know what to do, God."

"Dear Jesus, we don't deserve your help. But if you would be willing, would you please show us which way we should go?"

"We don't know how you could do this, God, but would you please give us certainty about which way we should go on the trail?"

"Thank you, Jesus, for helping us. Amen."

The last student had barely said, "Amen," when one of my kids said, "Look!"

Down the trail, we saw a middle-aged backpacker striding toward us. He held a walking stick and had his golden retriever alongside him. Overcome with joy, I literally ran to the guy.

"Can you tell me the name of the trail we're on?" I asked, hoping my voice didn't reveal my desperation. "We're kind of lost and in need of some help."

"I know," he said. "I saw you praying. I can do more than tell you the name of this trail. I can show you exactly where you are and which direction you need to go." With quiet confidence, he pulled out his GPS and half-a-dozen waterproof maps, then pointed to a map and spoke. "Here's where we're standing. You're *exactly* where you need to be. Just keep going in the direction you were headed, and you'll be at your bus in about an hour."

Shouts of joy and praise to Jesus rang out from my fellowship of junior high adventurers. We thanked our rescuer and set out down the trail.

WE REACT TO LIFE'S FRUSTRATIONS

Life is often like my wilderness experience in West Virginia. Your day's going well, and then something or someone frustrates your plans. One minute I was confident we were on the trail that would lead us home. The next minute I thought we were lost in the middle of nowhere. It seemed like life was designed to frustrate me. And then God graciously rescued me from going south into despair by inviting me to turn to him through the humble request of a young teenage girl.

God sent his angel that day to lead us out of the wilderness. But honestly, God doesn't often rescue me from my struggles in such clear and dramatic ways. In fact, God would have had good purposes for us had he allowed us to wander, lost, late into the night. But here's the point: if we don't take time to think about how we react to daily frustrations and difficulties, we'll typically go south when we encounter struggles. We easily and habitually default to despair, worry, anger, or bitterness.

Lisa and I moved to Grand Rapids, Michigan, nearly twenty years ago. Our first home was a fixer-upper. Many things needed work. Painting the garage was first on the list. I spent three weekends scraping old paint off and putting new paint on. Lisa had hung a decorative flowerpot by the garage door. One day as I was painting, I took the pot off the hook and set it on the ground near me. Lisa happened to look out the kitchen window that day and noticed I was splashing paint on her flowers. She responded by coming out of the house and saying, "You're getting paint on my flowers! Why don't you *ever* pay attention to what you're doing!"

Now if you're following my thinking, you can see this was a north-south moment in my life—a moment when I needed to be intentional about turning to God for my desire to feel loved and respected instead of going into an angry, self-centered reaction. And here's what poured out of my mouth in that snapshot in time: "I can't believe it! I spend three stinking weekends working in this hot, boiling sun, painting this garage, and I *never* hear *one* word of encouragement! But as soon as I make one mistake, you're out here telling me about it!"

Lisa was stunned and wounded by my rage. Because she's such a good lady, she chose to humble herself instead of pouring gas on the fire by reacting in kind. She asked me to help her understand what made me so upset. Facing her open and nondefensive spirit, my anger subsided. We sat on our screened-in porch and talked. We both came to see and admit how wrongly we had treated each other.

Our typical default mode is to go south when we experience offense and frustration. And when we keep going south day after day, we get discouraged with life, God, and ourselves. We hurt and even come to hate the people we love. Worst of all, we fail to reveal the goodness and greatness of God because of our demanding and self-centered reactions.

When trouble comes, we're always faced with a decision: Will we choose to turn north to God or go south and react in self-centered ways? "In times of frustration," wrote Larry Crabb, "our High Priest sometimes seems more callous to our needs than sympathetic. We pray, asking God to hear our cry, pleading with Him to let nothing else go wrong. I wonder if sometimes the passion in our prayers reflects more of a *demand* than a *petition*. Frustration is excellent soil for growing a demanding spirit. It is therefore important that we handle difficulties well, allowing them to mature us rather than to push us toward demandingness."[1]

GOD

SPIRIT

Groaning
hunger/thirst

FLESH

Satan

Learning how to turn to God and surrender to him in times of groaning is never easy. It can feel like death. But it's the pathway to life and spiritual transformation. It's a narrow road (Matt. 7:13–14), but it's possible to find it, and it's the only way to know and treasure Jesus.

SATAN HAS A PURPOSE FOR OUR PAIN

When life is pleasant, it's easy to believe God is good. When life is unpleasant, people often say, "We're under attack from Satan." Satan is the Enemy of our souls, yet God is always preeminent. Satan can do nothing without God's consent (Job 1; Luke 22:31–32). Therefore, our focus and faith should be more on God and his good purposes for our pain than on Satan. But with that said, it's important to understand that every day we wake up to a world at war. We are opposed. We have an Enemy who hates and hunts us. What is his purpose for our suffering?

Jesus said the thief comes only to steal, kill, and destroy; but Jesus has come that we might "have life, and have it to the full" (John 10:10). God is always working in every detail of our lives to help us turn our hearts toward him. The life we've always wanted is found in Jesus. Satan is always working to get us to doubt that life is in God. His destructive purposes are best served when we go south in response to the chaos and problems of life.

Satan has a very low opinion of us. He's convinced that we love Jesus only for the blessings we get from him—personal peace, good kids, good health, affluent lifestyle, reliable income, good friends, and meaningful job or ministry. Satan's purpose for bringing pain into our lives is to get us to curse God when we suffer. Listen in on his conversation with God:

> Then the LORD asked Satan, "Have you noticed my servant Job? He is the finest man in all the earth. He is blameless—a man of complete integrity. He fears God and stays away from evil."
>
> Satan replied to the LORD, "Yes, but Job has good reason to fear God. You have always put a wall of protection around him and his home and his property. You have made him prosper in everything he does. Look how rich he is! But reach out and take away everything he has, and he will surely curse you to your face!" (Job 1:8–11 NLT)

Here's what I hear Satan saying about Job, you, and me: "Let me rough them up, bring pain into their lives, and they'll go south! No one loves you, God, for you alone. They're all in it for your blessings. They just want a pleasant life. Let me bring trouble into their lives, and they'll curse you."

While we may not curse God with our mouths when we face daily problems, Satan is happy if we curse God in our hearts by doubting his goodness. The next step is to slowly harden our hearts toward Jesus and then live with greater passion for something, anything, other than him alone. In fact, Satan is pleased if he can get us to worship and serve God's gifts instead of the Giver. John Piper says:

> The greatest enemy of hunger for God is not poison but apple pie. It is not the banquet of the wicked that dulls our appetite for heaven, but endless nibbling at the table of the world. It is not the X-rated video, but the prime-time dribble of triviality we drink in every night. For all the ill that Satan can do, when God describes what keeps us from the banquet table of his love, it is a piece of land, a yoke of oxen, and a wife (Luke 14:18–20). The greatest adversary to God is not his enemies but his gifts. And the most deadly appetites are not for the poison of evil, but for the simple pleasures of earth. For when these replace an appetite for God himself, the idolatry is scarcely recognizable, and almost incurable.[2]

GOD HAS A GOOD PURPOSE FOR OUR PAIN

When God called Israel to be his chosen people, he miraculously delivered them from the bondage of Egypt and led them through the Red Sea. God's people burst into songs of gratitude. But following the miracles, God led his dearly loved children into a desert for forty years. When things went badly, they grumbled; when events went well, they were grateful. Up and down the story goes (Exod. 15–17; Num. 11–14).

Things haven't changed much over the last three thousand years. Most of us know what it's like to be in the wilderness, when our dearest dreams smash or almost smash, when all seems lost. We've been there: alone, afraid, confused, wondering if God even hears our cries. And if we live long, we'll be there again. More often than I want to admit, I've been a lot like Israel in those days of wilderness testing. I can be so happy when life goes well, sing-ing God's praise, and then quickly revert south into unbelief, anger, and rage when things go badly, doubting that God even notices me, let alone loves me.

Why does God take us, his dearly loved children, into the desert? In Deuteronomy, Moses looks back over those forty years and reflects on God's good purposes for Israel and for you and me. *Remember* is the first thing we're commanded to do:

> Remember how the LORD your God led you all the way in the desert these forty years, to humble you and to test you in order to know what was in your heart, whether or not you would keep his commands. He humbled you, causing you to hunger and then feeding you with manna . . . to teach you that man does not live on bread alone but on every word that comes from the mouth of the LORD. (Deut. 8:2–3)

In the desert, Israel was to remember how they had faced troubles and frus-trations of all kinds. At times they had no food or water. They feared death. Just like them, in the wilderness of West Virginia I had to decide if I would remember. Remember what? Remember God and trust in his faithfulness lest I forget him, panic, and try to seize control.

Would God's chosen people choose to turn to him in humble, grateful trust, or would they turn away from him and go south into unbelief, fear, and grumbling? The events they faced in the desert were not pointless, random acts. Neither are the events we face in daily life. We're to remember that God himself led them all the way in the desert in order to see what they would do in those difficult moments. Each experience in the desert presented them with an opportunity to turn north to God and make him the treasure and center of their lives, or with the temptation to forget him and go south into unbelief and anger. It's amazing that every moment of every day God gives us the choice to either remember, love, and trust him, or to forget him.

We really don't know where we're at with God until we face difficulty. Trouble and hardship, big or small, will expose what is truly in our hearts. We think we're pretty mature in Christ. Then someone suddenly criticizes us, and we quickly go south into depression or anger and slander. C. S. Lewis puts it this way:

Surely what a man does when he is taken off his guard is the best
evidence for what sort of a man he is? Surely what pops out before the
man has time to put on a disguise is the truth? If there are rats in a
cellar you are most likely to see them if you go in very suddenly. But
the suddenness does not create the rats: it only prevents them from
hiding. In the same way the suddenness of the provocation does not
make me an ill-tempered man; it only shows me what an ill-tempered
man I am.[3]

Those events and provocations are being used by God to bring to the surface
the lies we believe. They are God's agents of change. And in facing the lies, we
can come to believe the truth. The truth sets us free.

It's important to remember that there is always purpose to our pain. God
allowed me to get paint on Lisa's flowers. He allowed Lisa to criticize me. God
allowed us to think we were lost that day in the wilderness. Will we turn to him
and trust him in those moments, or forget him? Do we believe *God is enough* to
sustain and lead us in those painful moments of life no matter what happens, or
will we give way to unbelief and demand our own way? No matter how many
times we fail, God patiently works—perhaps encouraging us one moment,
then frustrating our plans through difficult circumstances the next—to help
us learn how to surrender to him so he can become our unshakable security.
While God doesn't cause people to sin against us, he does use everything that
comes into our lives for our good. Nothing touches us that hasn't been filtered
through the sovereign greatness and loving goodness of God's heart.

GOD IS IN THE BIG AND SMALL

Many people suffer in ways we might call "big," such as hearing the biopsy
is cancerous or losing a job. Through major victories, failures, and hardships,
David came to understand where life was found:

> My soul finds rest in *God alone*;
>   my salvation comes from him.
> *He alone* is my rock and my salvation;
>   he is my fortress, I will never be shaken.
>   (Ps. 62:1–2, emphasis added)

As David wrote those words, he had lost his kingdom; Absalom, his son, was trying to kill him. David was fleeing into the desert for his life.

Not everyone experiences the crushing weight of tragic events like being diagnosed with cancer or the death of a child. Such groaning deserves our deepest compassion. But everyone groans under the weight of daily problems, frustrations, and disappointments—a flat tire when you're late for work, a backed-up septic tank just as guests arrive, sleepless nights with screaming babies, marital and financial tension, or harsh and stinging words from a friend. Trouble comes in all shapes and sizes. But more often than not, it's the many little things of everyday life that pile up and get to us over time.

I'm ashamed to admit this: I've had a pet peeve. I can get ticked when people drive slowly in front of me. I've been known to grumble under my breath things like, "The speed limit's forty-five, not thirty-five. Being safe is one thing, being *stupid* is another!"

It's easy to assume those small events are just random occurrences without purpose. But I've learned and am still learning to see how God is lovingly pursuing me through even the smallest, daily, frustrating events. There is always a good purpose to our pain. God assures us, his dearly loved children, that he disciplines us as a father disciplines his son (Heb. 12:5–11). Discipline means training. God keeps working to grow us up so that "in the end it might go well with you" (Deut. 8:16).

As a result of God's discipline, a new song is growing in my heart. It's the song of knowing and treasuring Jesus in the midst of the daily grind. And this new song is translating into the ability to be kind and patient with others, even when they're frustrating or disappointing.

Fifteen years ago, I had a full-time, private practice as a Christian counselor. Each week I talked with many people who faced deep struggles. At a particular time in my counseling ministry, I was not doing well for several reasons. A former client was suing me. Two people I was working with were suicidal, and this weighed on me. In addition, after I had spent many hours working with and caring for a client, he told me he was going to see a different counselor. Last of all, I had several openings in my counseling schedule. I was concerned I wouldn't be able to pay the bills if the phone didn't start ringing.

One night as Lisa and I sat at the dinner table, she asked me how I was doing. Feeling overwhelmed with a sense of failure, I broke down and began to share honestly about my fears and discouragements. While I was talking, Lisa quietly stood up from the table, picked up her dinner plate, and walked to the sink a few feet away. My first inner reaction was to go south into anger. The self-talk that fueled my anger went like this: "Lisa doesn't care about me or what I'm going through." In my anger I wanted to tell her off by saying something like, "Do you realize how insensitive it feels to me when you just get up and leave when I'm sharing my heart with you?"

But this time I caught myself; this time I knew I was angry. I was coming to see that unrighteous anger was a signal, telling me I was going south by demanding love and respect from Lisa instead of turning north to Jesus alone for the longings of my heart. Therefore, I chose to hold my comments. I sat quietly at the table and prayed silently. *Father, right now I'm furious. I admit that I want to tell Lisa off. I acknowledge my anger to you alone and admit that I believe a lie. I believe I need Lisa to show care for me. But I repent. While I do legitimately desire a certain response from Lisa, I confess that I do not need anything from her. I turn to you alone, Jesus, for the hunger and thirst in my heart. It doesn't feel like you alone are enough to meet these needs, but I choose to believe the truth no matter what I feel. Right now I confess that you, Lord Jesus, are with me. I acknowledge in my heart that you are for me and you are gloriously enough to sustain me right now. You are my refuge and strength. I love you, Jesus.*

I sat there for another moment and embraced the truth of the greatness and goodness of God's grace and love for me. My anger began to subside. I didn't feel joyful, but by faith I sincerely thanked God for being with me in this moment of loneliness. Then, and only then, was I able to shift my focus from my needs to Lisa's needs. Instead of resenting Lisa for leaving the table, I began to honestly and sincerely wonder *why* she left. As I continued to focus my heart on Jesus as the center of my security, I tried to reach out to Lisa by asking some questions.

"Honey, what caused you to leave the table as I was talking? What were you feeling?"

After a moment of reflection, Lisa said, "I think I was feeling afraid."

"What were you afraid of, honey?"

She said, "I don't think you would do this to me and the kids (long pause and trembling voice), but I can't help but think about your dad . . . how when he was discouraged and depressed about his struggles at work, he tried to kill himself."

Lisa began to cry. My heart melted with compassion for her. I got up from the table, walked over to her, and put my arms around her. I thanked God for enabling me to stop my southward spiral into anger. I was so grateful that he helped me turn north to Jesus and listen to him so I could be a shelter for my dear wife instead of being her storm (Isa. 32:1–2).

Whether the daily problems I'm facing are big or small, I'm learning to stop and prayerfully ask myself questions like these: Do I believe God is sovereign and in control in this painful moment? Do I believe he is good right *now*, that his love is enough to sustain me no matter what happens? Do I believe God has a good purpose for allowing that car to go slow in front of me, for allowing Lisa to get up from the table and leave? Will I remember God, surrender and submit to him right now, and stop grumbling? Will I stop going south into anger and unbelief and pray for help to go north to Jesus so I can love God and love people from my heart?

Many times I've struggled to believe the truth about God's goodness and greatness in the middle of my problems. And I'm sure this will continue to be a battle for me. But as I'm growing in my understanding of God's character and unfailing love, I must conclude he's ordained that moment and that he has a good purpose for me. God uses *everything* for my good (Ps. 37:23 NLT; Rom. 8:28). I believe God means it when he says *everything*. He's not just in the big things. He's in the smallest, daily things too. And what is the "good" that God is working in me? He's always working to help me treasure him as he treasures me and to conform me into the very likeness of Jesus. He's working to bring forth the fruit of the Spirit: love, joy, peace, patience, kindness, goodness, faithfulness, gentleness, self-control (Gal. 5:22–23). Therefore God says, "Endure hardship as discipline. . . . No discipline seems pleasant at the time, but painful. Later on, however, it produces a harvest of righteousness and peace for those who have been trained by it" (Heb. 12:7, 11). God is always working in every detail of every day of my life—pleasant and unpleasant—to help me see and savor Jesus Christ so he becomes the love of my life. Then I can deeply and confidently say, "My soul finds rest in God alone" (Ps. 62:1).

Since God is so involved with even the most "insignificant" details of life (Matt. 10:29–30), we can be certain he's involved when the dishwasher breaks, an unexpected bill arrives, or a health issue comes into our lives. We tend to think God is working when things go well, but we rarely stop to consider that he's working when problems come and life is falling apart.

So I must be intentional about viewing daily life with the wide-angle lens of God's bigger purposes. Will I choose to fight against God and go south, making my family endure my anger? Or will I choose to acknowledge God in that moment and submit to his goodness and greatness as I prayerfully reflect on what his good purpose may be? God may not show me his good purpose in the moment of crisis or frustration, but the question remains: Will I remember him, talk to him, and trust that he alone is enough to sustain me in that moment? *That* is the good he's working in me. Choosing to trust God can enable me to respond to frustrating people with gentleness rather than impatience. Through the coming chapters, you'll see how God uses daily problems and frustrations in your life to draw you into a soul-stirring relationship with him so you can live out the double-love command: loving God and loving others (Matt. 22:37–40).

QUESTIONS FOR SELF-EXAMINATION AND DISCUSSION

1. What are some common tensions, frustrations, and disappointments you face in daily life? Can you name some you are currently facing?

2. Our suffering in life often seems random and without purpose, especially the little, daily things. Do you agree or disagree with that statement? Why or why not?

3. How would you handle daily frustrations differently if you believed God had good purposes behind them?

4. Describe a time you went north as you faced difficulty. What helped you choose to turn to God?

5. Describe a time you went south. Why do you think you chose to go there?

6. Would you say you typically go north or south when you face hardship and frustration in life? Why do you think that is true?

7. How would you like to grow and be different as a result of this study?

3

GROANING

GOD'S PASSIONATE PURSUIT OF YOUR HEART

GARY

For we know that all creation has been groaning as in the pains of childbirth
right up to the present time. And we believers also groan, even though
we have the Holy Spirit within us as a foretaste of future glory.
Romans 8:22–23 NLT

It was the first toilet I'd ever installed. I was pretty nervous because I really
didn't know what I was doing. But I could imagine what might happen if I
did it wrong. Thoughts of raw sewage spewing up from the floor haunted me.

The bathroom was small and cluttered with tools. Everything was covered
in sawdust. The sweltering heat made beads of salty, stinging sweat stream into
my eyes. Many things had gone wrong that morning, but my real frustrations
began with a black rubber ring that went over the drain hole in the bathroom
floor. The toilet sat over the ring. With the toilet and ring in place, I tightened
the bolts on the toilet base. The wrench kept slipping off the bolt, and my
knuckles continued slamming against the toilet. With the bolts tightened, I
sat on the toilet, but the toilet swiveled back and forth on the rubber ring. As
I tightened the bolts one more time, one of them snapped off. I was fuming.
Another trip to Home Depot.

Back again, I tightened the bolt once more; the toilet still swiveled. My
frustrations mounted. *Maybe it would be a good thing if the toilet swiveled*

back and forth, I reasoned. *It could be helpful when you turn and reach for the paper.*

To check out my theory, I ran upstairs and sat on the other toilets in the house. Not one of them swiveled back and forth. Coming back to reality, my deep-seated feelings of failure, inadequacy, and helplessness swept me south into an odd mixture of anger and near despair.

"God," I said quietly, trying hard to contain my emotions, "you created heaven and earth. With just *one* word from your mouth, you made it all happen. Bam! Just like that. You *could* help me. You *could* make this toilet stop swiveling! You *could* do *something,* but you don't! Why won't you help me?"

Just then I heard a little voice, "Daddy, can we help?" My two children stood at the bathroom door.

God, I thought, *you know that's not what I had in mind.* I took a deep breath, got control of my frustrations, and reluctantly agreed to some help.

"Okay," I said to seven-year-old Brandon. "Pick up the tools lying around and put them in that corner. Then sweep the floor."

Not even looking at my daughter, who had recently turned five, I said, "Kailie, the room's too small for all of us to be in here. You'll have to leave."

Kailie replied, "But Daaad, I want to help too!"

I was coming to a boil, but with as much self-control as I could muster, I turned to my daughter. "Kailie, this room's too small, and I'm really frustrated right now. *Please leave.*"

"But Daaaaad!"

Her whining tone sent me over the edge. I exploded, "*Kailie!* I'm not going to say it again!"

I'll never forget that moment. Before my very eyes, I saw the life drain from my little girl. Her shoulders slumped, and her little head hung low as she silently and obediently walked out of the room. Instantly, my anger turned into guilt and my guilt into sorrow. Knowing I'd hurt my daughter, I gently said, "Kailie, come here, honey." She turned and threw her little arms around me, sobbing and trembling.

"Honey," I said tenderly, "I'm so sorry for getting upset with you. You just wanted to be with us, didn't you?" Her head nodded as she cried and held me tighter. Her body quivered as she gasped for breath between sobs.

"Oh, sweetie, you feel like I don't want you, don't you?" I asked. Her little head went up and down. Her tears soaked my shoulder. "Dad's been a *real jerk*, hasn't he?" Her little head went up and down again. I assured her how much she was loved and wanted. Admitting I was wrong for the way I'd handled things, I asked for forgiveness. We talked more, and I could see in her eyes and in her smile that our relationship was restored.

WHY DOES GOD ALLOW US TO BE SUBJECTED TO FRUSTRATION?

Over the years, my relationship with Brandon and Kailie has been characterized by love and thoughtfulness. The way I reacted to my little girl that day would not define our relationship. Even though that's true, I have frustrated my kids many times, and they've frustrated me. But I don't *try* to frustrate them. Yet the Bible says God intentionally subjects his creation to frustration (Rom. 8:20). The Bible also tells us we're God's dearly loved children (Eph. 5:1). If God dearly loves us, why does he intentionally frustrate us? In order to understand God's good purposes, we have to go back to the beginning. Because the way we experience life now is not the way he created it to be.

IN THE BEGINNING...

Every moment of our lives unfolds as a story. I just told one story of my life: the story of the swiveling toilet. It had a beginning—I was installing my first toilet. In the next scene, things didn't go well. I got frustrated. Instead of turning north to God, I went south and hurt my little girl. I'm so glad that the story didn't end there. Kind words and forgiving hearts won the day. Yes, life is a story. We live scene by scene, day by day.

The Bible is God's story. The first scene in Genesis tells how everything got started. "In the beginning God created the heavens and the earth" (Gen. 1:1). The Bible says, "All things were created by him and for him" (Col. 1:16).

"Then God looked over all he had made, and he saw that it was very good" (Gen. 1:31 NLT). Like an artist stepping back from his easel to delight in his painting, God enjoyed the excellence of his creative work.

"Then God said, 'Let us make man in our image, in our likeness'" (Gen. 1:26). Man was God's creative masterpiece—a representation of God himself on the earth.

Why did God create mankind? Was he lonely, in need of companionship?

No. The life of God overflows in an explosively joyful, life-giving, others-centered, community of Father, Son, and Holy Spirit. And overflowing with life and generosity, God decided to make people so we could get in on their fun. It's like God the Father, Son, and Holy Spirit said, "We're so alive with life and having so much fun together, let's make our joy complete by creating people so they can enjoy this fellowship of soul-stirring, life-giving friendship with us."

God placed Adam and his wife, Eve, in a honeymoon paradise that transcended our wildest vacation dreams. The Garden of Eden was a home perfectly suited for them.

SHALOM

Adam and Eve were so secure in God's love that they freely and naturally loved each other with an understanding, sensitivity, and kindness that flowed so consistently; they were as *one* in spirit, soul, and body. They knew no sin, fear, or shame. Therefore, the Bible says they were naked and not ashamed (Gen. 2:25).

Adam and Eve experienced deep satisfaction by accomplishing the meaningful work God had given them to do (Gen. 1:28). Everything pointed back to the greatness and goodness of God: the grand Designer, Creator, and Sustainer. He was the glorious, life-giving center of it all. It was a world of wholeness and peace—*shalom*.

> The vision for wholeness and peace . . . is wonderfully gathered up in the Hebrew word *shalom* . . . a full-bodied concept that resonates with wholeness, unity, balance. Gathering in (but much broader than) peace, it means a harmonious, caring community with God at its center as the prime sustainer and most glorious inhabitant. This great vision of *shalom* begins and ends our Bible. In the creation narrative, God brought order and harmony out of chaos; in the Apocalypse of John, we have the glorious wholeness of a new heaven and a new earth.[1]

EVIL ENTERS THE STORY

Like our stories, God's story has a villain. Satan hates God, and he hates you and me. The Evil One hates oneness. He wants to breed distrust, conflict, and isolation. He wants to destroy shalom and blind us from seeing the glory of God. Therefore, the Serpent cast a spell of deceit over Eve by asking a question: "Did God really say you must not eat the fruit from any of the trees in the garden?" (Gen. 3:1 NLT).

With one question, the Serpent gets Eve to think what she's never thought before. *Eve, can you really trust what God said?*

Eve replies to the Serpent, "We may eat fruit from the trees in the garden, but God did say, 'You must not eat fruit from the tree that is in the middle of the garden, and you must not touch it, or you will die'" (Gen. 3:2–3). Without realizing the gravity of the conversation, Eve has become engaged in a war for her heart. She's teetering.

Then the Serpent calls God a liar. *"You will not surely die.... For God knows* that when you eat of it your eyes will be opened, and you will be like God, knowing good and evil" (Gen. 3:4–5, emphasis added).

I hear the Evil One saying, "Eve, God isn't as good as he looks. He's keeping the best tree from you."

How might Eve have felt in that moment of testing? Imagine your best friends invite you to their house for coffee and dessert. You're deeply warmed by their thoughtfulness. But as you're traveling home, you realize you forgot your Franklin Covey Planner. Knowing you can't survive a day without it, you turn around and drive all the way back to your friends' house. Pulling up to the house, you're surprised to see cars parked everywhere, and walking up to the front door, you hear music. You hear people laughing. You knock on the door and your friend opens it. All your friends are inside having a party.

You walk to the deck to find your planner. Steaks are sizzling on the grill. Baked potatoes and luscious salads are decoratively arranged on the table. The sting of rejection takes you south. You struggle with anger and jealousy. Your best friends saved their best for everyone but you.

I think that's how the Serpent wanted Eve to feel. "Yeah, God looks generous, Eve, but you're only getting coffee and dessert. He's keeping the steak for himself. You can't trust him. Don't let him get away with that! Assert yourself, Eve! Eat from this tree. You can be godlike. You can discern good from evil for yourself." Satan sowed seeds of doubt and discontent in her heart.

In that moment of testing, I think God was asking, "Adam, Eve, will you remember me *now*? Will you trust and obey me *now*?" In spite of all the evidence of God's goodness, Eve bought the lie. Driven by her lust to be like God, she reached out, took the fruit from the tree, and ate it (Gen. 3:6).

And here's the shocker: Adam was there watching it all. He should have protected his wife by speaking up. "Get out of here, Serpent! No, Eve! Don't eat that! God said we shouldn't."

But instead of loving God and courageously loving Eve, Adam doubted God and passively followed Eve. Adam goes south. He too turns from God and eats from the tree (Gen. 3:1–7).

Their rebellion unleashed a firestorm from hell. Everything that's wrong with this world finds its roots in the Fall. We read about it in the newspapers and see it every night on TV: a drunk driver takes out a school bus; pornography is a multibillion-dollar industry; child abuse, domestic violence, divorce, human trafficking, the killing of unborn children . . . Life is broken. It's not the way God created it to be.

TRAGEDY

Since that tragic day in the Garden, we naturally and habitually make ourselves, and whatever we think will make us happy, the passion and pursuit of our lives. "Since the fall of man," wrote Francis Schaeffer, "we do not want to deny ourselves. Actually we do everything we can . . . to put ourselves at the center of the universe. This is where we naturally want to live."[2] Just as the Serpent predicted, we live as if we're our own little gods.

> The inner, basic . . . defilement of fallen man is his profound
> and illusory conviction that he is a god and that the universe
> is centered upon him.
>
> THOMAS MERTON, *The Silent Life*

Because of our sin nature, passed on to us by Adam and Eve, we don't naturally delight in loving, serving, and celebrating God and one another. Instead, we forsake God and manipulate others for our own advantage. When we live self-centered instead of God-centered lives, our lives become chaotic and never make sense:

The search for the purpose of life has puzzled people for thousands of years. That's because we typically begin at the wrong starting point—ourselves. We ask self-centered questions like What do *I* want to be? What should *I* do with *my* life? What are *my* goals, *my* ambitions, *my* dreams for *my* future? But focusing on ourselves will never reveal our life's purpose. . . . You were made *by* God and *for* God—and until you understand that, life will never make sense. It is only in God that we discover our origin, our identity, our meaning, our purpose, our significance, and our destiny. Every other path leads to a dead end.[3]

The greatest lie Satan wants us to believe is that life is a story about us, about me, and that I play the leading role. The greatest truth God wants us to believe is that life is a story about Jesus Christ and that we play an important supportive role. Fully embracing this truth sets us free to live for God and the good of others. To embrace the lie brings us into the worst and darkest bondage possible. As Donald Miller said, "There is no addiction so powerful as self-addiction."[4]

God banished Adam and Eve from the Garden (Gen. 3:23–24). How many times over the years, after another fight with Eve or while mourning over the murder of his son Abel, did Adam climb a tree near the wall and look in on the Garden, longing for the days gone by. As much as he yearned for the cool afternoon walks with God, those days were over. Because of Adam and Eve's rebellion, life—as we experience it today—is tragic.

THE REST OF THE STORY

While tragedy is Satan's story, salvation is God's story. God's story began in the Garden of Eden. It ends in the glory of the new heavens and the new earth. Those cool afternoon walks with God will be restored. "'Now the dwelling of God is with men, and he will live with them. . . . He will wipe every tear from their eyes. There will be no more death or mourning or crying or pain, for the old order of things has passed away.' He who was seated on the throne said, 'I am making everything new!'" (Rev. 21:3–5).

As a woman groans in birth pains, yearning for the moment her child will be born, creation groans in birth pains, waiting in eager expectation for the glory of the new heavens and new earth.

In that day, greed, hatred, arrogance, and evil will not exist in the community of God's treasured and contented people. Disease, oppression, and poverty will not be found in the reign of God's shalom. God will again be the blazing center of his world: "The city has no need of sun or moon, for the glory of God illuminates the city, and the Lamb is its light" (Rev. 21:23 NLT).

In that day, we *will* live happily ever after. Our hope is not a fool's dream of blind optimism. Our hope is objective, firmly rooted in the gracious promises of God through Jesus Christ. God is leading history to a joyful and glorious destiny. The Bible says, "Long before he laid down earth's foundations, he had us in mind, had settled on us as the focus of his love, to be made whole and holy by his love. . . . Long before we first heard of Christ and got our hopes up, he had his eye on us, had designs on us for glorious living" (Eph. 1:4, 11 MSG).

Though God gives us good things to enjoy—such as healthy marriages, thriving churches, dear friends, meaningful jobs or ministries—life never lets us feel like we're *home.* "Home," wrote Timothy Keller, "is a powerful but elusive concept. The strong feelings that surround it reveal some deep longing within us for a place that absolutely fits and suits us. . . . Yet it seems that no real place or actual family ever satisfies these yearnings."[5] Sooner or later, something or someone has a way of messing things up. Life just doesn't work the way we want it to, and for good reason. As C. S. Lewis noted, "Our Father refreshes us on the journey with some pleasant inns, but will not encourage us to mistake them for home."[6] Truth is, we're not home. We're exiles from Eden, refugees in a foreign land, traveling through a wilderness toward our new home in the day of glory.

God dreams of that day when we'll be safely home with him. "'In that day,' says the LORD, . . . 'tears of joy will stream down their faces, and I will lead them home with great care'" (Jer. 31:1, 9 NLT). J. R. R. Tolkien paints a picture of what our joy may look like:

> "Is everything sad going to come untrue? What's happened to the world?" [asked Sam].
>
> "A great Shadow has departed," said Gandalf, and then he laughed, and the sound was like music, or like water in the parched land; and as he listened the thought came to him that he had not heard laughter, the pure sound of merriment, for days upon days without count. It fell upon his ears like the echo of all the joys he had ever known. But he

himself burst into tears. Then, as a sweet rain will pass down a wind of spring and the sun will shine out the clearer, his tears ceased, and his laughter welled up, and laughing he sprang from his bed.

"How do I feel?" he cried. "Well, I don't know how to say it. I feel, I feel"—he waved his arms in the air—"I feel like spring after winter, and sun on the leaves; and like trumpets and harps and all the songs I have ever heard!"[7]

To live faithfully in God's story amidst all the groaning, grieving, and disappointments of this fallen world, we must remember and hold on to this truth: we're not home yet. Philip Yancey wonderfully reminded us that "the Bible never belittles human disappointment . . . but it does add one key word: temporary. What we feel now, we will not always feel. Our disappointment is itself a sign, an aching, a hunger for something better. And faith is, in the end, a kind of homesickness—for a home we have never visited but have never once stopped longing for."[8]

GOD'S GIFT OF GROANING

The Garden of Eden is our past. Glory is our future. Groaning is God's gift in our present.

Groaning involves frustration (Rom. 8:20). The daily experience of frustration is so common, we often don't "name it"—flooded basements, wayward kids, wounding words, illness, conflict, annoying people, computer problems, financial stress, congested traffic, the list goes on. Now we're back to our question. Why does a good God intentionally subject us, his dearly loved children, to frustration? Truth be told, it's a gift from God. It's meant to direct us to him. If God did not frustrate us, we'd be hopelessly lost. While this truth can be hard to see in the face of pain and adversity, when we see it, we'll embrace it as our ally instead of our enemy. This is the truth: God subjects us to frustration because of our longings, the lies we believe, and his relentless love.

LONGINGS

Before the Fall, Adam and Eve were secure and happy in the life and love of God. But we've been separated from the life of God through sin. Fallen man is left with a gaping emptiness in his heart. Yet we long and ache for the fullness of unconditional love.

While Sandy talked with me, she recalled a memory from her early childhood. Her mom was often mean and harsh. One day while Sandy was brushing her hair, her mom came in her bedroom and scolded, "You're not doing that right!" Her mom grabbed the brush from her hand and hit her on the head with it. I felt sad as Sandy told me this story. Her eyes moistened. I asked her what she wanted from her mom in moments like that. She sobbed. "I so wanted her to be gentle with me. I just wanted her to say, 'Here, honey, let me help you.'"

We so long for kindness, wholeness, for shalom. Many people are aware of these deep longings; others are not. Those yearnings are windows into our soul. *They* are who *we* are. Admitting and embracing our longing to be loved, to be enjoyed, to please, and to be praised is part of being humble and human. C. S. Lewis wrote:

> No one can enter heaven except as a child; and nothing is so obvious in a child—not in a conceited child, but in a good child—as its great and undisguised pleasure in being praised. Not only in a child, either, but even in a dog or a horse. Apparently what I had mistaken for humility had, all these years, prevented me from understanding what is in fact the humblest, the most childlike, the most creaturely of pleasures—nay, the specific pleasure of the inferior: the pleasure of a beast before men, a child before its father, a pupil before his teacher, a creature before its Creator . . . when the redeemed soul, beyond all hope and nearly beyond belief, learns at last that she has pleased Him whom she was created to please.[9]

The Bible has a lot to say about longing—this deep and legitimate hunger and thirst within our aching souls. Here's a sampling:

Come, all you who are thirsty,
    come to the waters;
and you who have no money,
    come, buy and eat!
Come, buy wine [a metaphor for joy] and milk [a metaphor for nourishment]
    without money and without cost.
Why spend money [time and energy] on what is not bread [true soul food],
    and your labor on what does not satisfy [frustration/futility]? . . .
Give ear and come to me;
    hear me, that your soul may live. (Isa. 55:1–3)

Because your love is better than life,
    my lips will glorify you. . . .
My soul will be satisfied as with the richest of foods;
    with singing lips my mouth will praise you. (Ps. 63:3, 5)

> "Everyone who drinks this water will be thirsty again, but whoever drinks the water I give him will never thirst. Indeed, the water I give him will become in him a spring of water welling up to eternal life." (John 4:13–14)

> "I am the bread of life. He who comes to me will never go hungry, and he who believes in me will never be thirsty." (John 6:35)

The Bible talks a lot about food and water. It begins and ends with the theme of hunger and thirst. In Genesis, God invites Adam and Eve to eat freely from the trees of the Garden. The Serpent brings mankind down by getting them to eat forbidden fruit. Because of the Fall, Adam and Eve cannot eat from the Tree of Life. In the closing chapters of the book of Revelation, the river of the water of life flows through the new heavens and new earth. On each side of the river stands the Tree of Life, from which everyone can freely eat. The final chapter of God's redemptive story invites us to drink deeply:

"The Spirit and the bride say, 'Come!' And let him who hears say, 'Come!' Whoever is thirsty, let him come; and whoever wishes, let him take the free gift of the water of life" (Rev. 22:17).

Admitting we're hungry and thirsty isn't selfish. Many Christians ask, "Isn't it selfish to think about my desires? Shouldn't I just care about others?" Deep down, we're afraid to face and feel how alone we are. Diversion is one way we avoid facing this painful reality:

> Diversion is the first and most effective way to hide the elephant. An elephant can be hidden by mice, if there are enough of them. So our world is full of thousands of little things, which keep us diverted from the one big thing. We are kept so busy that we have no time to think.
>
> PETER KREEFT, *Three Philosophies of Life*

Truth is the Bible tells us to embrace our hunger and thirst because God wants to be the one who satisfies those needs. Our problem isn't our hunger and thirst but our foolish ideas about who or what can satisfy those longings.

I recently talked with a young man who yearns for his father's affirmation but never receives it. I asked him to tell me what he longs to hear from his dad. He said he wants to hear him say he was proud of him. He's always wanted his dad to show interest in him by asking him questions about his life, work, and his new marriage. It never happens. I told him his desire for his dad's affirmation and interest was very legitimate. He began to tear up. I cried with him. Then I asked him if he ever brought those felt longings to God in prayer, asking the Lord to speak to him and tell him what he thought of him. That idea had never occurred to my friend.

Just as God designed our bodies to need food and water, he designed our souls to hunger and thirst for love and meaning. He made us this way so we would depend on him for our soul's delight. He longs to provide for our needs as we lovingly look to him as our shepherd, father, and friend. Christians often pray and ask God to meet their need for wisdom and direction as they face life's decisions, but rarely understand that their intimate longings for love and meaning are what they're most dependent upon God for. We rarely stop to face and feel the deep hunger and thirst in our souls that are meant for God.

It can make us feel weak and needy. Truth is we are weak and needy. But we're fallen and therefore determined to be "strong" instead of dependent.

We have this hunger and thirst, you and me. We're created in God's image. Because God is love, we too long to courageously love and be loved. Everything God does has purpose and eternal significance. We too long to know our lives count for something eternally significant.

Deep in the heart of every man lurks a question, a longing. Whether he knows it or not, every man is asking in one way or another, "Do I have what it takes?" Men long to know they're competent—to know they have what it takes to make a real difference in this world. A man experiences shame when his incompetence is exposed. He fears he'll lose respect. Every man's question goes back to his longing to know his life has meaning and that he can make a significant impact in life and in his relationships.[10]

Deep in the heart of every woman is a question. She asks something like, "Am I lovely?" or "Will anyone choose or cherish me?" The basis for every woman's longing is her yearning to relax, secure in the unconditional, protective love of someone important to her.[11]

Let's be clear. Men also desire to know they're secure in someone's love. They long to rest in someone's care. Women long to know they're competent and capable to do something that really matters in life. Men and women want the same things. But as I understand the Bible and have talked with thousands of men and women, I believe men are more characterized by the longing to feel adequate and respected while women are more characterized by their longing to feel loved and cherished.

I can't stress this truth enough: these longings are legitimate. We must not hate them or call them selfish. We need to face them and feel them. C. S. Lewis commented:

> If there lurks in most modern minds the notion that to desire our own good and earnestly to hope for the enjoyment of it is a bad thing, I submit that this notion has crept in from Kant and the Stoics and is no part of the Christian faith. Indeed, if we consider the unblushing promises of reward and the staggering nature of the rewards promised in the Gospels, it would seem that Our Lord finds our desires not too strong, but too weak. We are half-hearted creatures, fooling about

with drink and sex and ambition when infinite joy is offered us, like an ignorant child who wants to go on making mud pies in a slum because he cannot imagine what is meant by the offer of a holiday at the sea. We are far too easily pleased.[12]

Men and women are relational to the core. When we know we're secure in God's unconditional love and that our lives are bearing fruit that has eternal significance, we experience, if ever so briefly, wholeness and joy. Men feel masculine and women feel feminine. Jesus spoke about this joy:

I am the vine; you are the branches. Those who remain in me, and I in them, will produce much fruit. For apart from me you can do nothing. . . . Remain in my love. When you obey my commandments [love God and love others], you remain in my love, just as I obey my Father's commandments and remain in his love. *I have told you these things so that you will be filled with my joy.* (John 15:5, 9–11 NLT, emphasis added)

LIES

Okay, we're hungry and thirsty. Those longings are deep and legitimate. But here's the problem: *we're born believing lies.* Without God's intervention, we naturally and habitually believe the lie the Serpent told Adam and Eve in the Garden. We believe that life—love and meaning—are found in this world instead of in knowing God. The Bible says that fallen man "exchanged the truth of God for a lie, and worshiped and served created things rather than the Creator" (Rom. 1:25). We worship created things when we live for people's approval, love, and respect more than God's; when we spend our life energy pursuing things like money, friends, popularity, power, and sex. While many of these things can be good in and of themselves, they have tragically taken God's place within our hearts. "The roots of our hearts have grown down into things. . . . God's gifts now take the place of God, and the whole course of nature is upset by the monstrous substitution."[13]

Thomas Merton has well said that, "In our desire to be 'as gods'—a lasting deformity impressed in our nature by original sin—we . . . demand that all our wishes be satisfied and that our will should never be frustrated or opposed."[14]

That is a profound observation. Demanding our own way is at the heart of trying to be our own god.

Try to imagine living in a world where you always got your way, where your will was never frustrated or opposed. Suppose you had your dream home overlooking the Rocky Mountains. And suppose you could drive "new every two." Imagine having so much money you never worried about bills. You could afford most anything you wanted. You had a secure retirement savings, an intimate and romantic marriage, good kids, good health. You always looked beautiful, had many close friends, had a nice church, and had a meaningful job or ministry that was deeply fulfilling. Left to ourselves, we'd forget God and call that life. We would be content to make this world home. And if we doubt that, listen to God's warning to his treasured people as they're about to enter the Promised Land:

> Be careful that you do not forget the LORD your God, failing to observe his commands [Love the Lord your God with all your heart]. . . . Otherwise, when you eat and are satisfied, when you build fine houses and settle down, and when your herds and flocks grow large and your silver and gold increase and all you have is multiplied, then your heart will become proud and you will forget the LORD your God. (Deut. 8:11–14)

What God predicted might happen did happen:

> "As they had their pasture, they became satisfied,
>   And being satisfied, their heart became proud;
> Therefore they forgot Me." (Hos. 13:6 NASB)

NEEDS VERSUS DESIRES

Longings are legitimate, but the biggest questions we have to ask ourselves every day are these: "*Whom* or *what* do we believe satisfies the hunger and thirst of our hearts? Whom do we depend on to satisfy our longing for love and respect? Do we believe satisfaction is found in Jesus or in people and things? Do we believe God alone is the source of life, or do we believe a lie? That is, do we believe the satisfaction of our heart's longing for life is found in our spouse, our boss, our father, our kids, or . . . you name it?

King David expressed his dependence on God alone in one of his psalms:

> O God, *you* are my God,
>   earnestly I seek *you*;
> my soul thirsts for *you*,
>   my body longs for *you*,
> *in a dry and weary land*
>   *where there is no water.* (Ps. 63:1, emphasis added)

Do you believe that? Do you believe this world is a dry and weary land where there is *no* water, or do you believe your thirst can be quenched in this world through your husband's or wife's response to you, or in your job, or through your kids, friends, or in sex, sports, grades, money, or something else? How does your heart seek the answer to your deepest question: Do I have what it takes? Am I lovely? Do you seek it from God or man?

This is very important. If we believe the food and water (love/security and respect/significance) we long for come from people, we will not fear God. If we believe it comes from God, we will not fear people, and our soul will find rest from the enslavement of the fear of man and the constant striving to get people to satisfy our longings. The Bible says, "The fear of the LORD leads to life: Then one rests content, untouched by trouble" (Prov. 19:23). *Untouched* doesn't mean we'll never struggle or get hurt. It means in the core of our heart lies a trust and security in God that cannot be shaken or destroyed. The bottom line is always good. Our souls will taste the rest that can never be shaken if our security is in Jesus Christ alone.

Some ask, "If God is all we need, what's the point of being married? Isn't my spouse supposed to meet my needs for security and significance?" Marriage gives us unique opportunities to enhance one another's experience of *feeling* secure and significant, but marriage was never meant to *be* our security and significance. Our souls find rest in God alone (Ps. 62:1).

Let's call our hunger and thirst a *need* when it comes to depending on God for it and only a *desire* when we look to people for it. Of course we naturally and legitimately desire that people will treat us with love and respect. And we should enjoy it when they freely give it to us. But the truth is we don't need them to. While rejection can deeply and legitimately hurt, we don't need to demand that people come through for us if the eternal, transcendent, living God has chosen to befriend us and dwell within our hearts. "If God is for us," asked Paul, "who can be against us?" (Rom. 8:31). Let this diagram show how our hunger and thirst for love and respect are *needs* as we depend on God for them and how they must be held as *desires* when we look to fallen people to satisfy those longings.

Our greatest problems in relationships come when we turn this diagram around, when we say, "I *desire* to know God's love, but I *need* it from people." For example, I legitimately desired that Lisa speak to me with respect that day when I splashed paint on her flowers; she legitimately desired that I show her love by being careful with the things that mattered to her. But we both believed lies that day. We believed we needed each other to meet our needs. Had Lisa and I been focused on the truth of God's love that day, we both would have known that our needs for love and respect were already met by faith in Jesus Christ. While we still would have felt the pain of one another's failure to show love and respect, we would not have gone south by demanding these things from each other. We could have treated one another with the dignity an image bearer of God deserves. We could have responded by speaking the truth in love instead of speaking with self-centered anger.

We go north to God when we look to Jesus alone to meet our hunger and thirst for love and respect. We're going south when we demand that people meet those needs.

Many men and women fear and/or resent their spouses, parents, kids, and others because they're looking to them, instead of God, to satisfy the hunger and thirst in their hearts. Both Lance and his father are good examples.

Lance was always in a bad mood when he thought about his dad. *Nothing is ever good enough for him! The lawn, the garden, his workshop—nothing makes that man happy.* Lance tried to earn his father's love and respect, but nothing worked. Last week Lance mowed the lawn carefully, trimmed all the bushes, and edged along the driveway and sidewalks. He hoped his dad would notice when he came home.

But as usual, his dad just grumbled on his way into the house, "Lance! Why don't you ever remember to put the rake and lawn mower away? How many times do I have to tell you? You *need to respect me* by doing what I say! Get it done! Now!"

And let's tune into Ashley's self-talk as she paces the floor, feeling a mixture of worry and frustration. She's waiting for Jake. He's thirty minutes late to pick her up for their date . . . again. *I should just call him and tell him the date is off! But what if he's been in an accident? I wish he'd just call me and let me know what's going on. If he gets here in one piece, I'm going to kill him. I don't think I mean very much to him if he can't pick me up on time or call. Maybe he's losing interest in me. I've gained a few pounds. I'm getting on a diet. That should keep his attention.*

Like Ashley, Lance, and his father, we Christians face a choice all day, every day. To whom will we turn to satisfy our hunger and thirst for love and respect? When we put people in God's place, we'll fear the significant people in our lives who may not meet our needs. We'll resent them when they fail to meet our needs. And people will fail us. The best father, mother, sister, brother, child, friend, or boss will fail us. It's impossible for a finite, fallen, self-centered person to meet the hunger and thirst that's designed for an infinite God. While the Bible affirms that "what a man desires is unfailing love" (Prov.

19:22), it also says, "Many a man claims to have unfailing love, but a faithful man who can find?" (Prov. 20:6). Only God loves with unfailing love. But without thinking about all this, we habitually try to pressure and manipulate broken, finite, people into satisfying the hunger and thirst in our souls. And in so doing, we sin against God just like Israel did:

> "My people have committed two sins:
> They have forsaken me,
>   the spring of living water,
> and have dug their own cisterns [wells],
>   broken cisterns that cannot hold water." (Jer. 2:13)

GOD'S RELENTLESS LOVE

So what does God do with us as we forsake him by chasing lies and delusions? Because he's so in love with us, his dearly loved children, he won't let our lies and broken cisterns work. If he did, we would grow arrogant, eventually forget God, and call this world home. *So God has graciously rigged life in such a way that anytime we're requiring people and created things to satisfy our hunger and thirst, those efforts will sooner or later be frustrated.* This frustration is a "severe mercy" from God.[15] Recall the curse God placed on the earth following the fall of Adam and Eve. For the woman, the curse involves relationships, especially with her husband (Gen. 3:16). Women will try but will not be able to find satisfaction for their longing for love in human relationships. They'll experience rejection and loneliness. For the man, the ground was put under a curse. It will bring painful toil and sweat as he tries to provide food from the soil (Gen. 3:17–19). Men's longings for competence will be frustrated by the "thorns and thistles" of life. They'll try but not be able to find lasting satisfaction through their work. They experience failure and inadequacy. These curses are meant to frustrate our idolatrous determination to find life/fulfillment in this world. Men and women *must* turn to God for the answer to their deep questions: Do I have what it takes? Am I loved? We'll only experience frustration and emptiness if we seek our answer from this world of created things.

But we're foolish and stubbornly determined to make this life work. We work to make human relationships and pleasant circumstances answer our deepest questions. When God frustrates our efforts, he is actually pursuing our hearts. God's good purpose is to turn our devotion back to a humble and grateful dependence on him alone for our deepest needs.

> "She [God's people, Israel] said, 'I will go after my lovers
>> [false gods], who give me my food and my water [life]. . . .'
> Therefore, I [God] will block her path with thornbushes;
>> I will wall her in so that she cannot find her way.
> She will chase after her lovers but not catch them. . . .
> Then she will say,
>> 'I will go back to my husband [God] as at first,
>> for then I was better off than now.'" (Hos. 2:5–7)

IT'S OKAY TO LAMENT

We legitimately hurt when people fail us, when friends betray us, when children disobey, when we sin, when life doesn't work. That's groaning. When we groan, God invites us to express our sorrow. That's called lament. Lament means voicing our pain and grief to God. Most of the psalms are lament psalms. They're written by godly people who wept deep tears.

> I am worn out from groaning;
>> all night long I flood my bed with weeping
>> and drench my couch with tears. (Ps. 6:6)

> My God, my God, why have you forsaken me?
>> Why are you so far from saving me,
>> so far from the words of my groaning? (Ps. 22:1)

The ability to cry and grieve is a gift from God. Lament is one of the most realistic expressions we can offer to God because suffering is so common in this fallen world. The human race experiences fear and abuse, loneliness, futility, homelessness, old age, abortion, poverty, corruption, conflict, human trafficking, failure, and more. Many people feel their lives are without purpose. Jeremiah, the prophet, once cursed the day he was born (Jer. 20:14–15). There is a lot of pain and groaning in our world because of the Fall. Until we acknowledge that, there's no need for the gospel. The Bible is realistic. It acknowledges the sorrows of life. The lament psalms give us language to express our groaning to God. Rather than grumbling against God, they guide us to come to him in trust and find hope in his goodness and greatness.

> O my God, I cry out by day, but you do not answer. . . .
> Yet you are enthroned as the Holy One;
>   you are the praise of Israel.
> In you our fathers put their trust. . . .
> You who fear the LORD, praise him! . . .
> For he has not despised or disdained
>   the suffering of the afflicted one. (Ps. 22:2–4, 23–24)

Lament is sorrow that is mixed with faith in God. God wants us to come to him honestly with our pain, to seek him and find him in the hour of trouble. But too often when we experience the pain of groaning, we doubt God's goodness. We go south and grumble against him. Grumbling is sorrow mixed with unbelief. Choosing to go north to God or to go south to the false gods of this world is a daily battle we must learn to face as we experience the pain of groaning.

QUESTIONS FOR SELF-EXAMINATION AND DISCUSSION

1. Which relationships and/or circumstances cause you the most frustration and why?
2. Identify two relationships or circumstances from which you try to get satisfaction for the hunger and thirst in your soul, for example:
   I need to get my husband to share his heart with me.
   I need my wife to be more sexually responsive to me.
   I need to get my boss to affirm me.
   I need to get my kids to do what I say.
3. While we may legitimately desire love and respect from the people mentioned above, they become our false gods when we *need* them to do something for us. Which of the questions in the lists below are you trying to get answered by the relationships you identified above?

Security	Significance
Am I desirable?	Do I have what it takes?
Am I wanted?	Am I important?
Am I loved?	Am I respected?
Am I cherished?	Do I matter?

4. Explain how God could be pursuing your heart's devotion for him by not allowing these two relationships to "work" the way you want them to.

5. What might God be saying to you right now as you reflect on these things?

6. What might you want to say to God as you reflect on all of this?

PART TWO

GOING SOUTH

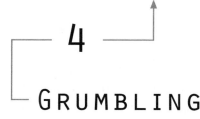

4

GRUMBLING

THE FIRST SIGN YOU'RE HEADED SOUTH

LISA

In the desert the whole community grumbled.
Exodus 16:2

As I stood washing dishes at the kitchen sink, I glanced out the window and across our tiny backyard to where I could see Gary on the ladder next to the garage with paintbrush in hand. It was gratifying to see what had been a chipped and peeling eyesore transforming into something clean and bright. Suddenly I noticed something else. The beautiful basket of bright pink *Impatiens* that I had so carefully chosen and hung from the eave of the garage was now on the ground next to the ladder, splotched with white paint.

My gratification over the painting project instantly turned to indignation. With barely a second's hesitation, I turned from the sink of dishes and marched, soapsuds flying, to confront my husband. Feeling justified in my cause, I let him know my disgust. "Look what you've done to my flowers! Why are you being so careless? Why don't you watch what you're doing?" I grabbed the planter and shot Gary a withering look.

Groaning, albeit minor, had intruded on my ordinary Saturday morning, and I went south in response to it. Choosing to turn toward God and to love my husband in the face of my disappointment did not even enter my mind. Instead, I wounded Gary with my harsh words, which were meant to shame

61

him. I felt unloved by his failure to take care of something I valued, and I wanted him to know it. I cared more about those flowers and what they represented in that moment than I did about my husband. Thankfully, the Lord has helped me over the years and continues to help me learn what it means to turn toward him in my groaning and to respond to such events with more patience and grace.

While we don't all react in the same manner, many of us, perhaps most of us, handle the groaning that comes into our lives with a similar knee-jerk reaction. Rarely do we stop to think about what's happening inside our hearts and to realize that we do have a choice about how we'll respond to people and situations that hurt, frustrate, or disappoint us. Perhaps that's why the Lord admonishes us through David: "Don't sin by letting anger control you. Think about it overnight and remain silent" (Ps. 4:4 NLT). Through the apostle Paul, God warns, "And 'don't sin by letting anger control you.' Don't let the sun go down while you are still angry, for anger gives a foothold to the devil" (Eph. 4:26–27 NLT).

The Scriptures teach us to think about our anger. With awareness and recognition of our emotions, we can become aware of turning south, away from God. For our purposes, we'll put all destructive emotions that arise in response to groaning in a general category called *grumbling*. Unrecognized and unchecked, grumbling will always lead to destructive behavior. Rightly understood, these emotions can tell us much about our heart's longings, our lies, and what we truly believe about God's relentless love. When we learn to tune in to our grumbling, we can become aware of when we are turning away from God in our response to groaning.

GOD'S PEOPLE BECAME GRUMBLERS

God's people have an amazing history of going south. Exodus 15–16 tells us the story of one such episode. Having just been delivered from four hundred years of slavery in Egypt and having witnessed firsthand the miracles of the Passover and the parting of the Red Sea, Israel is fresh off a celebration of God's love and faithfulness. Exodus 15 records a worship song expressing joy and confidence in God's power and provision. But only three days later, when Israel faced groaning in the form of thirst, God's faithfulness is forgotten: "For three days they traveled in the desert without finding water. When

they came to Marah, they could not drink its water because it was bitter.
. . . So the people grumbled against Moses, saying 'What are we to drink?'"
(Exod.15:22–24).

In spite of their grumbling and lack of faith, the Lord was patient and faithful to the Israelites. He miraculously turned the bitter water of Marah into
sweet, drinkable water and led them on to the oasis of Elim where they could
camp in the shade of palm trees and enjoy fresh water (Exod. 15:25–27). Still,
Israel's memory was short. Only a few weeks later, they found themselves in
the desert with little prospect of fresh food or water. This time, the whole community turned on Moses and Aaron: "If only we had died by the LORD's hand
in Egypt! There we sat around pots of meat and ate all the food we wanted,
but you have brought us out into this desert to starve this entire assembly to
death" (Exod. 16:3).

Again, God showed patience and mercy as he rained down manna and
quail to fill the stomachs of this faithless people (Exod. 16:11–17). Moses
made it clear that while Israel's grumbling was directed at Moses and Aaron,
it reflected a deeper reality. He said, "Who are we, that you should grumble
against us? . . . You are not grumbling against us, but against the LORD"
(Exod. 16:7–8). Anytime we descend into unchecked grumbling, we are ultimately questioning God's goodness and sovereignty. Israel's grumbling had
not only led them to accuse Moses and Aaron of unthinkable evil but even
more insidiously, in their hearts, to accuse God of the same. Grumbling is
the first evidence of stepping away from loving God and loving people in the
face of groaning. In fact, all grumbling left unexamined and unchecked will
result in damage to our relationship with God as well as our relationships with
people.

THE VALUE OF HUMAN EMOTIONS

In 1965, Duane Pearsall and Stanley Peterson invented the first battery-
powered smoke detector for home use. In a recent survey, 96 percent of homes
claimed to have at least one of these lifesaving devices. However, surveyors
also found that smoke alarms sounded in only half of the home fires reported
and that 65 percent of fire deaths occurred in homes with missing or disabled
smoke alarms.[1] So much sorrow and difficulty could have been avoided had an
alarm been kept ready to do its job and its warning heeded.

In the beginning, God created man with a similar built-in alarm system. When properly utilized, this system can alert us to the possibility that we are in danger of moving away from God—the same way a smoke alarm blares loudly to warn of a life-threatening fire. Like the smoke alarm that goes off in the middle of the night, emotions, properly understood, can warn us to escape the burning house of our own idolatry. Like many smoke alarms, however, at any given time this God-given alarm system has been either disabled or never used by a huge percentage of us.

Emotions are a valuable and important part of who we are as human beings. They are part of what it means to be made in the image of God. The Scriptures portray God as feeling all sorts of emotions—from joy and delight to anger and jealousy. While God's emotions are always pure, holy, and righteously motivated, ours have become tainted as a result of the Fall. Still, they can serve a redemptive purpose when we choose to use them to see what is in our hearts, instead of simply allowing them to control our behavior.

Sadly, many Christians have never been taught the value of emotional awareness. Some, if they are aware of experiencing difficult emotions, are concerned mainly with the proper expression of those feelings. Others have been taught that it is simply wrong for a Christian to feel difficult emotions such as anger, fear, jealousy, or worry, so they work hard to suppress those emotions. Still others are aware that these emotions control too much of their lives but have no idea how to use and tame them. Maturity in a fallen world, however, is not about living without troublesome emotions. It is learning first to understand what they are telling us about the deeper issues of our hearts. It is important to realize that these painful emotions are not *the* problem. *The lies that fuel the emotions are the real issue we must learn to face.* It is only in dealing with those lies that we will find freedom from being controlled by destructive emotions and freedom to respond to the groaning of life in ways that reflect movement toward God by loving him and others.

THE EMOTIONS OF GRUMBLING

The awareness of our emotions, or grumbling, in response to the groaning events of life is our first clue that we are going south and moving away from God and his purposes for us. Adding the category of grumbling to our diagram looks like this:

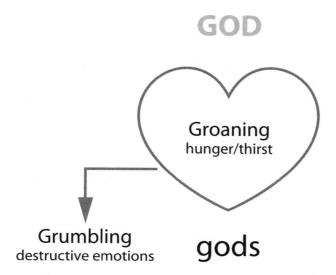

The first and most obvious emotional component of grumbling is anger. Of course, not all anger is movement away from God. There is righteous anger. It is good to be angry about sin and evil and the impact they have on people. There is truly something wrong with us if we don't feel angry about such things. But keep this in mind: righteous anger will always move us toward righteous behavior. It is always consistent with love for God and love for people. Therefore, any anger that gets in the way of a response that would glorify God and seek the best for others is grumbling anger. It is safe to say that given the pull of our fallen natures to go south, the anger we typically experience in response to groaning events of life is not righteously motivated. Even what starts out as righteous anger can go sour and turn to unrighteous anger if not carefully managed.

In Genesis 4, Cain experienced groaning in the form of critical feedback from the Lord. Both Cain and Abel had brought some of the fruit of their labor as a gift to the Lord. While Cain brought "some of his crops," Abel brought "the best of the firstborn lambs from his flock" (Gen. 4:3–4 NLT). The text goes on to tell us that the Lord accepted Abel's gift, but not Cain's. The inadequacy of his gift exposed, Cain immediately went south into grumbling. He got angry.

In Genesis 4:6, the Lord asks Cain two questions: "Why are you angry? Why is your face downcast?" Now when God asks someone a question, it isn't because he needs information he doesn't have. When God asks a question, it's always for the benefit of the person asked. Here, God was making Cain aware of his anger by speaking about it directly and calling attention to Cain's facial expression. He was asking Cain to do some self-examination, pointing out that sin was dangerously close to controlling him (v. 7). Of course the rest of the story exposes the fact that Cain did not stop and listen to the warning alarm of his emotion; he allowed his anger to control his behavior. The results were disastrous for both Abel and Cain.

Unexamined and unchecked anger is fertile soil for all sorts of self-centered behavior. Ephesians 4:26–27 tells us that anger that is unrecognized or not dealt with actually gives Satan a foothold in our lives. His mission is to kill, steal, and destroy all that is good (John 10:10). Clearly, Cain allowed Satan to gain a strong foothold in his life, which resulted in the murder of his brother. While few of us may resort to murder, we too can become unwitting servants of the Enemy. When we aren't aware of our anger, we can't use it for self-examination. Gordon MacDonald shared his experience:

> As a young pastor, I began to deny some of my emotions. It became less important for me to know how I was feeling and more important to deal with the emotions of others. . . . But my own emotions? I ignored them as much as possible.
>
> I suspect that this failure to respect and then to discipline my emotions . . . led me toward some midlife difficulties that could have been avoided. How many times I had read (and preached on) God's question to Cain, "Why is your face downcast? Why are you angry?"! I hear God saying to Cain, "Listen to your emotions; listen to your feelings! They're sending you a message. Now do something about it!"[2]

ANGER

The silence in the car was darker and colder than the winter night as Sam and Jennifer made their way home from the dinner party. Jennifer's habit of correcting the details of everything he talked about had Sam boiling inside. *Why does she have to do that to me? What does it matter if I don't get some insignificant details right? She just makes me look like a complete idiot in front of my friends.* Inwardly, Sam vowed that in the future he would keep his thoughts to himself if she were around. Back home, Sam took control of the remote and ignored Jennifer for the rest of the evening.

Josh lay facedown on his bed, pillow pulled over his head. Try as he might, he could not block out the memory of the looks on his coworkers' faces when he told them that the deal they had all worked so hard to put together had fallen through as a result of his mistake. *I'm such a worthless loser. I won't be surprised if they decide to fire me after this. Let's face it: nobody's ever going to want me working on their team after this stupid move.* There was just no point in getting out of bed.

Sarah jerked the video game controller from her fifteen-year-old son Ben's hands. "I've had enough of this!" she shouted as she threw the controller across the room. "You have no right to treat me like a slave and let me do all the work around here while you sit around and play games. Why can't you be more like your cousin Jon? At least he treats his mother with respect. Now get upstairs and clean your room—and don't even think about going out with your friends tonight because it isn't going to happen!"

What do Sam, Josh, and Sarah have in common? First, they're all experiencing groaning in some form. Life is just not working for them in the way they want it to. Sam's and Josh's inadequacies had been exposed. Sarah felt used and unappreciated. Second, they are each angry about it. They are going south. Sam's anger is taking the form of passive withdrawal, while Sarah attacks. Josh's anger is turning in on himself, and he is sliding down into depression. What is probably less obvious to each of them, and to us when we're angry, is the real reason for their anger. This point is extremely important to understand so we don't miss the message of our anger.

Most of us would blame our anger on the person or situation that we feel is responsible for our groaning. Sam would point to Jennifer. Sarah would point to her son. Josh would point to his own failure. What we don't realize is that this perspective puts other people and circumstances, or even our own inability to be perfect, in control of our emotions. And of course we cannot be held responsible for what we cannot control. But the Bible *does* hold us responsible for our anger: "Do not let the sun go down while you are still angry" (Eph. 4:26). This instruction implies that we have the ability to control our anger, which in turn implies that the source of our anger is internal rather than external. Grumbling anger points to something inside of our hearts that needs to be understood and corrected.

Grumbling anger reveals the lies we believe in our hearts. What we really believe often remains hidden from us until brought to the surface through the groaning of life. *We will always be controlled by what we really believe, even if we are not consciously aware of those beliefs.* In this sense, groaning is a blessing in that it exposes false beliefs and gives us the opportunity to align ourselves with the truth. Our emotional response to groaning is our lie detector and is meant to aid us in that process.

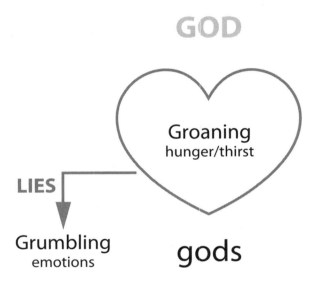

The first lie was introduced by the Serpent in the Garden of Eden and continues to be a stronghold in the lives of many of us today. In his beguiling style, the snake was able to convince Eve that fellowship with God and enjoyment of what he had provided for them in the Garden was simply not enough. Though God had freely given Adam and Eve the fruit of every tree in the Garden and withheld only the fruit of the Tree of the Knowledge of Good and Evil, Eve was convinced that she needed to have the one thing that had not been given to her. Trusting the Enemy's lies and doubting

God's goodness, Eve took control of getting that need met, and her husband followed suit. In doing so, they took the whole human race south with them.

Since that fateful day in the Garden, the human heart has been prone to believe lies. In fact, apart from God's intervention to reveal truth to us, it's impossible for us to believe otherwise. Like Eve in the Garden, we believe that there is something in this world that we *need* to be fulfilled and happy, to be significant and secure. When someone or something prevents us from having what we think we need, the inevitable emotional response is anger. You only have to observe normal two-year-olds who have their favorite playthings taken away to realize that this is not a learned response. Rather, it is the natural response of our fallen nature when our access to what we believe we need is blocked. This is what our anger tells us: *we are believing the lie that we need something other than God himself and what he chooses to provide for us in that moment.*

It's important for us to be able to identify specifically what we believe we need in order to recognize the lie, begin the process of needed repentance, and ultimately be set free to walk in the truth. Sam, in our earlier example, believed that he *needed* his wife not to make him look bad in front of his friends by correcting his mistakes. He believed he *needed* to look good to others. Josh believed that he always *needed* to perform like a winner and never make mistakes. Sarah believed she *needed* her son's cooperation and respect to be significant and secure. While it may be appropriate to address the sin of others for their sake, when we believe we need them to change for our own security and significance, we have crossed the line from legitimate desire to coveting.

Coveting is defined as believing we need something that God has chosen not to provide for us in the immediate moment. It often results in us feeling that we have the right to take or demand those things without giving much thought to the desires, feelings or needs of others. It's a word we don't often hear anymore, but perhaps we should, for the reality of coveting has never gone out of fashion in the fallen human heart. The Ten Commandments warn us against coveting our neighbor's possessions (Exod. 20:17), and James 4:1–3 explains that these excessive desires are the core reason for quarrels and fights even among believers.

> There is within the human heart a tough, fibrous root of fallen
> life whose nature is to possess, always to possess. It covets
> things with a deep and fierce passion. . . . God's gifts now
> take the place of God, and the whole course of nature is
> upset by the monstrous substitution.
>
> A. W. TOZER, *The Pursuit of God*

Truly, it is the gifts of God we have come to covet, to believe we need, in our time and in our way, for life to be what we want it to be. We have taken legitimate objects of *desire* and shifted them to the category of *needs*. We live self-centeredly to possess what we believe we need and react in anger toward others or ourselves when it doesn't come our way. The gifts from God that we may falsely believe we need include:

> I *need* to be loved/accepted/respected/liked/valued/honored by people.
> I *need* to have the cooperation of other people.
> I *need* to have people do things my way—the right way!
> I *need* to be seen as competent and successful/right.
> I *need* to have certain possessions.
> I *need* to have circumstances work out the way I want them to.
> I *need* to be treated fairly.
> I *need* to be able to perform up to my/others' expectations.
> I *need* financial security.
> I *need* physical health/beauty/abilities.
> I *need* _____.

Of course there are countless things and circumstances that could be placed in the blank after the word *need*. Whenever you find yourself grumbling, stop and ask yourself what you believe you need in that moment that is being denied you. Often these beliefs about our needs are multilayered. For example, Stacy came to counseling, struggling with a lot of frustration and anger toward her young children. As we peeled away the layers, we found that her anger revealed that she believed she *needed* her children's cooperation in keeping the house clean because she *needed* to prove to the world that she was competent. She *needed* the approval and acceptance of anyone who might come into her home.

Randy, on the other hand, believed he *needed* to impress his boss, because he *needed* to get a promotion, because he *needed* to make a certain income in order to prove to himself and others that he wasn't a loser. As a result, he was struggling with a lot of anger toward his wife, who objected to the long hours he felt he *needed* to be putting in at his job.

In most situations when we peel back all the layers of false beliefs, we eventually get down to our core beliefs about what will satisfy our needs for security and significance, love and respect. Stacy believed her security and significance as a woman was dependent upon her own ability to get others to see her as competent. Randy believed his security and significance was dependent upon being successful in his career. These were deep-seated lies that each of these individuals had to face and reject in order to begin to go north to God for those needs to be met and to respond to the people and circumstances of their lives in an authentically loving way. By listening to the message of their anger, both of these individuals, with honest, prayerful reflection, can know right away when they are being controlled by lies.

ANXIETY

Anger is not the only emotion that can reveal the lies we believe. Sometimes we get angry because we are first deeply afraid. Fear, or forms of fear such as anxiety or worry, can also tell us that we believe lies about what we need. Fear is a powerful emotion that can prompt us to make choices that we would not ordinarily make. The media and advertisers know this fact well and use it to their full advantage. If they can create fear, they can create and maintain an audience hungry for any tidbit of information that might be important to its health and well-being. They can also convince us to buy and use goods and services to keep ourselves from harm or avoid those things they claim have potential to bring us harm. The 2009 swine flu pandemic scare is an example of a media frenzy that had people flocking to buy masks and hand sanitizer, shutting down schools, and cancelling flights to Mexico. At this writing, the swine flu has turned out to be no more dangerous than the usual strains of flu we have each winter, which the media rarely report with such intensity.

Of course in the fallen world in which we live, there is always a place for legitimate concern and even fear that reflects our love for God and others and moves us to act in the best interest of others. Legitimate fear can help us take appropriate care of ourselves in the face of real and present danger. But a great deal of the anxiety and fear we experience in our day-to-day lives goes beyond what is legitimate and drives us to make choices to do and say things that reveal our lack of faith in God's ultimate provision and protection.

Anxiety is one of the most prevalent personal struggles that affect people's lives. Approximately twenty-five million Americans struggle with some form of anxiety disorder in any given year and as many as 25 percent of Americans will suffer from an anxiety disorder at some point in their lifetime.[3] Even if we don't have an actual anxiety disorder, many of us struggle with a level of fear or worry that robs us of peace and joy, threatens our physical health, and interferes with our relationships. The annual monetary cost for health care, medication, and decreased productivity related to anxiety is estimated to be upwards of sixty-five billion dollars per year.[4] Such high numbers reveal that even those of us who have peace with God through our belief in Christ may struggle to experience the "peace of God, which transcends all understanding" (Phil. 4:7). Though we may be trusting God in many areas of our lives, our anxiety and worry reveals that we likely remain captive to lies that we are unaware of.

The experience of fear was one of the first emotional impacts of the Fall. There is no reason to believe that Adam and Eve experienced anxiety of any kind prior to their act of disobedience. They walked with God and had full confidence in his provision and protection. But as soon as Adam ate from the forbidden tree and their eyes were opened, it was a different story. Adam and Eve then saw that they were naked, and they experienced shame. It seems that one of the most immediate effects of the Fall was that they both lost sight of the character of God even though they had experienced intimate fellowship with him. They no longer trusted in the relentless love of their Creator. Driven by fear, they trusted in their own ability to manage the situation by sewing together a few fig leaves and hiding in the bushes.

In the cool of the day, as the Lord walked in the Garden, he called to the man, "Where are you?" (Gen. 3:8–9). Obviously the all-knowing Lord of creation was not ignorant of Adam and Eve's location as they cowered behind the trees. The question was not one of physical location but was meant to expose the hearts of the wayward couple. An expanded version of the Lord's question might have gone something like this: "Where are you? Do you trust in me and my goodness right now or in yourself? Are you moving toward me or away from me, Adam and Eve?" This is the same question that God is asking each one of us when we experience anxiety, fear, or worry.

Fear, as well as anger, can reveal that we believe a lie about what we need in order to satisfy our longing to be secure and significant. While anger indicates that someone or something is stopping us from getting what we believe we need, fear or anxiety reveals that we may be unable to get or control what we believe we need. Benjamin Franklin once said that the only things certain in life are death and taxes.[5] If we're honest, we know this statement is true. Anything of this world that we depend on to meet our ultimate needs of significance and security is, at best, uncertain. Therefore, anyone whose security or significance is dependent on someone or something other than the loving faithfulness and sovereignty of God is subject to a lot of anxiety, worry, and fear. Such a person will be driven, almost reflexively, to control persons and circumstances.

While both men and women may struggle with anxiety and worry and the urge to control, women in particular seem to have a unique difficulty with this as it relates to their marriages and children. Perhaps the Lord was referring to this struggle when he told Eve that she would desire to control her husband (Gen. 3:16 NLT). The apostle Peter also alludes to this struggle as he instructs women on the inner beauty of a gentle and quiet spirit and urges them not to give way to fear (1 Peter 3:4–6). True inner beauty cannot be expressed when we are driven by anxiety and worry.

Fear clouds our perspective and influences our response to the people we love the most. Linda asked to meet me to discuss a situation with her husband that was bothering her. Over coffee, she recounted her story. Two days earlier, her husband, Chip, had come to her to let her know that an old high school girlfriend had contacted him via his Facebook page and had made some very inappropriate and suggestive advances toward him. Chip assured Linda that he had taken the appropriate steps of blocking this woman from contacting him in the future as well as talking with his men's accountability group about the situation. While she appreciated the steps that Chip had taken to be accountable to good men and letting her know what had happened, Linda found it difficult to be satisfied. Chip had, on the advice of his accountability partners, purposefully chosen not to share with Linda all the details of the content of the email he had received, because they believed this was in her best interest. Linda, however, felt an urge to know everything and continued to pepper Chip with questions about his relationship with this woman and what she had said to him. This was creating a good deal of tension between them and had left Chip feeling hurt and distrusted in spite of the effort he was making to be as forthright as possible.

"Is it okay that I want to know more details?" Linda asked me. Knowing that there was more going on below the surface than a simple yes or no answer would touch, I asked Linda to tell me what she was feeling when Chip came to her to tell her about this email. She immediately recounted his past addiction to pornography, which had also involved a good deal of dishonesty. Though Chip had long ago repented, submitted to accountability, and worked hard to rebuild trust in their relationship, the pornography issue had had a profound impact on Linda and their marriage. What Linda didn't realize was that her urge to know more was being driven by fear of being betrayed again. Her questions were an attempt to reduce her anxiety by gaining more information. When Chip resisted giving more, her anxiety grew, and she redoubled her efforts. While gaining more information may or may not have lessened her fears, it would have left untouched the deeper issues of the heart to which her anxiety was pointing and that needed to be addressed for her to respond to Chip with a gentle and quiet spirit.

"Where are you, Linda?" is the question God was asking in that moment. "Are you going north, moving toward me as you face this situation with Chip? What do you believe you need other than me and what I have chosen to provide for you right now? What do you trust in for your security right now?" For Linda, the answers revealed that what she really believed she needed was the *absolute assurance* that she would never be betrayed or hurt as she had been in the past. Linda's level of fear exposed the fact that, without realizing it, she had made her husband, Chip, her false god and the source of her security. While Chip's past struggles were a source of legitimate concern for Linda, her misplaced dependency caused her to focus mainly on getting him to relieve her fears. As a result, she thought little about how to love and encourage Chip in the situation.

Paula, too, was a woman driven by anxiety and worry. She was a victim of childhood sexual abuse, and tragically, years later, was abused again at the hands of someone she trusted. Legitimate anger and concern over the abuse had been twisted by lies into depression and anxiety that deeply affected Paula's life and relationships. As Paula's daughter Julie approached the age that Paula had been when she was first abused, Paula became more and more obsessed with protecting Julie from any potential harm. She kept a tight rein on all of Julie's activities and never allowed her to be home alone after school—the time of day when Paula herself had first been abused. Since all of this was happening at a time in Julie's life when she legitimately desired more freedom and independence, it created a great deal of friction between mother and daughter. Further, it created tension with other family members whose cooperation was needed to ensure Julie's protection.

Even though Paula had a relationship with God, practically speaking she lived as though he did not exist. Her fear indicated that her legitimate desire to protect her daughter from abuse had become a *need* that she depended upon herself and her family to provide. She could only feel secure if she could be certain that Julie would never experience the kind of groaning that she had known. As a result, she went way beyond the normal precautions and lived with constant anxiety. As Paula processed her own groaning experiences and embraced the truth of God's relentless love and power to redeem what others had meant for evil in her life, she was able to go north and respond to her daughter's desires for more freedom with wisdom and grace.

ENVY

Jealousy and envy, destructive emotions that are a combination of both anger and fear, are also evidence of grumbling. They too expose the belief that there is something we believe we need that someone else has or could take from us.

> When the victorious Israelite army was returning home after David had killed the Philistine, women from all the towns of Israel came out to meet King Saul. They sang and danced for joy with tambourines and cymbals. This was their song: "Saul has killed his thousands, and David his ten thousands!" This made Saul very angry. "What's this?" he said. "They credit David with ten thousands and me with only thousands. Next they'll be making him their king!" So from that time on Saul kept a jealous eye on David. (1 Sam. 18:6–9 NLT)

Saul was jealous of his position as king over Israel and greatly feared losing it to the popular David; thus, he attempted to murder him (1 Sam. 18:10–11). How easy for us, too, to go grumbling in envy and jealousy when someone else has the power, position, opportunities, finances, possessions, gifts, abilities, popularity, or relationships that we believe we need to really be happy. While our responses to others who have these things may be more subtle than Saul's toward David, they can be just as insidious. For example, we may think or speak slanderously of the people we envy or refuse to rejoice with any of the "Davids" in our life when they succeed.

I remember in high school being extremely jealous of a girl I'll call Mandy. She had a sweet and loving personality, was a popular cheerleader, and was well liked by everyone. She excelled at most anything she tried. I longed to be like her and have what she had. Lisa had her thousands, but Mandy had her ten thousands. Though, like everyone else, I liked and admired Mandy, my jealousy influenced the way I related to her. Once when I was paired up with her to work on a school project, I became a difficult and somewhat passive-aggressive partner to work with, dragging my feet and needing my ideas to be accepted and affirmed. It was a shameful and immature response that came from the lie that God and what he had provided for me wasn't enough. I needed to have what Mandy had, and she was potentially getting in the way of me having it.

SHAME

The focus of grumbling emotions is not always other people or outward circumstances. Sometimes we grumble against ourselves. We are not referring to the godly sorrow that comes as the result of conviction over real sin that leads to repentance, but to guilt, shame, and self-condemnation that gnaws away at the human soul and imprisons us in a self-focused world. It leads not toward repentance but toward self-destructive and relationally destructive ways of living.

As with anger and fear, such shame and guilt point to the fact that we believe a lie. We may believe the lie that we have not and cannot be forgiven for our sin, or we may be trusting in a false god for what we most deeply need to be significant and secure—and that god has failed us. Counselor Dan Allender wrote:

Shame arises when we feel deficient, yes. But far more, we feel deficient and ugly when the god we (covertly and at times unconsciously) worship lets us down and reveals the foolishness of our idolatrous trust. Shame is not primarily an experience of feeling bad or deficient as it is the exposure of foolish trust in a god who is not God.[6]

The Bible teaches us that shame is the inevitable result of idolatry: "But those who trust in idols, who say to images, 'You are our gods,' will be turned back in utter shame" (Isa. 42:17). Shame comes when we have failed to win the approval of our "god." If the Lord is our God, then we are freed from shame because we have his approval and acceptance—not based on our performance but upon the loving sacrifice of Jesus on our behalf. Any other god's judgment *is* based on performance. Those other gods may be self, parents, friends, employers, teachers, pastors, or community.

Several years ago I was involved in a minor traffic accident that was at least partially my fault. I felt intense shame as I drove around town with a mangled bumper for a few weeks before we were able to get it repaired. That bumper was evidence to the world of my failure. My pride was assaulted, and my imperfection was exposed. I see now that my shame was due in large part to my own idolatry. I believed that I needed my world to see me as competent. My security was dependent, not upon God's loving acceptance of me, but upon what other people thought of me. It was up to me to manage and control the opinions of others by my performance.

Shame exposes the belief that we need something from ourselves (often perfection) because we need the approval of others in order to be secure or significant. It is often related to our personal performance but can also be related to the performance of those we feel close ties with such as our children or spouse. We need, and therefore we *need them*, to be perfect, strong, wise, in control, on top of things, successful, attractive, and right. We need and *need them* to be smart enough never to be the victim of someone else's sin or failure. We need and *need them* to live up to our own expectations and what we perceive to be the expectations of others.

Our shame is even more intense when we believe our weakness or imperfections have been exposed to others. For this reason, many of us choose to hide from others behind masks of competence and control. Jason struggled with a deep sense of shame the day following his small-group meeting. For the first time he had allowed his small group to hear about the difficulties he was having at work and with his teenage daughter. Usually composed and confident, he began to weep as he talked. The compassion and concern expressed by the group overwhelmed his efforts to stay in control of his emotions. Even though the group encouraged him and appreciated being let into his struggles, Jason was haunted by guilt and shame over his weakness. He was strongly tempted to find an excuse to avoid the next group meeting. He wanted to retreat to the perceived safety of his false self and isolate himself from the community of believers. He was plagued with depression.

In *Deceived by Shame, Desired by God*, Cynthia Spell Humbert wrote:

> A false self is created as a cover-up from shame. If in the true self, I feel damaged and flawed, I need a false self, which appears to be acceptable. However, when a false self is adapted, I no longer exist as a genuine human being. . . . I become separated from the true person, the unique individual that God intended for me to become. Shame has destroyed the lives of many in this way. In fact, most emotional illness happens as the byproduct of a shame-filled life lived in the false self.[7]

Of course, the core problem here is not the false self or even the shame but, rather, the lies that provoke both of those.

Only as Jason took the time to listen to the message of his shame was he able to identify the lie that he believed: he needed to be seen by others as a man who is competent and in control in order to be acceptable and wanted. His father had modeled that to be a man was to never openly admit failure or weakness. This lie had shaped Jason's false self as well as his behavior toward his family and at work. As Jason repented from these lies and embraced the truth, he was able to enter into relationships in the freedom of God's love and acceptance. He was able to risk being honest about his failures. Over time, the need to maintain his false self was slowly replaced by a growing freedom to be honest about his failures in a way that helped others to feel accepted and safe as well.

WE MUST GET TO THE ROOT

Last summer I found an extremely large and prickly thistle growing in one of my flower beds. Donning my gardening gloves, I yanked and pulled. But alas, I only succeeded in breaking off the top of the plant. The root remained firmly in place. For a little while the garden appeared to be clear of the ugly weed, but within a few weeks the thistle was back, uglier and thornier than ever. Destructive emotions are a lot like that. They look and feel ugly, and we often work hard to get them out of the garden of our lives but without ever extracting the deep and hidden root that lies below. As a result, those emotions keep on returning and taking over more of our lives and leading us to say and do things that do not reflect Christlike character.

In order to deal with our grumbling emotions, it's imperative that we come to understand the belief system that's setting them off. When we begin to put words to the lies that we've believed, we're then able, with the power of God, to reject those lies and choose to believe the truth. As the apostle Peter said, "His [Jesus'] divine power has given us *everything we need* for life and godliness through our knowledge of him who called us by his own glory and goodness" (2 Peter 1:3, emphasis added). Since this is true, then no person or circumstance is really able to prevent us from having everything we need to be whole, secure, and loving people. Though there is much that we desire from this world and the people in it, their failure to come through for us does not condemn us to a life of insignificance or insecurity.

Of course, lurking behind the lies we believe about what we really need to be significant and secure, fulfilled and happy is the deadly sin of human pride. Pride supports and maintains the lies that our grumbling exposes. While on one level we may claim to be deceived by these lies, it's our pride that *wants* to believe them. Human pride will not tolerate groaning of any kind. It dictates and demands what we must have, what we need for relief. It demands to be in control of getting those needs met and always puts self first. Going south is, in and of itself, a function of pride at work. Lies are the servants of pride. In order to reject lies, we must also reject pride, and vice versa. As we surrender our pride to God, allowing him to determine what we need and when we need it and to supply as he sees fit, we root out lies that fuel our grumbling emotions. If we fail to engage in this process, our grumbling emotions will lead to harmful and destructive behavior designed to get control over people or circumstances. We call this behavior *grasping,* and it's the topic of our next chapter.

QUESTIONS FOR SELF-EXAMINATION AND DISCUSSION

1. How do you typically handle difficult emotions like anger, fear, worry, jealousy, guilt, or shame?

   I get busy or do something to distract myself from feeling them.

   I let those emotions control me and I react.

   I ask God to take those feelings away.

   I reflect and get to the root belief behind the emotion.

   I _____.

2. Think of a situation where you felt one of the emotions mentioned above. What were you believing you needed at that moment that God may not have provided?

3. How does pride make you hang on to that lie?

4. Do you believe that God has provided and will provide all that you really need for life and godliness? Why or why not?

5. How do you think it would affect your emotions if you were to move your answer to question 2 above from the category of need to the category of desire?

5

GRASPING

YOUR ATTEMPTS TO GAIN CONTROL

GARY

A man's own folly ruins his life,
yet his heart rages against the LORD.
Proverbs 19:3

Two men were rushed into an emergency room. The first man asked the doctors, "Can you give me something for the pain?" The second man asked, "What's wrong with me?" The first man wants *relief* from pain, while the second wants to *understand* what's wrong with him. The first question represents our typical response to suffering. We lurch into the emergency room of life and ask for painkillers *first*, and once they begin to work, pain loses its ability to instruct.

When you're struggling with the pain of life and you're going south into grumbling, which question do you tend to ask? Pursuing the answer to the first question, "How can I feel better?" makes us shallow and self-centered people who live for no higher purpose than feeling good. Seeking the answer to the second question, "What's wrong with me?" can take us on the journey to knowing God. Deep faith, hope, and love are forged in the fires of pain and adversity—not through a comfortable and pain-free life. So in this chapter, we'll continue to grapple with the question, "What's wrong with me?" In the next chapter, we'll begin to look at the solution to our problems. It's called *grace*.

GRUMBLING LEADS TO GRASPING

Previously, Lisa helped us understand the importance of emotions. Just as smoke detectors alert us to the danger of fire, our grumbling emotions—such as anger, worry, jealousy, shame, and self-hatred—alert us to the dangerous lies we believe, idolatrous lies about who or what can satisfy our heart's deepest longings. If left unchecked, grumbling always influences our behavior. We call those behaviors *grasping*. We're literally grasping for life from the false gods of this world. Grasping is anything we think, do, or say that's motivated by grumbling. Grasping can take many forms, but most can be categorized as either passive or aggressive.

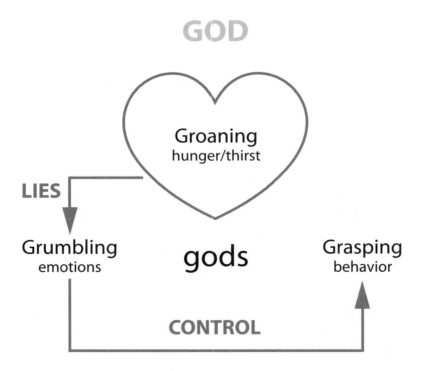

People who have a more *passive* style of grasping tend to seek control by stuffing their negative feelings. They avoid situations where they fear conflict, failure, or rejection. They work hard to comply to others' expectations in order to avoid rejection and gain acceptance. People with this passive style of grasping are often nice, thoughtful, accommodating, and easy to get along with. While such characteristics can be good, they are often mixed with self-centered motivations.

A friend of mine is passive. He grasps for control by excessively checking with his wife and others whenever he wants to make a decision. On the surface it appears he wants to please and respect others, but he's coming to see that his real motivation comes from a fearful demand that he never face the pain of disapproval and failure. He puts the responsibility of decision making on his wife. If the decision turns out to be a bad one, he can put some of the blame on her; after all, she approved it. He passively expresses his anger through procrastination, avoidance, excuses, and "forgetting." He reverts to these grasping behaviors instead of having the courage to be honest and forthright with others.

People who have a more *aggressive* style of grasping are quick to let others know their thoughts and feelings. These people are often in leadership positions. Their strength can be good; they keep leading when others would flee. But they can be prone to lead with a demand that others comply with their agenda. "It's my way or the highway." They stay in control by always being "right." They'll reject others before others can shame or reject them. People who aggressively grasp for control can be quite domineering. They're like steamrollers. At their worst, they can be verbally or physically abusive to people who stand in the way of getting what they want.

Some people are a combination of the two styles. They may be passive in public, grasping for the approval of others by being socially compliant, but at home they shift to being aggressive, demanding that their families give them the love and respect they want.

There are literally thousands of ways to grasp for control, but because it's driven by self-centered energy, all grasping behavior violates the command to love God and to love others. All grasping behavior communicates, "God is not enough to sustain me in the groaning of life. I must step outside his presence and provision and take control of what matters most to me."

Think of a time when you were angry (grumbling) at someone because they disappointed or hurt you. Maybe a parent criticized you in public, or a coworker frustrated you because of something they didn't do. Remember the time your spouse forgot your birthday or the time a friend left you waiting for hours? Take a minute and consider how your grumbling influenced the way you responded (your grasping behavior). Did you raise your voice and dump your frustrations on them? "Where have you been? Did you forget me again?" Or did you punish the person by withdrawing into a sulky silence? "No. I don't want to talk. Just leave me alone." Or maybe you gossiped about that person with your friends. What do you do when you're angry about the groaning and frustrations of life? Make no mistake. Grumbling, if left unchecked, will lead to grasping behavior. Let's unpack that statement a little more by looking at three examples from the lives of everyday Christians.

KERRIE

Kerrie was almost frantic with worry. *How am I going to get everything done?* she asked herself. She'd promised to bake cookies for her daughter's kindergarten class, bring dinner to a lady in her small group who was recovering from surgery, and visit her mother in the nursing home. Kerrie also needed time to prepare her lesson for the ladies Bible study. The pressure mounted. *Why do I do this to myself?* Then the phone rang.

Kerrie answered, "Hello."

"Hi Kerrie! This is Susan. How are you?"

"I'm doing just fine!" Kerrie replied in a buoyant and confident tone.

"Is this a bad time to talk?" Susan asked.

"Not at all," Kerrie said, feeling guilty for telling such blatant lies.

Susan went on. "Well, I have a favor to ask. I have to run a bunch of errands, and I wondered if I could drop my baby off at your place for an hour or so while I get things done. Are you busy right now?"

"No," Kerrie replied. "Drop Sarah off. I'll be glad to take care of her."

Susan was delighted, "Thank you so much! You're such a wonderful person! I'll be there in a few. Bye."

As Kerrie hung the phone up, she took a deep sigh, broke into tears, and screamed, "When is it going to be my turn?"

SCOTT AND DEBBIE

Scott arrived home from a business trip. He had one thing on his mind. That night he started rubbing Debbie's back.

"Don't" she said. "I'm not in the mood."

A shock wave of anger surged through Scott. "Fine!" he said. "Thanks for the *warm welcome* home." He turned his back to Debbie.

Debbie was furious. She shot darts back at Scott. "You're such a *jerk*. I can't believe how selfish you are! I've been taking care of three kids, paying bills, and holding down the house for nearly a week while you're off doing your dream job. And when you come home, there's not one question about how my sister's doing since her surgery yesterday or how I'm doing. It's always about Scott and his 'needs.' Well *I need* something more than that."

Scott cursed at Debbie, got out of bed, and slept on the sofa.

MASON

Mason's graphic design business was floundering. He couldn't sleep. He went to his computer to check his e-mail. He was supposed to hear from a client yesterday. *Is he going to sign that contract or not?* No e-mail. His father's words taunted him: *"You'll never make it on your own."* Feelings of shame, powerlessness, and failure flooded his soul. Just then, a picture of a beautiful woman shot up on his computer. "See all you want to see" danced back and forth on the pop-up. "She's looking for *you*," the caption read. Mason's finger hovered over the mouse. *One click to paradise.* Then he threw the mouse across the room. *No! That road takes me to hell.* He didn't want to have to tell Steve and Craig that he went there again. They cared enough to ask, and Mason wouldn't lie to them. It was a real friendship where they spoke the truth in love. Mason got up from his computer and paced through the house. *What am I going to do?* he asked himself as he gorged himself on his third bowl of Cinnamon Toast Crunch.

Let's take a look inside the souls of our everyday Christians to see how their grumbling leads to grasping.

KERRIE

Kerrie legitimately longs for acceptance, but she believes a lie. She believes she *needs* to meet everyone's expectations in order to gain people's acceptance and avoid their rejection. She's depending more on people than she is on God for her need to feel loved and wanted. Therefore, she's fearful of refusing people's requests. Kerrie's form of grumbling is *fear*. Her grumbling influences her behavior. Instead of resting in God's love, she fearfully grasps for people's acceptance by performing for them—she compulsively tries to please everyone.

SCOTT AND DEBBIE

Scott believes a lie. He believes he needs Debbie's compliance in order to feel like a man. He depends more on Debbie than he does on God for his need to feel adequate and respected. Therefore, Scott went south when Debbie refused to have sex. His grumbling—*rage*—led to his grasping behavior. He turned his back to Debbie, and his sarcastic comments were intended to make her feel guilty for not coming through for him. He cursed at her and slept on the sofa in order to punish her and make her feel abandoned.

Debbie felt very alone in her marriage. When Scott missed every opportunity to touch her loneliness by spending some quality time with her, his request for sex seemed like too much. Debbie believed a lie too. She believed that she needed Scott to love her well before she could respond to him. Therefore, Debbie went south into grumbling—*anger/resentment*—when she felt used, which influenced her grasping behavior. She spoke in a harsh tone with the intent of belittling Scott for not thinking of her needs.

MASON

Mason believes lies. He believes he needs his father's approval, and he believes he can get it by being successful as a graphic artist. Therefore, Mason feels shame and self-contempt when his hope of success is thwarted. In his grumbling—*fear, shame, and self-contempt*—he almost grasped for relief from his inner feelings of failure and inadequacy by clicking on the porn sight. Though he chose to say no to that temptation, he grasped for another temporary pain relief by gorging himself with food.

WHAT LIES BENEATH ALL GRASPING

What do Kerrie, Scott, Debbie, and Mason all have in common? What do we all have in common when we're going south into grumbling and grasping?

THIRSTY

We all want something. Kerrie longed for acceptance; Scott wanted to feel like a man through Debbie's warm, sexual responsiveness; Debbie wanted to feel loved and treasured by Scott instead of feeling used; Mason wanted his father's respect. At any given moment, whether we're aware of it or not, we're all thirsting for love and respect, acceptance and meaning. It's normal to long for love and respect. It's not immature to feel pain when we're sinned against or when our desires go unmet. That's all part of groaning.

FOOLISH

We're all thirsty but we're also foolish. Each person in our examples did not turn to God for their needs when they felt the sting of rejection and failure. Instead, they forgot God and went south into grumbling and grasping. Grumbling is very different than groaning. We legitimately groan, or hurt, when we experience the pain of unmet desire. But when we grumble, an alarm is going off telling us we have, in that moment, forsaken God as the source of our security. We're demanding that people, sex, food—you name it—make us feel good. We're making those things our gods. Instead of loving God and loving others, we're forsaking God and manipulating others. That's grasping, and that's tragic.

Jesus was God, yet he never considered his equality with God as something to be grasped or held on to. Instead, he humbled himself and made himself as nothing in order to save us (Phil. 2:5–11). But we who are "nothing" desperately try to be our own god through our grasping. Because our grasping is so pervasive and sometimes subtle, we often don't recognize it. Moreover, we easily justify ourselves when we do it: "Yeah, I shouldn't have cursed at Debbie, but do you realize how disrespectfully she spoke to me?" When we keep saying, "Yeah, but," we're using our pain to justify our sinful reactions. But someone's sin never justifies our sin. When we go south into grumbling and grasping, we're forsaking God and sinning against others.

FORGETFUL

Whenever we go south into grumbling and grasping, we're choosing to forget God in that moment. Whenever Mason chose to fantasize over pornography, he had to put God out of his mind. Retaining thoughts of God while looking at a naked woman would have provoked guilt and destroyed the pleasure he was seeking. Mason also had to forget what was dear to his heart—his wife and children. Mason, like all of us, literally had to suppress the truth of God in order to embrace sin (Rom. 1:25). Like a little child exerting strength to push an inflatable toy beneath the water, we exert strength to suppress and forget the knowledge of God when we go south and grumble and grasp for control. Sin always requires an active refusal to remember God. When we forget God in order to embrace sin, we also forget our purpose for living: to reveal the heart of God to this world by caring for people who groan.

GRASPING FOR CONTROL IS IDOLATRY

When we forsake God, we'll feel pressure to control what matters most to us. It will seem like everything rests on our shoulders to make life work and to make people give us the love and respect we're desperate for. When our car breaks down in the middle of nowhere, when people insult or disappoint us, or when our best efforts fail, we realize we're not in control. That threatens us. As if we're drowning, we panic and feel small, inadequate, alone. We don't like those feelings. When we forget God in those moments, our deepest commitment is to our own safety and emotional survival. Desperate to stay afloat, we succumb to the pressure of trying to regain control by manipulating people and circumstances.

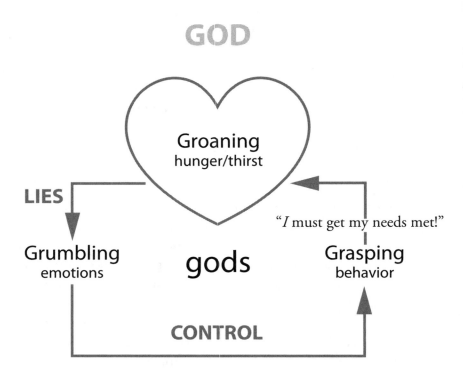

The invitation to relax and surrender to God when we feel small, poor, weak, and needy feels impractical, if not impossible, to a proud person who demands to be in control. Jean Vanier develops this thought:

> The problem is that we refuse to admit our weakness, our needs,
>   our poverty
> because we are frightened of rejection.
> We have been taught to be strong, to be "the best," to win
>   in order to become "someone."
> Since society tends to marginalize those who are weak
> we think that weakness means rejection.
> So we try to hide our poverty for as long as we can
> and to pretend that we are strong;
> we build up an appearance of being in control.[1]

In the days of the Old Testament, God's people often forsook the Lord by worshipping false gods. Israel often served Baal, the fertility god of the ancient Near East. Being the fertility god meant that Baal alone had the power to send the rain on your land and cause your crops and vineyards to grow. He could make your sheep, oxen, and chickens multiply like rabbits. Since the more crops and livestock you had, the wealthier you were, Baal was the big kahuna who could put you on the road to the "good life." And if for some reason Baal was ticked at you, he could turn the faucet off and stop the rain. He could dry things up and make everything you had wither and die. So if you bought into Baal worship, you wanted to know how to stay on his good side. That is, you wanted to know how you could control Baal so he would give you what you wanted.

To appease and please Baal, you had to visit one of his local temples, which were as common as McDonalds and Starbucks. But instead of being greeted by a smiling waiter or barista, you were greeted by a temple prostitute. Yep. Having sexual intercourse with the prostitute was supposed to excite and arouse Baal, and then his sperm—the rain—would fall to the ground and make your crops, vineyards, and herds grow and multiply. Since God's people were farmers and shepherds, they needed rain. Going to temple prostitutes to get on Baal's good side gave Israel a false sense of control. In so doing, Israel often forgot God and committed flagrant adultery against him. Some Israelites even became temple prostitutes. They wore the special clothes, earrings, and jewelry that all temple prostitutes wore in order to attract their "lovers" to the temple. Hosea was one of the Lord's prophets who exposed the willfulness of Israel's adulteries and prostitution with the hope of turning Israel back to God:

> "She [Israel] said, 'I'll run after other lovers
> and sell myself to them for food and water,
> for clothing of wool and linen,
> and for olive oil and drinks.' . . .
> "She put on her earrings and jewels
> and went out to look for her lovers
> but forgot all about me,"
> says the LORD. (Hos. 2:5, 13 NLT)

Kerrie, Scott, Debbie, and all of us are guilty of "putting on our earrings and jewels" and chasing after our lovers by trying to get control over people.

On the surface, who would fault Kerrie for all the nice things she did for her friends? But Kerrie feared being weak. If she couldn't be strong for everyone, she expected their rejection. That terrified her. She succumbed to the compulsive need to control what people thought of her since she depended more on them to quench her thirst for love and acceptance than she did on God. She put on her "earrings and jewels" of people-pleasing in order to attract "her lovers" to give her the "food and water" of love and acceptance. She tried to control what others thought of her by always appearing happy, competent, and able to meet everyone's expectations. She never asked for help. She was always the "giver." Everyone thought she was wonderful because they knew they could count on Kerrie if they needed something. That crumb of acceptance kept her going. In a small way, Kerrie's false gods worked, but the price was overwhelming.

Mason longed for his father's respect. Mason believed he could earn it if he was a successful graphic artist like his dad. Therefore, he worked ridiculous hours under great pressure to succeed. Mason was grasping for control of his dad's opinion of him. Dad's opinion became more important than God's and thus became a god Mason worshiped. When the pressure became overwhelming,

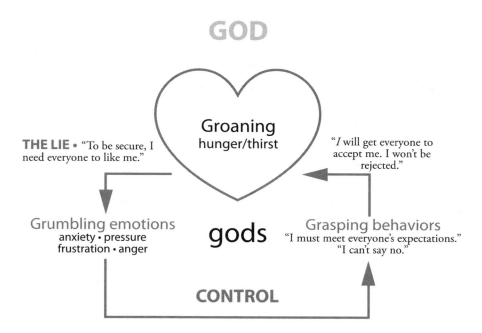

he grasped for comfort through pornography. Fantasy had been his magic carpet ride to a world where he was in control of all that happened. The woman in the picture saw Mason the way he wanted to be seen—no flaws, no failures, no incompetence. She was always smiling and fully responsive. Everything in his fantasy went exactly the way he wanted it to. There, Mason could feel like a man without needing to take the risk of being one. And when Mason stopped using porn to assuage his inner loneliness, he developed a new addiction to food.

FIVE WAYS WE GRASP FOR CONTROL

POWER

Grasping is about power. When we forget God, we believe the lie that we're in control of managing our own lives. Moreover, we believe the lie that we need people to give us our "food and water." Therefore, we seek power through various ways in order to manage and manipulate people and circumstances so they meet our needs and treat us the way we want. This kind of power wounds and destroys people, but it's so common that we're often blind to how and when we're doing it.

Consider the stereotypical CEO. He has no problem making decisions and telling people what he thinks or what they should do. He elevates task over people. Rather than serve others, he demands that others serve him. His words and actions say, "Just get it done or you're gone." King Herod was such a man. When he heard that the Magi from the East were looking for Jesus, the King of the Jews, Herod feared for his position as king. He believed he needed that position in order to be significant. Notice how Herod's grumbling—his terror and rage—influenced his grasping behavior:

> When word of their inquiry got to Herod, he was *terrified*. . . . Herod lost no time. . . . Herod then arranged a secret meeting with the scholars from the East. Pretending to be as devout as they were. . . . [Herod] said, "Go find this child. . . . As soon as you find him, send word and I'll join you at once in your worship." . . . In a dream, they [the scholars] were warned not to report back to Herod. . . . Herod, when he realized that the scholars had tricked him, flew into a *rage*. He commanded the murder of every little boy two years old and under who lived in Bethlehem and its surrounding hills. (Matt. 2:3–4, 7–8, 12, 16 MSG, emphasis added)

Anger can be used as a form of power to control people. What parent hasn't strong-armed a child with anger at some time? "If you don't stop crying, I'll give you something to cry about!" I've used the power of anger to get control. Just yesterday I was enjoying my early morning devotions along with a good cup of coffee. It was a peaceful time with Jesus. Then Mario, our cat, began whining at the front door just a few feet away. He wanted to go outside so he could eat grass and throw up on my carpet. Mario is very old. Most of his teeth are gone. He can't see. In fact, you have to put his nose in his food so he can find it. Mario's been neutered and declawed. He's kinda pathetic. Needless to say, he can't be outside without supervision.

Anyway, Mario wanted out, and I wanted peace and quiet. Our agendas clashed. I resorted to power to get control over Mario. I spoke in a loud tone of voice, "Mario! Be quiet!" He ran away. Peace was restored . . . for two minutes. Mario was back at the door, making deep and pathetic meowing noises. This time, I increased my power surge. I yelled louder and with a harsh tone.

"*Mario!* Be quiet!" He ignored me and kept meowing. Then I pulled out all the stops. I came out of my chair, chased him through the house, and threw a sofa pillow at him. Peace was restored through power. I went back to reading my devotional—*The Imitation of Christ*. (Please, no calls or e-mails from PETA. I've repented.)

Grasping for control over people is not funny. Our ungodly use of power comes in many forms: sarcasm, rage, physical and verbal abuse, shaming, intimidation, always being right, never admitting we're wrong, holding a grudge—the list goes on. Anything we do that uses force or intimidation to manipulate and control people is a misuse of power. It destroys people's dignity. It disrespects their freedom to choose. It's a violation of love and respect. We're driven by the same energy as King Herod.

PERFORMANCE

Since the Fall, everyone lives with a distorted view of God. Adam and Eve fled from God because they didn't trust in his grace. Like our first parents, Christians often believe God is holy but doubt he is good. Many Christians assume God's primary attitude toward them is disappointment, anger, or disgust due to their failures and sins. When we see God this way, we'll try to perform for God in order to earn his love. It's a form of Baal worship. We'll put on our earrings and jewels of performance in an attempt to appease or please God. We see God as a harsh and demanding taskmaster instead of our patient and loving husband (Hos. 2:16). David Benner commented:

> The central feature of any spiritual response to such a God will be an effort to earn his approval. Far from daring to relax in his presence, you will be vigilant to perform as well as you possibly can. The motive for any obedience you might offer will be fear rather than love, and there will be little genuine surrender. Surrender involves relaxing, and you must feel safe before you can relax. How could anyone ever expect to feel safe enough to relax in the presence of a God who is preoccupied with their shortcomings and failures?[2]

When we perform for God in order to earn his love, we're going south into grasping. We're trying to control God's opinion of us by our performance. We try to appease and please God with the expectation that God will bless our lives and make things go the way we want them to. When God doesn't do what we expect him to, we wrongly assume that he doesn't love us or that we need to work harder to make him happy.

Patrick's story is a good example of someone who tried to control God through performance:

> I found it easy to trust God when he blessed my business with increased profits and sales. But when the business struggled, I assumed God was punishing me for some sin I had committed or because I wasn't doing something right. I prayed for God's favor and tried to look into myself so I could find and fix the problem. Maybe I wasn't working hard enough; maybe I wasn't focused enough.
>
> This past quarter was the worst my business has ever had. As usual, I tried to figure out what I had done wrong to cause God to withhold his blessing. Why was God punishing me? I took inventory of all areas of my life. But all this was very confusing because for the past several months I had been walking closer to God than ever before. By God's grace, I had been growing in significant ways. Yet my business had its worst quarter. Money was tight. In the face of growing financial pressure, I was tempted to take matters into my own hands by handling these problems in the same way I did before I was a believer.
>
> Before I was a believer, on occasion I would charge personal expenses through my rental properties. If my house needed paint, I charged it through my rental properties. Over the past many years, I had not done this because the Holy Spirit convicted me of this sin. But with this recent bad quarter, the temptation to charge some personal expenses through my rental properties was stronger than ever.
>
> My battle with temptation raged until I told my accountability partner about my struggles. He said that sometimes God does discipline us through painful events like a bad quarter, but we can't assume that is always the reason for such things. Just because life goes bad, doesn't mean we did something wrong. He talked about a man in the Bible whose name was Job. God allowed everything to be taken

away from Job—not because Job had sinned but because God loved and trusted Job to stay faithful no matter what the circumstances (Job 1–2). Then God showed me my real sin. I was not trusting in God when things got difficult. Since I saw this, I have found new energy to follow God. I *want* to trust him, and I *want* to tell him I love him by staying faithful to him no matter what happens.

Most people work harder at performing for people than they do for God. Because we see and relate to people every day, we tend to give them more power to define us than God, whom we can't see. People can say nice things to us and make us feel good about ourselves. They can applaud our good deeds like Susan did for Kerrie: "You're such a wonderful person!" We like that feeling, and we work hard to perform for people so they'll give us more. "The tongue has the power of life and death" (Prov. 18:21). Indeed. When people bless us with their words and deeds, it can feel like life.

People can also wound us with "death" words. Kerrie, for example, grew up with an alcoholic father. During her childhood, she felt like she was always walking in a minefield when her dad was drunk. Anytime she made a wrong step such as dropping a dish or talking too loud, her father exploded in rage. His abusive words tore through her soul like hot shrapnel. "You're such a worthless, clumsy kid!" From an early age, Kerrie felt so afraid of her father's angry and shaming words that she succumbed to the pressure of performance. Who could blame that little girl? She worked hard to be a good girl with the hope of appeasing and pleasing her dad. She made every effort to do things right and to never say no to his requests. Kerrie never deserved her dad's abuse. Yet she grew up as a fear-driven perfectionist and a people-pleaser in order to gain approval and avoid rejection.

In one way or another, we all try to be in control of our lives by performing for God and people instead of freely loving them from our heart. Performing is significantly different from loving or being responsible. True love wants to give because we know we are dearly loved by Jesus, and therefore we want to bless others. When we love, we know our limitations and can draw appropriate boundaries. We're secure enough in God's love to be able to say yes and no to people's requests. On the other hand, when we perform, we hide behind masks of what we think people want us to be because we're grasping for their love, approval, and acceptance instead of resting in God's; we're giving people more power than God in defining who we are.

Needing to be good at something—athletics, academics, career, music performance—in order to prove our worth is another way we perform. We're putting on our earrings and jewelry when we use those gifs and talents to impress people for the purpose of gaining their applause or avoiding their rejection. Jesus said when we do our good deeds with the motivation of being seen and admired by people, we have received our reward in full (Matt. 6:1–2).

Furthermore, when we perform to gain the applause of people, we'll be jealous of those who outperform us. When the people sang about Saul slaying his thousands and David his tens of thousands in battle, Saul was instantly jealous of David's success. He saw David as the competition. Saul's jealous grumbling drove him to grasp for control by attempting to take out the competition—ultimately trying to kill David (1 Sam. 18:6–11). There will always be a "David" in our lives. There will always be someone who can do what we do better. And like Saul, if we're worshipping the god of self and people's applause, we'll be jealous of those people who outshine us. Our jealousy will lead to acts of punishment. We'll look for their flaws and faults in order to make ourselves look better. Instead of rejoicing with the Davids in our life, we'll fear, hate, and envy them.

PUNISHMENT

No matter how hard we work to get people to meet our needs, sooner or later they'll fail. It's inevitable. People are finite and fallen. Moreover, God won't let our false gods work for long. He wants to use their failure to drive us to him. But when our use of power and performing fail to work, we often resort to punishment.

People who fear conflict will commonly punish others by emotional withdrawal. They hide or "stuff" their thoughts and feelings behind a self-protective wall of silence. They can literally be smiling on the outside and furious on the inside. Stuffers are usually nice people, but they tend to be fearful of ever speaking the truth. Yet even if they stuff and hide their anger, their anger always finds a way to punish the one they're angry with:

1. Passive-aggressive behavior: "Oh, I'm sorry for not helping you. I didn't see you carrying those groceries in from the car."

2. Forgetting: "I didn't mean to keep you waiting, I just forgot." Forgetting is an especially subtle means of punishment.

3. Sarcasm: "Oh come on. I was only joking." Sarcasm punishes through shame.

4. Physical and emotional isolation. We avoid people we're angry with by spending hours watching TV, playing video games, engaging in a hobby, or just staying in another room. Abandoning a relationship altogether is an extreme form of this.

5. Suicide. In the worst case scenario, feeling hopeless and helpless of ever getting people to respond to their needs, stuffers seek to punish their loved ones by leaving them with feelings of confusion, guilt, sorrow, and unanswered questions.

"Dumpers," unlike stuffers, punish people by lashing back when they're hurt and angry. Instead of stuffing their thoughts and feelings, they tend to dump them out on others.[3] A typical comment from a dumper could sound like this: "Why don't you ever talk to me! I'm getting sick and tired of this marriage!" Screaming, slamming doors, putting a fist through the wall, breaking or throwing things are obvious behavioral attempts to control and intimidate people by letting them know they've let you down. Like a bull in a china shop, the dumper can do a lot of emotional damage with words and actions. While dumpers often pride themselves in being able to speak the truth, they typically do so with zero love. In the worst case scenario, dumpers may resort to punishing others by physical abuse or even homicide.

POSSESSIONS

A billboard featuring the face of Kermit the Frog read: "He eats insects. He dates a pig. He's a Hollywood star—live your dream." We all have dreams. We dream of who we want to be, how we want to live, and how we want others to perceive us. Hollywood, TV, and marketing companies know how to capture, even create, our dreams. They bombard us with advertising for the right medication, vacation package, body image, automobile, and cell phone to make our dreams come true. In our broken culture—where people's value is often assessed by their earning power, the prestige of their occupation, the size of their home, their physical appearance, possessions, and education instead of the fact that they've been created in the image of God—discontent is bred. People grasp for a sense of security or significance by what they have or by trying to impress people with their possessions.

PLEASURES

We try to deny our inner pain and desperate need for God through addictive behaviors. Whether we realize it or not, we're all addicted to something. Anything we compulsively grasp for is a form of addiction. I'm tempted to live for people's affirmation instead of trusting in God's. Others are addicted to popularity, ministry, work, money, power, beauty, clothes, TV, video gaming, sex, grades, food, or gambling. . . . The gods of this world are legion. I recently heard a woman on television say, "Whenever I feel rejected or abandoned, I go shopping!" Her closets and drawers were jammed with clothing, makeup, and trinkets. Her addiction to shopping was her way of coping with the pain of groaning. But these addictions only offer temporary relief. When we grasp for life from created things, sooner or later, we'll be left with greater emptiness. As Jeremiah says, they are "*broken* cisterns that *cannot hold* water" (2:13, emphasis added). Nothing created can ever satisfy us; we were made for God alone.

> Dear children, keep away from anything that might take God's place in your hearts.
>
> 1 JOHN 5:21 NLT

THE CONSEQUENCES OF OUR GRASPING

Does grasping relieve our groaning? Sometimes. But sooner or later it will always increase our groaning. Grasping has consequences. Passivity and avoidance of problems usually leads to bigger problems that can't be avoided. Compulsive shopping, to big debt. Compulsive eating, to obesity and health issues. Refusing to pay our bills, to phone calls from collection agencies. Though we avoid the pain of rejection by being compliant and never saying no to people, our stress levels go off the charts from increased pressure and responsibility. Those who use power to get others to meet their needs often end up alone and rejected as others resent and avoid them. Many men and women live under the crushing weight of secret sins. The more they use illicit sex, pornography, drugs, or alcohol to ease their groaning, the more their guilt, shame, and loneliness eats them alive. And a fear of being found out constantly haunts them. As the psalmist says, "The sorrows of those will increase who run after other gods" (Ps. 16:4).

Tragically, grasping causes conflict and destroys relationships. I believe that was Satan's ultimate intention when he tempted Eve to grasp for control in the Garden.

One of my counseling opportunities was with a couple named Steve and Carol. They're born-again Christians, but they're destroying their marriage. It was my first counseling session with them. Carol shared first.

"I just can't talk to Steve!" Carol said as she cried angry tears. "Every time I tell him how alone I feel, he just gets angry and defensive. He tells me to stop nagging him. But if I don't nag, he'll just work late, watch TV, or play video games till two o'clock in the morning. I feel invisible . . . like thin air! He doesn't touch me, talk to me, or notice I'm around. I've tried being nice. I've tried talking, praying, yelling. *Nothing* gets through to him! Nothing ever changes. I can't stand it any longer!"

Then Steve spoke up. "It's true. . . . I don't talk to Carol. I avoid the problems in our marriage. She probably does feel alone." Then, with rage in his eyes, he said, "But can anyone blame me for not talking to her? Just listen to her. *That's* what I get all day long! Anytime I try to talk, she just criticizes me—tells me what I'm doing wrong. You'd think I'm the laziest loser of a husband in the world. If just one time, and I mean it, *one time*, Carol would affirm how hard I work to provide for this family, I might feel like talking. But do I ever hear a 'thank-you'? *Never!* I don't want a divorce, but I don't know how I can go on in a marriage like this."

When we're struggling with conflict, the book of James is helpful. James asks us a crucial question: "What *causes* fights and quarrels among you?" (James 4:1, emphasis added). Steve believed Carol's negativity and lack of respect was the cause of their fights. Carol believed Steve's passivity and rejection was the source of their quarrels. It's so easy to assume the cause is "out there." We typically and habitually believe the person who hurts us is the cause of our fights. But the book of James won't let us shift blame onto others. It continues. "What causes fights and quarrels among you? Don't they come from your desires that battle within you? You want something but don't get it"

(James 4:1–2). James is clear. The cause of my fights and quarrels come from the desires that battle within me. I want something, but I can't get it so I fight, kick, and scream. What did Steve and Carol want? What do we all want when we're fighting?

Carol legitimately longed for Steve's love. She wanted to feel cherished by him. She longed for his protective, spiritual leadership. And Steve legitimately wanted Carol's respect. He wanted her to appreciate who he was and all he did for the family, instead of just pointing out his failures. While these desires are legitimate, James gets to the heart of the problem when we're grasping for them from each other: "You want something [love and respect, for example] but don't get it [painful groaning]. You kill and covet [you go south into grumbling and grasping for what you want]" (James 4:2).

When the book of James says we kill each other, it's referring to unrighteous anger. Jesus said that anger is like murder (Matt. 5:21–22). And the apostle John wrote, "Anyone who hates his brother is a murderer" (1 John 3:15). When James says we covet, it means we're lusting after something, demanding something. Steve and Carol didn't just desire love and respect from one another; they demanded it. They lusted for it. As a result of their coveting, they were breaking the tenth commandment: "You shall not covet." Consequently, they were also breaking the first commandment: "You shall have no other gods before me." Moreover, they were breaking the sixth commandment ("You shall not murder") by killing each other and destroying their marriage with anger. They were actually doing the work of Satan. With these thoughts, and after compassionately acknowledging what they each longed for from the other, I asked Steve and Carol a question.

"Steve and Carol," I began, "you both *desire* love and respect. That's good. We all legitimately desire those things. But when you're not getting the love and respect you want from each other, how often, in those moments of conflict, do you turn to God and pray?"

They both said, "Never." They were convicted and saddened as they realized they never turned to God for the desires of their hearts. Just as James says, "You do not have, because you do not ask God" (4:2). It's like Steve and Carol were walking past God and grabbing each other by the throat, screaming, "Give me life! Give me love and respect!"

Larry Crabb has likened such an approach to marriage as a tick-on-a-dog relationship.[4] A tick has one central purpose in life—to suck the lifeblood out of another creature. When two people, such as Steve and Carol or you and me, approach marriage or any relationship with the primary purpose of getting life from one another, we have a tick-on-a-dog relationship. The problem, of course, is there are two ticks with no dog!

Conflict that's caused by grasping certainly isn't confined to marriage. When we approach any relationship like a tick, conflict is inevitable. Shannon B. Rainey, for example, described how fights and quarrels developed in her singles group:

> Most of us women were interested in being treated as special by the single men in our fellowship. The "desires that battled within us" for love and enjoyment of relationships were natural and God-given. After all, there was nothing wrong with wanting to be chosen. But what we often did with our desires was utterly selfish.
>
> When we couldn't rejoice with an engaged friend, when we bickered in meetings to have the upper hand in planning social events, and when we griped about how wimpy the men were because they didn't ask us out, our desires were anything but warmly inviting. Instead, we were consumed with self-centered energy that ignited anger and jealousy, distanced the men, and alienated the women into competitive factions.
>
> When we tired of the "fights and quarrels among us," we'd go through stages of denying our desires, hiding our jealousy, and disguising our anger behind an exasperated façade of thinking, *Men! Who needs them anyway?!*
>
> Ultimately the motives underlying our desires were self-seeking. When we did not get our way, we wore our anger in its various guises, with no real concern for how we could encourage our brothers or rejoice with our sisters who were dating frequently.[5]

Anger is easier to feel than sorrow. Anger gives us a false sense of power. Feeling our disappointment can make us more aware of our dependence on God, but that feels weak and helpless. Proud people would rather grumble and grasp for the illusion of control instead of humbly trusting and surrendering their needs to God.

GRASPING FORMS A FIST IN GOD'S FACE

There may be many times when we do turn to God and pray in the midst of conflict. Yet God doesn't seem to answer. Why? The book of James continues. "When you ask, you do not receive, because you ask with wrong motives, that you may spend what you get on your pleasures" (4:3). The Greek word used for *pleasures* is the same word we use for *hedonism*. Often when we pray for God's help in the midst of our grumbling and grasping, we're saying something like this: "God, please make my false gods work! Change them so they'll give me the love and respect I *need* and covet from them!" Steve and Carol were making one another their gods. James then exposes the heart of the issue: "You adulterous people, don't you know that friendship with the world is hatred toward God? Anyone who chooses to be a friend of the world becomes an enemy of God" (v. 4).

When we grasp for life from people or things, we're making friends with the world. In that moment, we're showing hatred for God. We've become his enemy. Jesus said we can't serve two masters. We'll love one and hate the other (Matt. 6:24).

When our hand grasps onto something, it forms into a fist. When we grasp onto the world, we're forming a fist in God's face. Grasping behavior says to God, "Who you are and all you've provided for me isn't enough! I need that person to give me what I need!" We are, as the books of Hosea, Jeremiah, and James say, adulterous people! We are whoring after other gods.

When we, with the convicting help of the Holy Spirit, humble ourselves and take a hard look at the idolatrous lies we believe, evidenced by our grumbling emotions and grasping behaviors, we begin to see how ugly and self-centered we are. We see how we're trying to control and manipulate people and circumstances through power, performance, punishment, possessions, and pleasures instead of trusting in God for our heart's deepest longings. When we honestly face ourselves, we see how we habitually live for ourselves and the avoidance of groaning. And we hurt people in the process. We're stunned to silence by how rarely we think about the fears, wounds, and longings of others who groan. We try to suck the life out of one another. In so doing, we wound and destroy people we should love. We have their blood on our hands. Our self-centeredness is worthy of God's severest judgment. The Lord laments:

My people have forgotten me,
days without number.
How skilled you are at pursuing love!
Even the worst of women can learn from your ways.
On your clothes men find
the lifeblood of the innocent poor. (Jer. 2:32–34)

WOUNDING GOD'S FAME AMONG THE NATIONS

Why does it ultimately matter if we go north or south? What's at stake when we're grumbling and grasping? From Genesis to Revelation, God has one central purpose for creating you and me: it's all about his glory. John Piper has eloquently said:

> The created universe is all about glory. The deepest longing of the human heart and the deepest meaning of heaven and earth are summed up in this: the glory of God. The universe was made to show it, and we were made to see it and savor it. Nothing less will do. Which is why the world is as disordered and as dysfunctional as it is. We have exchanged the glory of God for other things (Rom. 1:23).[6]

The root meaning for the Hebrew word *glory* means "heavy" or "weighty." God's glory contains the *full weight* of all his attributes. The Lord wants to draw all men and women to himself by revealing his glory. We're naturally drawn to beauty, and we'll be drawn to God when we see his glory. Nothing so glorifies his greatness and goodness as when we love him with all our hearts and when we love each other in tender, sacrificial community. We glorify God when we say with our life, "Nothing is more gloriously satisfying than God!" Being contented in God, rather than coveting created things, says that the Lord is a good and satisfying God. As image bearers of God, our true significance is experienced when we enhance God's fame by setting our heart's affections on him as the one true love and treasure of our lives. Furthermore, we make God famous when we gladly and humbly love and serve one another from our heart.

God chose Israel to be his treasured people. One purpose for doing that was to spread his fame among the nations. As Israel made God the blazing center of their lives and lived in lavish, tenderhearted devotion and harmony with each other, the surrounding nations would be drawn to the goodness and greatness of God. Israel's visible lifestyle would draw everyone's attention to the invisible God.

But Israel failed. The Lord says, "They profaned my holy name" (Ezek. 36:20). Because of Israel's self-centered lifestyle and adultery with foreign gods, God seemed ordinary and even worthless to an onlooking world. There was nothing in Israel's lifestyle that elevated God's name above the false gods of their day. The Hebrew word *profane* can also mean "to wound."[7] Israel wounded God's reputation among the nations as they exploited one another and went whoring after other gods.

We too have profaned and wounded God's fame as we've gone whoring after our false gods. Too often we've grumbled and grasped for life from people and things. We suppress the truth and glory of God through our unrighteousness whenever we demand that people give us love and respect. Too many times I've demanded that Lisa or my kids or friends or colleagues give me life by treating me the way I demand to be treated. I covet and kill when I do that. I'm an idolater and a murderer when I want anything more than God. I commit sin of the worst kind because I'm saying in my heart and through my behavior, "There's something more glorious and essential to my well-being than God."

Today, too many Christians are going south into grasping for life by engaging in sexual perversions, promiscuity, and affairs. Too many of our marriages are embroiled in bitter conflict and ending in divorce. Too many husbands abuse their wives; too many of our churches fight and split over personal preferences instead of biblical truth; too many pastors seek relief from their groaning through pornography; too many Christians gossip against their neighbor and harbor an unforgiving spirit; too many are killing their unborn children through abortion. All of us, in our own ways, have done too much to profane and wound the name of God in our homes, our neighborhoods, and among the nations. When we, by the Holy Spirit's work, begin to see the depths of our sin, the damage it has done to God's reputation, and how it wounds others, we begin to see that what we deserve is the wrath and judgment of a holy God. We deserve eternal hell. It's then we realize that our greatest need is not for people to change and treat us better. What we need most is God's undeserved forgiveness that comes by his amazing grace.

QUESTIONS FOR SELF-EXAMINATION AND DISCUSSION

1. Describe three ways you grasp for control. What do you think, do, or say? Be specific.

2. How are these behaviors trying to gain control over people or circumstances in order to get what you want such as love or respect (or to avoid what you don't want—such as rejection)?

3. How does your behavior negatively impact or hurt people? Our sin always has an impact on others (example: withdrawing our heart's involvement from people has an impact on them whether they're fully aware of it or not). Try to imagine what people experience from your grumbling emotions and grasping behaviors.

4. How often do you sincerely consider what others experience from you, instead of what you experience from others?

5. How is this sin against God and others? That is, how does your grasping violate the double-love command of loving God and loving others?

6. Think of a time when you went south and embraced something you knew was sin. What was your relationship with God like in that moment?

7. Do any of these questions provoke godly sorrow in you or do you tend to feel justified in doing what you do? What other responses are you aware of?

PART THREE

GOING NORTH

6

GRACE

THE POWER TO TURN NORTH

GARY

Your worst days are never so bad that you are beyond the reach of God's grace.
And your best days are never so good that you are beyond the need of God's grace.
Jerry Bridges, *The Discipline of Grace*

Palm branches sway and dance, bending toward the ground. Howling wind blows down as the chopper hovers over the landing zone. Three men jump to the ground. Unloading their gear, they shout goodbyes over the deafening noise of the aircraft. The chopper roars and lifts away. Its noise fades to silence as it disappears into the morning sky. The men stand in the jungle in search of local tribesmen who have never heard the gospel. Moments pass. Then the jungle's silence is shaken by beating drums and blood-chilling screams. The tribesmen have found the missionaries. A hundred terror-stricken natives cautiously step into the clearing, brandishing spears and shields. The tribesmen believe the men have come to kill them.

If you were one of those three men, what would you most want the tribesmen to know about you? I'd want them to know I am good. I've come to love them—not to harm them. I believe that's what God wants us to know when he exposes the idolatry beneath our grumbling and grasping. Though we deserve death for the ways we've defamed his name, God doesn't want to condemn us; he wants to convict us. He convicts us because he loves us. He wants us to confess our sin and helplessness so we can experience his life-changing grace. Nothing has the power to change our sinful, fear-stricken hearts like an encounter with God's loving-kindness.

JUSTICE OR GRACE

Steve's parents were gone for the evening so we hung out at his house that Friday night. Steve and I were friends in middle school. We were bored and looked for something to do.

Steve opened the doors of his dad's liquor cabinet. "Take what you want but don't tell anyone who gave it to you."

I wondered what it would be like to get drunk as I took a quart of Canadian Club whiskey. The next day I found out.

Days later I was at home when the phone rang. "Gary!" my mom shouted over the blaring music of Jimi Hendrix as she knocked on my bedroom door. "The phone's for you!"

I went to the kitchen and answered the call. "Hello?"

A middle-aged man replied, "Hello. Is this Gary Heim?" He spoke in a serious and deliberate tone of voice.

"Yes it is." I wondered why this stranger was calling me.

"My name is Mr. Johnson. I'm Steve's father. I understand you took something from my house last Friday that belonged to me. Do you know what I'm talking about, Gary?" My heart pounded with terror. Steve's dad was a big attorney in town. I knew I was caught.

"Yes, sir. I know what you're talking about."

Steve's dad went on. "I want you to come to my office tomorrow. I want to talk about what you need to do to make this right."

The next day I sat in Mr. Johnson's office. He began the conversation. "Do you know you could go to jail for what you did? You're only fourteen years old, but I could have you arrested for stealing and possession of alcohol!" As Steve's dad lectured me, I was ashamed and speechless. It was like an out-of-body experience. Mr. Johnson continued. "I'm giving you twenty-four hours to tell your parents what you've done. I want them to call me. If I don't hear from them, I'm calling the police."

I wasted no time. My parents made the call to Steve's dad.

Now, Steve's dad would have acted justly had he turned me over to the police. Justice is getting what we deserve when we do wrong. Mr. Johnson didn't turn me in, and I'm grateful.

Grace is getting what we don't deserve when we do wrong. When I walked into Mr. Johnson's office, I braced myself for anger, rejection, punishment. I didn't expect kindness. But when I've blown it and someone does respond with kindness, my heart softens. My defenses relax. Experiencing the grace of God's kindness in the face of our sin is the beginning of real change.

Imagine that Steve's dad had confronted me with what I did and then said, "Gary, I'm not sure why you took that whisky, but there's one thing of which I am sure. I care about you. When I was your age, I did the same kind of thing. But someone cared enough about me to help me find something better in life than drinking. I want to pass that on to you too. But first, let's get a burger and some fries at McDonald's so we can get acquainted. I want to be your friend."

THE LIFE-CHANGING POWER OF GRACE

Steve's dad didn't offer me grace like that, but a few years later, someone else did. Before that happened, however, my problems got worse. My drinking led to smoking pot, which eventually led me to doing LSD. In those days, I often came home drunk, stoned, or high. I was arrested three times for possession of alcohol. My mom was frantic. She worked hard to change me by grounding me, lecturing me, crying, praying, screaming, and everything else a parent could do. But the more she tried to control me and turn me to God, the more I hated her. One day one of Mom's sisters said to her, "Jan, you've got to stop trying to control Gary. You've got to surrender him to God." My mom loved God and she loved me. She listened to her sister.

In the midst of all the chaos, our pastor, Daryl Kraft, at Sunrise Chapel in Plymouth, Indiana, reached out to me. Daryl knew about my drinking, drugs, and anger. He knew I was a mess, but Daryl wasn't shaken by that. He befriended me. He was kind to me. He gave me an IQ test and told me I was smart. I could hardly believe it. His time and interest told me I mattered to him. He was a living example of God's grace. My fist at God relaxed, and my heart began to open. One Saturday night when I was out with my friends, I took a double hit of Yellow Microdot (LSD). During that "high," I saw how self-centered and ugly I was. It seemed like I was covered with filth. For weeks following, I struggled with guilt for the way I was living and for how I was hurting my mom.

One Sunday morning, Daryl was preaching. He explained how Jesus Christ died on the cross for our sin. "For God so loved the world that he gave his one and only Son, that whoever believes in him shall not perish but have eternal life" (John 3:16). I'd heard it a thousand times, but that morning God opened my heart. I was hearing it again for the *first* time. I saw how my hatred, drugs, and alcohol were sins against Jesus Christ, God's Son. I was trying to find happiness without him. I deserved his wrath. Yet I could see that Jesus loved me. His heart overflowed with kindness for me. Tears streamed down my face. Jesus died for *me*. He wanted friendship with *me*, right where I was.

I was haunted by Jesus for days. I couldn't wait any longer. I told my mom I wanted to talk with Pastor Daryl. Her jaw dropped to the ground. That was the last thing she expected to hear. We drove to the church, and I found Daryl. There I stood—long hair, black leather jacket, strung out on drugs, and reeking with cigarette smoke. "I want to ask Jesus to forgive me," I said. "I want him to be the leader of my life." I think Daryl's jaw dropped to the ground. God's grace is so full of surprises. Daryl and I knelt down and prayed together,

"God, I've sinned against you," I said. "I've hurt a lot of people. I ask for your forgiveness. I do believe Jesus died on the cross for my sins so I wouldn't have to be condemned to hell. Please forgive me and come into my heart, Jesus. I want you to be my leader."

I walked out of that church forgiven. I was head over heels in love with Jesus. I asked for my mom's forgiveness, and our relationship was healed. I was so ecstatic about Jesus that I couldn't help but tell my friends about him. I was passing out Bibles left and right at my high school. Several of my friends believed in Jesus too. We formed a Bible study. Many friends came; others thought I had flipped out on acid. But I knew I had experienced the life-changing power of God's saving grace. I was moving north for the first time in my life.

THE HEART OF CHRISTIANITY

Grace and forgiveness are at the heart of Christianity. While God has every right to condemn us to hell for the ways we go south into grumbling and grasping, he longs to forgive us. The Bible says, "The wrath of God is being

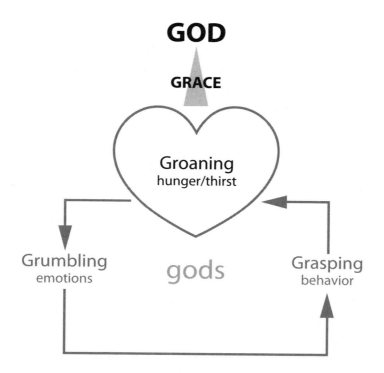

revealed from heaven against all the godlessness and wickedness of men who suppress the truth by their wickedness. . . . But God demonstrates his own love for us in this: While we were still sinners, Christ died for us" (Rom. 1:18; 5:8). Jesus died so we could have a soul-stirring, life-changing, love relationship with him. Thank you, Jesus! And that's the reason God gave us the Bible:

> The Bible is not an end in itself, but a means to bring men to an intimate and satisfying knowledge of God, that they may enter into Him, that they may delight in His Presence, may taste and know the inner sweetness of the very God Himself in the core and center of their hearts. . . . The continuous and unembarrassed interchange of love and thought between God and the soul of the redeemed man is the throbbing heart of New Testament religion.[1]

Through God's free gift of salvation, offered by God's grace, we *immediately* go from being God's enemies to being his friends and dearly loved children

(Rom. 5:10; Eph. 2:1–5; 5:1). Think about that. We're God's dearly loved children. We belong to his family, the church. We're no longer on the outside looking in. We're accepted, known, and loved. We are, to use Jesus' terminology, spiritually born again (John 3:3–8). The Spirit of God comes into our hearts, and from deep within we cry, "Abba, Father," meaning "Daddy" (Rom. 8:15). But this rebirth is only the beginning. Just as new parents dream about the tender love relationship they'll have with their baby through each stage of life, God dreams about the intimate relationship he longs to have with you and me through each stage of our lives.

> Only two things have ever changed the human soul:
> the fall and grace.
>
> LARRY CRABB, *Connecting*

But as cute as babies can be, they poop their diapers and scream through the night. They want what they want when they want it. Neediness and demands characterize babies when they experience the pain of unmet needs. Babies simply don't care about the impact they're having on their parents. They're self-absorbed. They quickly and habitually go south when they groan. Many Christians live like babies when they experience pain and frustration. We so quickly and habitually grumble and grasp for whatever we believe we need from people, while ignoring the impact we're having on them. Every day we're in great need of God's grace.

God wants so much more for us. He wants to help us grow up into maturity. Maturity doesn't mean we'll have it all together or never need forgiveness again. Jesus said the greatest in the kingdom is like a little child (Matt. 18:4). Children are needy, and they're always dependent on someone to provide for their needs. Like children, we all have struggles. To struggle well, we have to admit our neediness and then learn how to find contentment in Jesus Christ alone. That's, in part, what it means to be mature.

THE TREASURE OF YOUR HEART

Finding our contentment in God alone isn't easy. As long as we live in this fallen world, we'll struggle with disappointment, frustration, lies, and self-centeredness. Hopefully you're seeing some of the lies you believe and the specific ways they take you south. The ability to resist the allure of those lies will not happen by just trying harder to stop going south. It comes by growing our heart's affections for Jesus Christ. As our affections grow stronger for Jesus, we'll find the desire and will to say no to other competing affections. Those lesser affections may always nag at us, but they'll lose their attraction and power to take us south as we make Jesus the treasure of our heart. We'll start saying, "Sneak a peek at pornography? Gossip behind my friend's back? No. I don't want to do that. Jesus loves me and I love him. I *want* to stay faithful to him."

My friend Dan Lokers says, "When we understand how much Jesus treasures us, we'll treasure him." Like stoking the coals of a fire helps increase the intensity of that fire, stoking the coals of our heart's affections for God is the pathway to increasing our intensity of love for Jesus—thereby helping us to resist our attraction to false gods.

Joe, for example, sincerely says he wants to make God first in his life. Yet deep down he believes the lie that becoming the president of a large bank will satisfy his need to feel significant. Therefore, Joe *wants* to spend his life energy at the office. Working early and staying late feels more like a "get to." If the treasure of Joe's heart is defined by impressing people with his power and position at work, taking time for devotions with God and being in a small group at his church will feel more like a "have to." His heart will not be in it. It's not what he treasures. Trying to discipline himself to do things like devotions will not last, or if it does, it won't produce spiritual fruit.

Joyce is a different story. She was in a troubled marriage and habitually went south whenever her husband failed to love her. When she and I talked together, she felt hope as she began to see how she was grasping for life from her husband, Bill, instead of turning to Jesus for her heart's deepest longings. She gave me an example of how she had caught herself doing that. She had recently shared some exciting news with Bill: she had been accepted into a nursing program. But as she talked, she noticed Bill's blank and passionless stare. As usual, he was checked out. His lack of interest in her dreams felt like a bucket of cold water in her face. She instantly went south into rage and vowed to herself that she'd never tell him anything that mattered to her again.

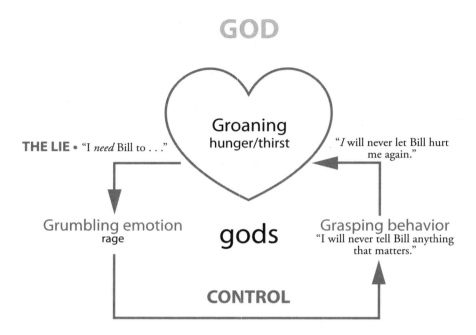

But this time, Joyce caught herself going south. She admitted she was furious. She remembered that grumbling was a signal telling her she believed a lie. She asked the Holy Spirit to help her put words to the lie that fueled her rage as she listened to her self-talk. Joyce came to see that she believed she *needed* Bill to show interest in her dreams in order to make her feel loved and not alone. She realized that her vow to never tell Bill anything that mattered to her was her grasping behavior. Her motive was to punish Bill. She also wanted to be in control to prevent getting hurt again, instead of entrusting her deepest longings to God. She saw that Bill's rejection was being used by God to reveal her lies. She saw how God was pursuing her through Bill's lack of responsiveness. As Joyce acknowledged and repented from the lies and embraced the truth of Christ's unfailing love for her, she realized she was taking new steps toward wholehearted devotion to Jesus. While Bill's continued lack of passion still hurt, she saw how God was using that pain to help her turn to Jesus and say, "You are with me, Jesus. You love me. You are all I need to be secure as a woman." Indeed, Jesus was becoming the true lover of her soul who was enabling her to be less fearful and angry at Bill's failure to meet her needs. Loving God and loving Bill felt a little more like a "get to" than a "have to."

Just like Joe and Joyce, we will pursue what we believe will satisfy our longing for love and meaning. Blaise Pascal has well said:

> All men seek happiness. There are no exceptions. However different the means they may employ, they all strive towards this goal. . . . The will never takes the least step except to that end. This is the motive of every act of every man, including those who go and hang themselves.[2]

Pascal echoed the words of Jesus, "Where your treasure is, there your heart will be also" (Matt. 6:21). What do you treasure deep in your heart? Treasure is what people think will make them happy. Jesus likened his kingdom to treasure. "The kingdom of heaven is like treasure hidden in a field. When a man found it, he hid it again, and then in his joy went and sold all he had and bought that field" (Matt. 13:44). When we understand in our hearts as well as our heads that God is the greatest soul-stirring treasure we can have, pursuing God will feel more like a "get to" than a "have to." It is *in his joy* that the man in Jesus' parable went and sold all he had.

At this point, you might be feeling guilty, thinking something like, *I don't treasure Jesus like that. I don't know how to get there. I'm more aware of wanting my marriage to work than I want God. I'm such a failure. Does God hate me?* Guilt is the last thing we want to put on you. God loves us right where we are, not where we should be. God is for us, not against us (Rom. 8:31). He wants to help each of us take our next step toward treasuring him no matter how far away that seems. Trust him. He'll take you one step at a time if you want him to.

How can we stoke the affections of our heart for Jesus so we'll *want* to go north and choose God in the frustrations of life? How can pursing God feel more like a "get to" than a "have to"? *We will only follow God to the degree we believe he is good.* Children don't need to be told to eat what tastes good. Once they've tasted it, they want more. Once we taste and see that God is good, we'll want more.

TASTE AND SEE THAT THE LORD IS GOOD!

God is a living person. Theologically we know this, yet we relate to God as if he were just an idea or set of principles and rules to follow. But the Bible is clear. Jesus can be known just as any person can be known: "*Taste and see* that the LORD is good" (Ps. 34:8, emphasis added); "My sheep *hear* My voice" (John 10:27 NKJV, emphasis added). David again wrote, "I have *seen* you in the sanctuary and *beheld* your power and your glory" (Ps. 63:2, emphasis added). And Paul said, "I pray also that the *eyes of your heart* may be enlightened" (Eph. 1:18, emphasis added). These and other passages speak of the spiritual senses through which we can know and personally experience God. God walked and talked with Adam and Eve in the Garden. God's grace and forgiveness have paved the way for us to have an intimate, heart-throbbing love relationship with him (Heb. 10:19–22).

The biggest obstacle to tasting and seeing that God is good is our foolish assumption that it's all up to us to make it happen. We so naturally try to live the Christian life in our own power that we don't realize we're doing it. When we fail and go south, we just keep trying harder to do the right thing. We berate ourselves and work harder to stop grumbling and grasping. We think thoughts such as, *I'm grumbling. Stop doing that!* Or, *I'm trying to get their approval again. Cut that out! I don't need their approval.* But we keep failing. We get discouraged and give up. Good grief. Who wants to live in this kind of cycle? While growth is most often a slow process, we'll never know God by just trying harder. But relinquishing self-effort comes hard because by nature we're proud and self-reliant. We hate feeling powerless and dependent.

The apostle Paul wrote, "Live by the Spirit, and you will not gratify the desires of the sinful nature" (Gal. 5:16). "Living by the Spirit" sounds so mysterious that we tend to gloss over Paul's words. Or we assume that living by the Spirit means praying, having devotions, and trying to please God by doing what he tells us to do. We feel pretty good about ourselves when we manage to check those things off our Christian to-do list, and we feel a chronic, low-grade sense of guilt when we keep failing. Please tell me there's more to the Christian life.

Yes, the Christian life does involve prayer, Bible study, and hard choices to stay faithful in tough times, but those things will not bear fruit. Christianity is not defined by choices but by affections. While true love for God is demonstrated by our obedience to what he tells us to do (Deut. 6–8; John 14:15), we make choices based on what we love and hold as our supreme value. We will always choose what we value most. Many psalmists have expressed their affections for God and his Word.

I *delight* to do Your will, O my God,
And Your law is within my *heart*.
(Ps. 40:8 NKJV, emphasis added)

Whom have I in heaven but you?
I desire you more than anything on earth.
(Ps. 73:25 NLT, emphasis added)

I'm ecstatic over what you say [God's law],
like one who strikes it rich.
(Ps. 119:162 MSG)

That's Christianity. That's heart change. That's heart-throbbing, belly-laughing, knee-slapping relationship with God. God wants the affections of our hearts, not just our good behavior. When God says of his people, "They honor me with their lips, but their hearts are far from me" (Isa. 29:13 NLT), he's saying that they're doing all the right things, but they're just going through the motions. He doesn't have their hearts. When rules and doing right things takes priority over personal, intimate relationship with God, we're committing the soul-deadening sin of legalism.

Good behavior is not enough. In fact, learning to walk by the Spirit will bring us to the painful awareness that we're powerless to change our hearts or even make ourselves want God. These are all gifts given to us by God's grace.

OH, WHAT A MISERABLE PERSON I AM!

When Paul tried to live the Christian life by trying harder to live up to God's expectations, he ended up saying, "Oh, what a miserable person I am!" (Rom. 7:24 NLT). This is the confession of a broken, helpless man. He's come to the end of himself. "I've tried everything, and nothing helps. I'm at the end of my rope. Is there no one who can do anything for me?" (Rom. 7:24 MSG). I suggest reading Romans 7 before you read the next paragraph.

Paul was a born-again Christian. He said, "I love God's law with all my heart" (Rom. 7:22 NLT). No one loves God's law unless the Spirit of God lives in him or her. Though Paul loved God's law, he was locked in a bitter struggle. He sincerely wanted to obey God and live north, but he kept failing and going south. He lamented, "I want to do what is right, but I don't do it. Instead, I do what I hate" (Rom. 7:15 NLT). Ever been there? Paul, like most of us, was trying hard to please God by his own efforts, but he kept failing. Examining the Romans 7:6–25 passage, Andrew Murray commented:

> The man is wrestling and struggling to fulfill God's law. . . . You will find the little words, *I*, *me*, and *my*, occur more than forty times. It is the regenerate "I" in its impotence, seeking to obey the law without being filled with the Spirit. This is the experience of almost every saint. . . .
>
> *God allows that failure that the regenerate man should be taught his own utter impotence.*[3]

This is a painful but crucial lesson in learning how to live north by God's enabling grace. Nearly every person I've known who has come to see the lies they believe and the ways they go south into grumbling and grasping has tried to stop their southward spiral through their own efforts. A man's self-talk may go like this: "Taking another look at that woman is grasping for relief from your loneliness. That's sin, you idiot. Stop doing that. Stop doing that . . ." He keeps failing, and he keeps trying harder—only to fail again and again. Some people eventually quit trying and live for something other than God. Others face the end of themselves and see how God is leading them to a day-by-day dependence on him for their ability to change. Life really is all about fostering a personal, loving relationship with Jesus.

I'm grateful when people I'm counseling gain insight into their struggles and really want to change. But real change, genuine love for God and love for others, will never happen until they realize they're powerless to change themselves. We can't stop going south without humbly and intentionally turning to God for help in our helplessness.

When the apostle Paul faced his utter helplessness to stop going south into sin, he cried out, "Oh, what a miserable person I am! Who will free me from this life that is dominated by sin and death?" (Rom. 7:24 NLT). Notice that Paul didn't go on to say, "I need more insight into my problems!" (Of course insight can be very important.) Paul didn't say, "I need more principles or steps to follow in order to stop sinning!" Nope. Paul realized he needed a real, living person to help him change! Paul needed Jesus, not more self-help. Paul is ecstatic when he says, "Thank God! The answer is in *Jesus Christ our Lord*" (Rom. 7:25 NLT, emphasis added). I too want to shout, "Thank you, Jesus! Thank you for making this all about a growing love affair with you, rather than a set of expectations to measure up to."

The Bible says that God resists the proud but gives grace, or unmerited favor, to the humble (James 4:6). Trying to earn God's love by doing everything right will never work. But when we turn to God for help, we will find his grace. Jesus is our lifeline to living north. By the grace of God, we begin to taste and see that the Lord is good. In God's time and way, he reveals himself to our hearts through the Word of God, the Spirit of God, and the people of God as we stay open to him. Rather than doing good things in order to earn his love, we discover that trusting God loves us is what pleases him. Our heart's affections are stirred. We begin to relax as we trust in his love. Then what we "ought to do" starts to feel a little more like a "get to." I *want* to read my Bible because through it I hear from Jesus. I want to obey God because he's good. I want to meet with spiritual friends so we can help each other stoke the fire of our heart's affections for Jesus.

HUMILITY AND HONESTY

Learning how to go north and choose God in the groaning of life begins with humility. The Bible says, "The first step in learning is bowing down to GOD" (Prov. 1:7 MSG). Pride takes us south; humility takes us north. Humility is the gateway into God's enabling grace. Ellen Vaughn elaborated:

> Pride isolates people from one another and from God. It is, as C. S. Lewis put it, the "anti-God" state of mind. It is mutually exclusive with gratitude, for cultivating a thankful heart is not about autonomy, self-sufficiency, and self-congratulation, but dependence and thanks to Another. . . . Gratitude to God is the manifestation of the fact that we rely on Him and trust Him, whatever comes. And it requires that we acknowledge we have needs, needs only He can fill.[4]

Therefore, God is irresistibly drawn to the weak, broken, and humble in spirit. Isaiah said:

> For this is what the high and lofty One says—
>   he who lives forever, whose name is holy:
> "I live in a high and holy place,
>   but also with him who is contrite and lowly in spirit,
> to revive the spirit of the lowly
>   and to revive the heart of the contrite." (Isa. 57:15)

Can you hear God's good heart in those words? He is kind and gentle with broken, fallen, struggling, sinful people. He wants to help us.

No matter how lost, confused, or sinful we may be, God favors us when we humble ourselves and tell him about all our weaknesses, failures, and need for his help. Hosea the prophet calls us to humbly trust in God's grace:

> Bring your confessions, and return to the LORD.
>   Say to him,
> "Forgive all our sins and graciously receive us,
>   so that we may offer you praises. . . .
> Never again will we say to the idols we have made,
>   'You are our gods.'
> No, in you alone
>   do the orphans find mercy." (Hos. 14:2–3 NLT)

C. J. Mahaney has well said that humility gets God's attention. Humility draws the gaze of our Sovereign God.

> God is decisively drawn to humility. The person who is humble is the one who draws God's attention, and in this sense, drawing His attention means also attracting His grace—His unmerited kindness. . . .
>
> What a promise! . . . "God . . . gives grace to the humble" (James 4:6). Contrary to popular and false belief, it's not "those who help themselves" whom God helps; it's those who *humble* themselves.[5]

We humble ourselves when we invite God and others to evaluate our lives in the light of God's truth and holiness. Honesty means facing the truth about ourselves and others—the bad and the good. We humble ourselves when we face and grieve the brokenness of this fallen world. We are all fallen, finite, broken people.

Our longing for love and respect is legitimate. Yet it's in those tender places of our hearts that we've been disappointed by one another. For many, facing and feeling this pain does not come easy. Proverbs 19:22 says, "What a man desires is unfailing love; better to be poor than a liar." We don't like being poor. We refuse to be poor when we believe our parents, pastors, or any human being has loved us unconditionally or with unfailing love. Proverbs again says, "Many a man claims to have unfailing love, but a faithful man who can find?" (Prov. 20:6). That's not to say our pastors and parents, friends and colleagues, haven't deeply and meaningfully loved us. I deeply love my wife and children, and they love me. But becoming poor, rather than being a liar, means facing the painful reality that no one—no matter how good they may be—has ever loved us with *unfailing* love. We're all self-centered people. The best parents, whether intentionally or unintentionally, have significantly sinned against their children. In this world no one loves us the way we want to be loved. We are lonely. Facing and mourning this painful truth is important. Jesus said, "Blessed are those who mourn, for they will be comforted" (Matt. 5:4). We'll either demand comfort from people by manipulating love from them, or we'll see our desperate need to trust in the one and only God who loves us with unfailing love.

Humbling ourselves also means facing and mourning our sinful responses to those who have not loved us well. We must grieve the ways we go south and hurt people when they disappoint us. We need to explore and learn how we specifically go south. What are the "buttons" that cause you to go south? Is it when people criticize you, correct you, mock you, disagree with you, ignore you, or fail to affirm you? What causes you to grumble? How do you specifically grasp for control?

We are truly victims in this fallen world. People sin against us. We groan. Face it. Feel it. Don't minimize it. But we easily use our pain to justify our sinful reactions. Just a harsh tone or glaring look from someone can cause us to go into a southward spiral for hours if not days. We keep record of what they've done, rehearsing it over and over. We nurse our bitterness. Honestly knowing and facing ourselves means we take full responsibility for what we choose to do with God: Do we turn to him or forsake him? We are also in charge of our response to the person who wronged us: Do we choose to grasp or forgive? When we remove our excuses and stop all our blame shifting, we're left naked and undone before a holy God. Either we cast ourselves on his amazing grace, or we harden our hearts and remain alone in our sin as we keep trying to justify ourselves.

We humble ourselves when we ask God and others to help us face the painful impact our self-centeredness has on people. Face it. feel it. Don't minimize it. Put yourself in their shoes. What do they experience when they relate to you? What do people long for from you that you rarely give? How often do you think about that? How often are you saddened over their pain instead of just feeling your own?

Louie Konopka, our senior pastor, often says, "The greatest day in your life is the day you face yourself. It's then you can experience God's grace." When he preaches, he often shares his own failures and struggles. Through his life and example, he invites us to honestly and humbly face ourselves.

While reflecting on Matthew 5:21–22, Haddon Robinson shared a snapshot from his life when he faced himself as a murderer:

My mother died when I was a boy, and my dad raised me. . . .

When he got older, he came to live with us. He became senile and began to lose track of time. . . . He was a child, and I became a parent to him.

One day we were home, and he wanted to go outside. I got him ready; but it was a cold day, and he quickly came back inside. Then he went out and came back in again. After about the third time out and in, I became very irritated. . . .

He wanted to go out again, but he had no sooner gotten out than he knocked on the door. I was furious. . . . He stood there in the door and didn't go either way, so I hauled off and swatted him. I could have punched him in the mouth, knocked him to the ground. . . . At that moment I could have killed him.

It is a horrible memory because of the ugliness inside me that day. . . . We can excuse my behavior and say, "Old people get that way; they can be irritating." The truth is, I had a flash—the flash of a murderer.

What happens when we truly see our lives? If we wash it from our minds, we travel alone in our self-righteousness. If we have a sense of bankruptcy, that poverty of spirit, we throw ourselves at His feet and cry out for mercy and forgiveness.

We all need the grace of a forgiving God. Those who understand this make it into the kingdom. As Samuel Rutherford said, "Bow low, man, bow low, the door into the kingdom is low."[6]

Face the truth: life is broken. We're all broken. God's grace will never be amazing until we face how much we need it.

LOCKED DOORS

Life is difficult. We experience disappointment, loneliness, failure. What will help us hear Jesus' lavish invitation to come to him when we feel like giving up?

One of my greatest mentors, Larry Crabb, tells a story that's given me a picture of what it looks like to turn north to Jesus when I'm overwhelmed by life's problems. When Larry was about three years old, he got locked in the bathroom. Thinking he was trapped inside for the rest of his life, he panicked and screamed in despair. Larry's dad got a ladder, climbed up to the bathroom window, crawled inside, and unlocked the door.[7]

There are times in our lives when we feel like we're "locked in the bathroom": the loss of a job, a troubled marriage, a wayward son, the discovery of a malignant tumor—you name it. We go south and panic. We get angry. We weep. We pray, "God, please unlock the door." Just as Larry's dad came through the bathroom window and unlocked the door, God sometimes answers our prayers in the way we want: we get the job, the marriage counseling works, our son turns to God and gets off drugs, the cancer is cured. We're grateful.

We should be grateful when God answers prayer and unlocks the doors of our problems. God loves to give us good gifts. But he knows how easy it is for us to set our heart's affections on those gifts. It's easy to believe that God is good when life goes well. But we've all had those times when the door doesn't unlock. Sometimes God allows our problems and frustrations to continue for weeks, months, maybe years. During one of my most frustrating years in private practice, I cried out to God for help and encouragement. I didn't think I could survive another month. The next day a courier from the courthouse showed up at my office. "Sign these papers," he said. I was being sued by a former client. What is God up to when he allows our struggles to intensify, when he refuses to "unlock the bathroom door"?

Imagine you're "locked in the bathroom." Maybe your locked door is an illness, financial pressures, or a difficult person in your life who hurts or annoys you. Maybe your locked door is a constant, crippling feeling of inadequacy. What frustrates you? What keeps you from getting what you want? A locked door is anything, big or small, that blocks our path to getting what we really want. Imagine the door stays locked for a long time. You're frustrated and angry, demanding that it open. As you're standing in front of the bathroom door, God comes in through the window. He sits on the floor and says, "Come to me. Sit here on the floor beside me. I want to be with you."

You turn your back to him as you're grabbing and twisting the doorknob. You continue praying, "God, I want you to make my husband be more sensitive to me! I need you to make my job go better! I need to get my wife to understand and respect me. God, what I *need* you to do for me is _____." You kick the door and scream in frustration.

Jesus continues to sit on the floor. He says, "I know you want that door to open. I hurt with you. I really do care about your pain. But what I want right now is to be with you. Please come to me. Come and sit here with me." God grieves over our refusal to come to him:

> "I reached out day after day
>   to a people who turned their backs on me,
> People who make wrong turns,
>   who insist on doing things their own way." (Isa. 65:1–2 MSG)

Our greatest problem isn't our locked door. Whenever we believe we *need* the door to open, our greatest problem is that we want something more than God. I shudder to think of what I could have become had God given me what I wanted in place of him. The Bible says one of the worst kinds of judgment from God is when he gives us over to our own way. Romans 1:26–32 and Psalm 73:3–12 describe the type of people we'll become when God gives us over to our own way. We've all known parents who let their kids have their own way. While Mom and Dad may think the little darlings are cute, no one else wants to be around those children. And deep down in their little hearts, those children long for Mom and Dad to be loving enough and strong enough to stand in their way and kindly but firmly say no.

Here's a life-changing truth we've discovered: *Frustration and locked doors are gifts from God. They are God's agents of change. Disappointments, annoying people, and difficult circumstances are all used by God to surface the lies we believe.* They are his severe mercies. For example, throughout much of my life, I depended on people's affirmation to make me feel competent. I felt so energized when I heard encouraging words. But guess what? Lisa does not have the gift of encouragement. By her own admission, she's more prone to see and point out what's wrong. For many years in our marriage, I resented Lisa for her lack of affirmation. I put a lot of pressure on her to encourage me when I did something well or when I struggled with feelings of failure. God used Lisa's lack of encouragement to bring my lies to the surface. Lisa was being used in my life as God's agent of change. Over the years, I've come to see that my grumbling emotions served as signals. My anger at Lisa and my jealousy toward others who got affirmed by people became so obvious and overwhelming to me that I had to face the lies they were alerting me to. I believed I *needed* people to give me life by speaking affirming words to me. I coveted recognition and applause. By facing my grumbling emotions and the lies they were exposing, I've been able to identify my lies and false gods. I've seen how I've forsaken Jesus by putting pressure on Lisa and others to give me life. I've mourned and wept over my sin. And by God's grace, I'm learning to intentionally make Jesus the treasure and center of my heart. He is with me! Jesus is for me! He lives in my heart! I don't want to tell Jesus he isn't enough for me. I don't want to forsake him anymore. He is more than enough for me whether people affirm me or not. Over the years as I've been learning to find my contentment in Jesus, Lisa has also changed. She is turning to Jesus too. She is softer and kinder. She blesses me with her support and yes, encouragement.

God uses our locked doors, disappointments, and frustrations to help us grow. They help us see if we believe truth or lies. Are we able to stay centered on and contented in Jesus when life is frustrating and disappointing, or do we go south and grumble and grasp for control? Locked doors of every kind are God's agents of change. They present us with opportunities to turn to Jesus in absolute surrender and say, "You are all I need." Whenever we face and feel frustration, whenever a door isn't opening, God is pursuing our hearts. He's inviting us in that very moment to draw near to him, to relinquish lies and embrace the truth of his sustaining presence. There, and only there, are we truly safe, truly free.

When David faced troubled days and locked doors, he knew what he needed most. He sought one thing:

> One thing I ask of the LORD,
>   this is what I seek:
> that I may dwell in the house of the LORD
>   all the days of my life,
> to gaze upon the beauty of the LORD
>   and to seek him in his temple.
> For in the day of trouble
>   he will keep me safe in his dwelling. (Ps. 27:4–5)

God is good when he opens doors. He's equally good when he keeps them shut. Will we humbly turn to him, seek him? Our primary motive should not be to get the door to open, although it's okay to ask him to do that. Our chief desire should be to hear his voice, to enjoy being with him, to treasure him as he treasures us—even when the door doesn't open. Philip Yancey wrote: "He [Job] was still sitting in a pile of rubble, naked, covered with sores, and it was in *those* circumstances that he learned to praise God. Only one thing had changed: God had given Job a glimpse of the big picture."[8]

Only when our souls are centered on Jesus and quieted by the transcendence of our good God can we begin to discern what a godly response to the locked doors of our lives might look like. Seeking solutions and problem solving are then legitimate. But until our hearts are right with God, anything we do will be wrong. We'll be grasping for solutions to gain control. The opposite of grasping—true giving—can only come when our hearts are centered on or quieted in God.

THE PRAYER OF RELINQUISHMENT

Prayer, or talking to God, is one of the first evidences that we're turning north in humble dependence. Our failure to pray isn't because we're busy; it's because we're self-reliant. If I'm not talking to God and seeking his help when I'm groaning or grumbling, I'm probably grasping for control.

When locked doors don't open, we often react with anger, fear, shame, or self-contempt. Remember, emotions are our lie detectors. As we become aware of those emotions, we must slow down and reflect on our self-talk.[9] What are we believing? We must ask the Holy Spirit to help us as we listen and discern the lie we're telling ourselves about what we believe we need and who we're depending on to meet those needs. All day long I'm often saying things like, "Father, I relinquish this lie that says I need this person to affirm what I just said." Other times my prayers are like this: "Dear God, right now I relinquish this lie up to you that says I need this situation to be different. I don't need that person to treat me differently. It doesn't matter what they might be thinking of me right now. It's okay if I look small in their eyes. You were willing to appear small on the cross for me. I love you, Jesus. I admit the truth: you're gloriously enough to sustain me right now."

Many of the psalms are like the prayer journals of people who fought to stay contented and centered in God. It's like reading their self-talk as they exhort themselves with the truth of God's sufficiency: "Find rest, O my soul, in God alone; my hope comes from him" (Ps. 62:5).

PEACE MAY NOT COME FOR A LONG TIME

Choosing to believe the truth of Christ's sufficiency won't make all the emotional struggles disappear. Our fallen natures stubbornly cling to lies. Lies run deep. They've often been forged in the fires of childhood disappointments, wounds, and trauma. Moreover, we are opposed by Satan and his demon hordes; the Enemy hates it when we turn to God.

Yep, the lies often pull at us even when we're turning to God and believing the truth about his sufficiency. God doesn't always give us good feelings as soon as we turn to him. If he did, we'd seek him for good feelings instead of seeking him because he's God. Like withdrawal from drugs or alcohol, we'll go through a period of painful detox. We're addicts to this world. The pain we've covered up with our grasping behaviors may hurt like hell when we stop going south. The transition from south to north is painfully lonely as we stop manipulating people to meet our needs and cling to the naked truth of Christ's sufficiency. Truth must sustain us, not experiences. Yet we must continue to listen expectantly for Jesus to speak to our wounded hearts. And as we wait for him, we must choose to believe the truth and resist the lies that scream in our ears. As Lisa says, "We must believe the truth even when it doesn't feel true."

While fly-fishing the Muskegon River, I waded into the high, rushing current. I had to intentionally brace myself to keep from being knocked over and taken downstream. Similarly, when we start to turn from our lies and embrace the truth of Christ's love and sufficiency, the power of the lies wants to knock us down and take us south. They seem so real. "You're worthless. No one would ever choose you. You failed *again*. God is disgusted with you. There's no way you could be his dearly loved child!" We mentally brace ourselves against the lies by clinging to the truth. Bringing every thought captive to Christ is a process. It may sound something like this: "The Lord is my Shepherd. I have all I need. It doesn't matter if my spouse spoke in a harsh tone of voice. I choose you, God. You are all I need to be okay right now. I will not go south and retaliate. Find rest, O my soul, in God alone."

It may take weeks, months, or years of fighting such currents. But as we learn to find our contentment in Jesus and embrace the truth of his unfailing love through the Word of God, the Spirit of God, and the people of God (more will be said about this in chapter 11), the lies, with time, begin to lose intensity. As we keep abandoning ourselves to God alone and this process becomes the habit of our souls (Ps. 27:8), inner peace and security grow.

But this process is messy! Growth comes slowly, fitfully, three steps forward—two steps back. There will be times we are confused out of our minds. Those moments are locked doors too. We come to God broken, confused, and desperate once again. We need him to speak. It's part of the way he forges a deep and intimate relationship with us. Deep faith, hope, and love are forged in the fires of adversity. It's truly a miracle of God that we get to the other side—but we do.

As we learn to walk with God, we are able to recover sooner. Offenses that used to take me days to recover from only take hours. What once took hours only takes minutes. Much that used to instantaneously take me south can now be overlooked in the moment. Instead of reacting in anger, I'm intentionally responding with gentleness. I fail often, but I see growth, and it's truly a miracle. Change is possible!

Be patient with yourself. Of all the ways Paul could define love, he begins with two words: patient and kind (1 Cor. 13:4). God, who is love, is patient and kind with you. He's committed to your growth and well-being one step at a time (Phil. 1:6).

SURRENDER OFTEN BRINGS SORROW

It's okay to grieve the loss of our false, yet treasured dreams. The deepest dream we can ever dream is that of knowing God. The pathway to getting there, however, is always painful. We will suffer. Our lies and stubborn self-centeredness won't die without pain. Jesus said, "Anyone who does not carry his cross and follow me cannot be my disciple" (Luke 14:27). The cross is not a piece of jewelry; it's an instrument of death. Larry Crabb has said that any time God allows a dream to be shattered, it's to awaken a deeper dream:

> Following Christ *must* take us through seasons of disappointment, because Christianity remakes our dreams before it fulfills them. The process is excruciating. It can include divorce, bankruptcy, accidents, murder, near apostasy—anything. . . .
>
> Disappointment, severe enough to be called death, is unavoidable in a true spiritual journey.[10]

I had lunch with a young man I'd been mentoring. He'd grown in humility, honesty, and surrender to Jesus as he struggled with locked doors in his marriage. "I've come to realize," he said, "that I need to grieve and lament as I relinquish some of my dreams of marriage. I always thought my wife would want to encourage and affirm me for working hard. I've so longed for her to welcome me when I walk in the door at night and say I'm a good man. I've come to realize that my love language is words of affirmation. That isn't hers. She rarely thinks to say encouraging words to me. I used to resent her for that. I think I went through a time when I even hated her. I've gone south so many times; I've been so needy and demanding. But I'm repenting from my self-centeredness. I'm letting go of the lie that tells me I *need* her to make me feel important. For me, part of repenting means feeling and grieving the painful loss of those broken dreams. It means feeling the loneliness as I let go of my demands and surrender my heart to God alone."

His sorrow was legitimate. He wasn't speaking out of self-pity but from genuine loneliness as he surrendered himself to God. I left that conversation remembering the difference between grieving and grumbling. Godly grief, or lament, feels the pain of broken dreams while entrusting one's soul to God. Godly grief is sorrow mixed with faith. Grumbling, on the other hand, feels the pain of broken dreams and raises a fist at God. It's sorrow mixed with unbelief.

My friend was legitimately grieving and trusting in God alone for his needs. I felt joy for him. In the face of his shattered dreams of marriage, he was finding a new security in Jesus that was enabling him to be patient and kind toward his wife. Instead of demanding that she speak his love language, he was learning to speak hers as he turned to God for his. God's amazing grace was at work in my friend's life, and he was in turn becoming a living expression of God's grace to his wife.

SURRENDERING OUR "PAPPIES" IS PAINFUL

We all have our lies, addictions, and false gods—the things we turn to for comfort and relief in the groaning of life instead of turning to God. Like little children, we scream and cry when we don't get what we want. Surrendering our dreams, desires, and longings to God is indeed a painful and often lonely process. We'll be forgotten by others, rejected, overlooked, and misunderstood. Others will get what they want and we won't. Life isn't fair. It's a dark night of the soul. We are much like little Mary Elise as she learned to relinquish her pappies:

> As my daughter approached her third birthday, my wife and I decided it was time for her to give up the pacifier. Used only at bedtime, Mary Elise's "pappy" was a security, a familiar way to lose herself to sleep. We prayed for parental wisdom, my wife did a little research, and we came up with a plan. We took all of Mary Elise's pappies, sealed them in a plastic bag, and let her hand them over to the woman behind the counter at ToysRUs. Then she picked out a toy in exchange for relinquishing one of her most beloved possessions. At the time, Mary Elise was unfazed, and quite happy about it.
>
> Bedtime was a different story. Mary Elise begged for her pappies and cried when we reminded her that she'd given them to the cashier

at the toy store. We prayed bedtime prayers, and at the end my wife said, "Jesus, please help Mary Elise. Comfort her as she grows up and gives up her pappies. Amen."

"Will Jesus bring back my pappies?" Mary Elise asked.

"No," we said. "But He will make you feel better. He'll comfort you with His presence."

Only a few sniffles as she turned this over in her head. We said goodnight. . . . About thirty minutes later we heard Mary Elise sobbing in her room. We went in, and she looked up at us and said, "I don't like Jesus very much."

We were speechless. Then we realized she was honestly confronting her pain and grief at a level of honesty most of us rarely face. . . . Part of me longed to burst into tears and grab my daughter and say, "I know exactly how you feel. Some days I don't much like Him either."

Instead I whispered, "That's okay," and hugged her close.[11]

When I think about this painful process of relinquishing our "pappies," I'm drawn back to Psalm 131. It's a song for pilgrims as they ascend to Jerusalem. We are indeed pilgrims. Banished from Eden, we're traveling to our new home in the heavenly Jerusalem. Through this psalm, God hugs us close and tenderly invites us to quiet our souls in his love. Until we're home in glory, we'll be forever learning new depths of this little song:

> Lord, my heart is not proud;
> my eyes are not haughty.
> I don't concern myself with matters too great
> or too awesome for me to grasp.
> Instead, I have calmed and quieted myself,
> like a weaned child who no longer cries for its mother's milk.
> Yes, like a weaned child is my soul within me.
> O Israel, put your hope in the Lord—
> now and always. (Ps. 131:1–3 NLT)

The humble no longer try to control the things they cannot change or understand. The life that's been weaned from the false gods of this world is a life of inner peace and quiet. Double-mindedness brings restlessness, while the pure in heart know peace. Humility occurs when we've learned to bond with the heart of God. It's the place of becoming little children. This humble, tender, childlike place of complete trust in God is the first and highest virtue of mankind. It's the place from which all virtues grow.

> The humble enjoy continual peace, but in the heart of the proud is envy, and frequent indignation.
>
> THOMAS À KEMPIS

A weaned child no longer screams for mother's milk. Though the weaning process was painful, the child has come to that place of being content to just be with mother—to rest in the security of her loving presence. There we discover the very purpose for our life: to live and love in such a way that invites others to taste and see that the Lord is good. "O Israel [O friends, spouse, children, coworker, enemies], put your hope in the LORD—now and always" (Ps. 131:3 NLT).

Going north to God, as pictured in Psalm 131, requires the painful process of letting go of our pappies, but it's far more. It's a coming to and learning how to rest secure in the arms of God, pictured as a kind and tenderhearted mother. Only here will we find freedom from the enslaving burden of needing to get our way. This is what it means to be pure in heart.

IT'S OKAY TO STRUGGLE WITH GOD

Problems, groaning, and locked doors tempt us to doubt God's goodness. That's the great battle of the ages. Evil grows when we doubt God is good. We're tempted to question God's love, his power, or both when he doesn't protect us from suffering. When I'm tempted to lose heart, John gives me hope.

John the Baptist was a great prophet. He announced the coming of the Messiah: "Look, the Lamb of God, who takes away the sin of the world!" (John 1:29). Like all God-fearing Jews of his day, John fully expected the Messiah would overthrow the kingdom of Rome and establish the kingdom of God on earth. But John was sitting in a dank, stinking, Roman prison. And those prison doors would never open for him. The day was soon coming when King Herod's wife, Herodias, would have John's head chopped off and served to her on a silver platter (Matt. 14:1–12).

While in prison, John sent his disciples to Jesus with a question: "Are you the Messiah we've been expecting, or should we keep looking for someone else?" (Matt. 11:3 NLT). Was John disillusioned by Jesus? Had he expected Jesus to break him out of jail, overthrow Rome, and establish the kingdom? Rome was still in power. Jesus was loving his enemies instead of destroying them. Did Jesus disappoint John's expectations, causing him to doubt that Jesus was the Messiah? I think so.

Like John, we've all had our expectations of what Jesus will do for us. We've had our cherished dreams of what life will be like when we follow him. You never expected he would allow your marriage to end in divorce, that you'd be fired from your job, or that your three-year-old would die of brain cancer. We never believed God would allow the things we've suffered to happen. As one of my seminary professors once said, when we signed up to follow Jesus, we thought we were getting on an airplane that would take us to a bright, sunny vacation place like Florida. But when we got off the plane, we found ourselves in the bitter, winter snows of Alaska.

How has Jesus disappointed your expectations? Jesus told John's disciples to go back to John and tell him about all the things they've seen Jesus accomplish: the blind see, the lame walk, the lepers are healed, the deaf hear, the dead are raised, and the gospel is preached to the poor (Matt. 11:5). As John's disciples began to leave, Jesus spoke to the people standing nearby. "I tell you the truth, of all who have ever lived, none is greater than John the Baptist" (Matt. 11:11 NLT).

I thank God for John. If the greatest man who ever lived could struggle with deep doubt and discouragement, we can too. John had the courage to trust Jesus enough to come to him (through his disciples) and ask the hard questions. John gives us permission to come to God humbly and honestly when we're struggling with doubts and confusion. Jesus revealed his power to John's disciples so they could reassure John that he was indeed the Messiah. He was worthy of John's trust even though John was sitting in a stinking prison. God will open his heart to us if we'll humble ourselves and pray, "God, I'm so afraid. I'm so discouraged. Would you be willing to talk to me? Just speak whatever I need to hear." Then wait in expectation. God will speak in his time and way so we too can have a renewed vision of who he is. And when Jesus speaks, no matter how simply and quietly it may be—through Scripture, the radio, a friend, a devotion, a sermon, a small group, in our heart—we'll find that we don't need him to unlock our prison door. We just need *him*.

Jesus sent another message to John through his disciples. "Tell him, 'God blesses those who do not turn away because of me'" (Matt. 11:6 NLT). That's an amazing statement. We can fall away from God *because of Jesus*. When Jesus doesn't meet our expectations, we may be tempted to turn away. God help us. What truth will keep us faithful to God's one and only Son?

In his book, *Lament for a Son*, Nicholas Wolterstorff chronicles his journey through grief. His son Eric was twenty-three years old when he was killed in a mountain-climbing accident in Austria. Nicholas asked the deep questions we're all asking but too afraid to say out loud:

> How is faith to endure, O God, when you allow all this scraping and tearing on us? You have allowed rivers of blood to flow, mountains of suffering to pile up, sobs to become humanity's song—all without lifting a finger that we could see. You have allowed bonds of love beyond number to be painfully snapped. If you have not abandoned us, explain yourself.
>
> We strain to hear. But instead of hearing an answer we catch sight of God himself scraped and torn. Through our tears we see the tears of God.[12]

Jesus disappointed people's expectations. Rather than powerfully over-throwing Rome, Jesus was crucified in weakness and surrender. Could anything have been more hopeless and discouraging than to see your Messiah die naked and bloodied beyond recognition on a criminal's cross? Yet Jesus' death was the very means through which God was rescuing the world. When we doubt God cares or that he's in control, we must remember that we do not see as God sees. We must wait for that day of glory when we shall know fully, even as we are fully known (1 Cor. 13:12). Until then, we must continually come back to the communion table and remember the truth. Through the torn body and shed blood of Jesus Christ, represented by the bread and the cup, we are reminded of God's amazing grace. He humbled himself to the point of death on a cross so we could live. "Do this in remembrance of me" (Luke 22:19). He is good. He is great. We must not forget. He can be trusted no matter what.

QUESTIONS FOR SELF-EXAMINATION AND DISCUSSION

1. Have you received God's forgiveness through Jesus Christ's death on the cross for your sin? If not, would you be willing to pray right now and ask God to forgive you and receive his free gift of salvation? You can pray a prayer similar to the one I prayed (see page 112).

2. Have you faced your sin of forsaking God and grasping for your security and significance from people, or are you trying to justify the ways you go south?

3. How confident are you that God dearly loves and delights in you? Are you confident that he cares about your longing to be loved and treated with respect, and that he wants you to bring those longings to him so he can care for you?

4. In what areas of your life do you try hard to please God but fail? What would it be like for you to admit you are helpless to change yourself (Rom. 7:14–26)? When you experience the pain of groaning, will you come to God and ask him to help you go north instead of south?

5. Does following God feel more like a "have to" or a "get to"? Why? What do you pursue to satisfy your longing for love and meaning more than pursuing God?

6. A locked door is anything, big or small, that blocks our path to getting what we really want. Describe a time you have experienced, or maybe are currently experiencing, a locked door. What does God reveal about your heart in that situation?

7. As you face your locked doors, what helps you move to godly grief and relinquishment instead of grumbling and grasping? How do you depend on God's grace to help you?

8. How do you imagine God responds to you when you honestly admit all the ways you go south? How does his response influence your response to him?

7

A GREAT GIFT

THE NEW IDENTITY WE NEED

LISA

*Anyone who belongs to Christ has become a new person. The old life is gone;
a new life has begun! And all of this is a gift from God, who brought us
back to himself through Christ.*
2 Corinthians 5:17–18 NLT

A Facebook friend of mine recently posted the charming YouTube video of a little girl named Jessica. Standing atop her bathroom counter, this blond, curly haired four-year-old looked straight in the mirror. With all the innocent joy and passion she could muster, she proclaimed how pleased she was with her life and herself: "I love my house, I love my dad, I love my mom, I love my sisters, I love my cousin, I love my aunt, I love my room, I love my hair, I love my haircut, I love my stuff, I love my whole house! I can do anything good! Yay! Yay! Yay!"

Clearly, in that moment, little Jessica meant every word she said and was absolutely happy and content with her life. Contrast Jessica with the excessively neurotic, middle-aged Bob Wylie in the film *What About Bob?* as he closes his eyes, rubs his temples, and repeats the mantra over and over again, "I feel good, I feel great, I feel wonderful!" Everyone knows that Bob is trying to convince himself of something that he really doesn't believe. Bob feels lousy. He's afraid of everything, and his best friend is a goldfish.[1] If Bob were to look in the bathroom mirror and make an honest evaluation of himself and his life, he would likely say something like, "I'm a failure, a worthless loser. I can't do anything right. I don't like who I am. I don't like my life."

What about you? When you look in the bathroom mirror, who do you see—Jessica or Bob? Admittedly, most of us are somewhere in between the two. The majority of us have lived longer than Jessica, and most of us have had the mirror of life reflect an image of ourselves that is less than flattering. As we have experienced the pain of life in a fallen world through failure, rejection, and disappointment, many of us have come to see ourselves as worthless, undesirable, no good, ugly nobodies. Even though we may have accepted Christ as our Savior long ago, this shameful self-image often remains entwined around our souls and continues to influence us to go south as we face the groaning of life. It isn't until we believe and receive the great gift of who we truly are in Christ that we begin to be set free to go north as we face the daily hardships and frustrations of life.

Even those who are prone to think and speak quite highly of themselves, if honest, discover that beneath the self-assured assessment lies deep insecurity. Someone who has developed an overinflated view of himself through parental affirmation or his own success will demand that his world keep on affirming him because without it he is nothing. He is at core insecure. Henri Nouwen has commented:

> Maybe you think that you are more tempted by arrogance than by self-rejection. But isn't arrogance, in fact, the other side of self-rejection? Isn't arrogance putting yourself on a pedestal to avoid being seen as you see yourself? Isn't arrogance, in the final analysis, just another way of dealing with the feelings of worthlessness?[2]

Driven by these shameful images, we live lives that are desperate attempts to avoid, fix, hide from, make up for, or disprove all that we fear is most deeply true about us. We put on masks designed to make us acceptable to our world, but they keep us distant and alone. Some of us seek to anesthetize the pain of a shameful image through compulsive eating, drinking, dieting, exercise, drugs, work, cleaning, or a thousand other grasping behaviors. When we're held captive to lies about our deepest identity, we live less for the kingdom of God and more for our own self-protection and enhancement. As our pastor, Louie, has said many times, "Everything we do, we do according to our self-image."[3]

GO TO THE SOURCE

A helpful step toward becoming free of a lie-based self-image is to understand its source. To be theologically correct, we must acknowledge that it all began in the Garden when Adam and Eve traded the truth of God for a lie. Before the Fall, the source of their personal identities was naturally their relationship with their Creator. They had value, worth, and purpose simply because they were God's creation, his children. Their relationship with each other and their work were given as gifts from God, as venues to live out their identity. There was no shame—only freedom and joyful relating with their God and each other. But after they disobeyed God, the center of their universe shifted. Because the relationship with God had been severed, they now looked to each other and to their fallen world to give them an identity. And so it is with us. The bent of our sinful nature is to look to the fallen world and to other sinful people to tell us who we are. But like the reflection from a broken mirror, these things can, at best, only send back a warped and distorted image. The world sends us messages about who we are through the wounds we have received, our failures, the sins we have committed, and the difficult circumstances we have had to endure; it tells us we're "somebody" if we look good or if we can impress others with our performance.

THE WOUNDS OF LIFE

It was just a birthmark: a dark, red spot on his neck no bigger than a quarter. No big deal. Until that day in the locker room when Tony was getting dressed for third-grade gym class. "Hey Tony, what's that on your neck?"

Feeling vulnerable, Tony tightened up inside. "What's what on my neck?"

Josh walked over and took a look at Tony's neck. Then Josh called out to the other boys in the locker room, "Hey, you guys, take a look at the hickey on Tony's neck!" The guys came running over.

"Ya been makin' out with your girlfriend, Tony? What's her name?" A song echoed from the locker room out into the hallway: "Tony and Susie sittin' in a tree . . ." The room howled with laughter.

That day was a turning point in Tony's life. It was the day he became painfully aware that something was shamefully wrong. And he started to learn how to hide in order to avoid shame and rejection. Better wear a shirt with a high collar. From now on you have to be on your guard. Life isn't safe.

Nobody gets through this life without being hurt or wounded relationally. Nobody. Because we're surrounded by fallen people, it's impossible not to be personally impacted by another person's sin or failure. While not all hurts and wounds are equal, all wounds—intentional or unintentional—can speak loudly about our value and worth. We long for our world to tell us we're loved and wanted, appreciated and needed, respected and important. But so often the messages we get through family members, teachers, peers, and employers are just the opposite. Even the love and acceptance of those who have been good to us are not enough to totally overcome the wounds inflicted by others. Those wounds are like cuts to the soul—sites where lies about who we really are enter like bacteria, creating a systemic infection of a negative and painfully distorted self-image.

My story is no exception. In first grade, I went to a new school, wanting to fit in, to be accepted and enjoyed by my peers. It wasn't long, however, before I got the message that I wasn't going to be part of the group of girls I had hoped to join. My attempts to play with them at recess were rebuffed, even mocked. A few of them surrounded me in the school hallway. "Are those *corrective* shoes?" one of them sneered, pointing down at the clunky black-and-white saddle oxford shoes I wore—so ugly compared to the shiny, sleek penny loafers the girls were wearing that year. It was true; they were corrective shoes. For me they created a bigger problem than the one they were meant to help. While the girls giggled and ran off, I spent the rest of that recess huddled against a brick wall, hating my shoes and myself. Though I could not have put words to it then, I knew deep inside that something must be wrong with me to bring about this rejection. The image reflected back to me by my world was that I was *undesirable*. How I longed to feel wanted, chosen, pursued, and delighted in by my peers.

Through the years as I continued to gaze in the broken mirror of my world, I kept getting the same message. I became more and more convinced of its truth, but with little awareness of the power and influence it was having in my life. Fearful of being further exposed as *undesirable*, I became shy and reluctant to reach out. Hungry for approval and acceptance, I was driven toward achievement and performance. Though all this looked good on the outside, it was selfishly motivated. I was desperately grasping for life from people. Self-absorbed, I was aware of the needs and desires of others only to the degree that meeting their needs and expectations was a way to make myself desirable.

The wounds that Tony and I received in elementary school pale in comparison to the wounds a great many have suffered. Over the years I have spent as a counselor, I have heard countless heartbreaking stories of abuse, neglect, and betrayal, often at the hands of someone who should have been trustworthy. Such wounds and disappointments are deep and significant, and it's easy to understand how they could go to the very core of one's identity. Those who have suffered lesser wounds tend to discount their experiences when others seem to have suffered so much more. But the power is not in the size of the wound itself but in the lie that comes to us through the wound. Deadly bacteria can enter the body through a small cut as easily as through a gaping wound. Though we may not be aware of it, this infection of lies influences our entire worldview. It infiltrates the way we think about ourselves, God, and others. When we believe lies, they determine the way we respond to life and relationships, and their pull is always to take us south.

Our sin and failure

Another significant influence on our identity is the memory we have of our own failure. Though we may understand the theology of confession and forgiveness through the blood of Christ for all of our sin, some of us continue to live under the shame of our past, especially if the past sin has ongoing ramifications in our present life. Such was the case for Nancy. In her latter teens and early twenties, Nancy had been sexually active with a number of boyfriends. Years later, though she had come to the Lord, sought forgiveness, and had become a faithful wife, she was reaping the consequences of this behavior. A sexually transmitted disease contracted during those earlier years led to a battle with infertility. Nancy was filled with shame and self-contempt, seeing herself as *dirty scum*. She pushed her husband, Joe, away with an angry and critical spirit, while seeking solace in pints of Ben & Jerry's Chunky Monkey ice cream. Everything she did, she did according to her self-image.

Like Nancy, many believers have difficulty letting go of the image they have of themselves that is based on their past sin. Memories of sexual immorality, adultery, abortion, abuse, or other self-centered behavior continue to haunt them. They often say, "I know God forgives me, but I just can't seem to forgive myself." Sometimes this stance is even mistaken as humility and is believed to be necessary to keep their behavior on the right track. I recently heard a well-known Christian leader admit that she continued to be haunted by her failure to witness to a particular group of people when she had the chance. In spite of repeated confession, she remained plagued by guilt and shame that was not relieved until she did better the next time she had the chance to witness. I wondered if her effort at witnessing was driven by her image of herself as a loved and forgiven child of God who, out of gratitude, wanted to give to others, or if she was driven by the image of herself as a failure, a person who needed to do better to be acceptable to God and to herself. I do know that when we hang on to a self-image that is based on our sin and our shame, we are likely to be motivated to live and respond to the events of life by working to hide or make up for things that seem to prove that image.

LIFE IN A FALLEN WORLD

Jesus told us in John 16:33, "Here on earth you will have many trials and sorrows" (NLT). If we are looking to this world to tell us who we are and what we have to offer, then the trials themselves can become powerful communicators of a negative and shameful self-image—even if they cannot be directly traced to our own sin or the sin of another. Singleness, a physical deformity or disability, a season of unemployment, financial struggles in spite of responsibility, a painful loss, or any area where we fall short of our culture's standards of beauty, intelligence, or success are life circumstances that can whisper to our hearts that we are a worthless failure—rejected, ugly, or alone. Even David apparently slipped into such a view in the face of a difficult and painful situation where God was not providing the relief he desired. In Psalm 22:6 he refers to himself as "a worm and not a man."

Sandy and James were two individuals who found their self-image in the mirror of difficult circumstances. Sandy was a kind and intelligent girl who was raised in a loving, Christian home. In spite of these positive qualities, one thing became clear to Sandy through her high school and college years: she was not the kind of girl that boys liked to date. Though she longed to marry and have children, she saw herself as unattractive and believed that she would always be alone. Expecting rejection, Sandy's image of herself fueled her fears, and she buried her hopes and dreams by focusing on becoming a highly educated and competent professional. While in and of itself this was not a bad direction, for Sandy it was a cloak of self-protection that kept her safe, but lonely. Outwardly successful and independent, emotionally she remained vulnerable to the pursuit of any man who gave her attention. Because she was so thirsty for love from a man, her ability to discern a man's character and motivation became clouded. As a result, she suffered even more heartache and rejection. Each rejection seemed to confirm her painful and deeply held self-image.

James struggled all of his life with a learning disability. Even though he worked hard in school and sought out extra tutoring, he was never able to achieve better than Cs and Ds on his report card. James saw himself as stupid and feared others would too. He was driven to find relief from this painful self-image by working to make his plumbing business successful. Through hard work he achieved the business success he craved, yet he still erupted in anger at employees or family members who exposed his mistakes or did something that made him feel stupid. James was proud of his achievements; but his success was not enough to erase the deeply held image of himself as stupid. Anyone who dared to bring that image to light paid dearly.

BOIL IT DOWN

Take what has been said to you through the wounds of life, your own sin and failure, and the difficult circumstances you have experienced, and boil it all down to a word or a phrase that describes you. That word or phrase describes your lie-based self-image that not only is painfully shameful but has great power to take you south into self-centered directions. It tells you who you should or shouldn't be and what you must do or not do to have any hope of gaining the love and respect you most long for and of avoiding the rejection you most fear.

If you see yourself as a loser, then you'll do whatever it takes to avoid having others see you that way too. The lies will tell you that you must be seen as competent, intelligent, together, right, in control, and pretty darn near perfect. You must be good at hiding those parts of you that don't measure up. The lies will tell you that you must avoid situations where your shortcomings could be exposed. They'll also direct you to spend your time and money on those things that enhance the way you feel about yourself and the way the world sees you. Rather than face the pressure, some may withdraw and live a passive existence, doing what's easy and indulging in whatever pleasure relieves the pain of feeling like a loser.

Sometimes even positive experiences, where we have tasted a bit of what we most deeply desire, serve to clarify what we believe we must be or do to overcome a painful self-image. For me, one of those events came in later elementary school. With the self-image of *undesirable* already in place, one day I found myself actually sought out by the "popular" group of girls. They were constructing a paper banner for the boys' basketball team to run through when they entered the gym for an important upcoming game. The project required some special artwork, and I had gained the reputation of being one of the better artists in our sixth-grade class. I, the *undesirable*, was suddenly chosen to hang out with the *desirable*. Wow. It felt good. It was a sip of cold water for my thirsty, young soul. But without realizing it at the time, I learned something that day. If I had any hope of being *desirable*, I would have to be able to do something that others valued and appreciated. If I couldn't do something well, I would likely remain alone and unloved—*undesirable*. It was all up to me. I needed to find a way to become desirable. I succumbed to the pressure of grasping for people's acceptance through my performance. That lie became a guiding force in the choices I made in relationships, ministry, and career for years to come.

If you believe that there is something you can do to improve or replace a negative self-image, then of course there is great pressure to find and to do whatever that is. Tastes we have had of success, affirmation, love, and respect have been sweet, and our souls are determined to find a way to keep them coming. The lie I believed as an elementary schoolgirl later found an expression during my teens when I decided to take guitar lessons. My desire to take up guitar had very little to do with enjoying the instrument and a lot to do with trying to prove something about myself by impressing my peers. In my foolish thinking, I thought if I could just do something that others found "cool," then maybe I would be "cool." I believed the lie that I *needed* to be good at this because I *needed* the acceptance and admiration of my peers to be whole. As you can imagine, I approached my lessons with a tremendous amount of pressure and anxiety. Ultimately, the anxiety was so counterproductive that I was unable to learn and eventually gave up the effort.

Not only did I put pressure on myself to perform in order to make myself desirable to others, I extended that pressure to others as well. Whenever we're operating from a negative and shameful self-image, we'll put expectations on others to come through for us in ways that tell us we are wanted, loved, valued, and appreciated. We may do it in ways that are obviously demanding, expressing anger and punishing others when they don't meet our expectations, or we may subtly obligate them by our own giving, followed by attempts to provoke guilt in those who don't come through in response. I know that I've been guilty of both. If we believe the world around us meets our needs and is able to give us a sense of worth and value, then that world must be manipulated either by our performance or by our demands. We may grasp for control by becoming, at least to some degree, needy, people-pleasing doormats with little sense of appropriate boundaries or angry, controlling dominants requiring life to be done our way. Either way, we're self-centered takers seeking to get a sense of identity from the world.

Unfortunately for me, the lies about what I needed and what I could do to make myself desirable did not die along with the attempt to learn the guitar. My efforts simply shifted to new areas of performance and new relationships. When I was successful at getting my world to tell me I was desirable through my performance, it bred pride and pressure to keep it up. When I failed, it bred self-contempt, shame, and anger. It wasn't until I was in my forties that I really began to see the lies that drove my performance mentality. Until what we believe about ourselves and our identity is exposed as lies, we will continue living by those lies.

THE LENS OF LIES

The lies that we believe about who we are become the lens through which we view and interpret all that happens to us. If we have come to see ourselves as worthless, incompetent, or undesirable, and we experience further pain or rejection, we'll assume—at least in some measure—that the reason is because we *are* worthless, incompetent, or undesirable. We may tend to anticipate and assume rejection, reading it into the words and actions of others, even when it isn't really there. Sometimes we even behave in ways that draw others to view us as we view ourselves.

Chuck, a young father of two, was on the cusp of a budding career as an electrical engineer. Though very bright and outwardly confident, Chuck was bound by a deadly core identity. Comparing his own life to the achievements of others, he saw himself as a loser and deeply feared others would as well. Any feedback that he interpreted as criticism affirmed that shameful identity and was met either with harsh anger or poisonous self-contempt.

One day, at the end of a staff meeting, Chuck's boss commented, "We're watching you, Chuck." Now, what the supervisor meant is, "Chuck, we think you have potential for advancement in this company. We're keeping our eyes open to those we see as having talent, and we're looking for the right time and place to promote them." But because the supervisor's words were filtered through Chuck's image of himself as a loser, that's not what he heard. He believed that what he most deeply feared had come to pass: the fact that he was a loser had been exposed, and his boss was watching and waiting for him to mess up. Chuck sank into depression. Eventually he resigned from his job and even attempted suicide. I can imagine that Chuck's boss was left wondering if his positive evaluation of Chuck had been correct after all.

Surely Satan comes to steal, kill, and destroy. He does so by getting us to believe, live by, and interpret life's events through his lies. I know how often I've been tempted to interpret the actions and words of others as evidence of my identity as undesirable—to be overly sensitive and take offense or sink into shame because I've perceived criticism or rejection that may not have been there at all. Or if the criticism and rejection were real, how often I've been deeply threatened and responded badly to it because I believed the lie that I needed to be seen in a positive light. I wonder how many friendships, marriages, families, churches, and individual lives have been thrown into turmoil and even destroyed because believers remain captive to the Enemy's lies. Surely this is no small matter.

IT LOOKS SO TRUE

Part of the deadly nature of these lies is that they're so close to the truth. The world can often be temporarily manipulated to affirm us. The world is impressed with success in business, politics, the arts, sports, and even ministry.

It values beauty and charm. "When we have come to believe in the voices that call us worthless and unlovable, then success, popularity and power are easily perceived as attractive solutions."[4]

Everywhere you go, the world is offering opportunities and products to enhance your popularity and power. Watch TV for just half an hour or glance through a magazine, and you'll see what I mean. Your local bookstore has whole sections of books that will gladly teach you the skills you need in order to get what you want in your career and relationships. Even well-known Christian authors have fallen into the trap of coaching believers in the art of popularity and power. "If you want to be loved, valued, and accepted by someone, then you must meet their needs," they say. Give the world what it wants, and you get what you want—at least for a while. The girl who loses one hundred pounds and gets a makeover will probably have the world telling her how beautiful she is. The man who has a successful business will likely gain a good measure of respect and admiration from his community. But gain the weight or lose the money and you're back to where you started. What the world gives, it can, and often does, take away.

The world's solution to a negative and painful self-image is enough experiences of success and affirmation. The idea is that if people are shielded from experiences of rejection and failure and only hear words of affirmation (true or not), they'll become people who feel good about themselves and live lives of love and responsibility. While I'm all for affirming people when it's appropriate and for celebrating true success for the right reasons, this theory has resulted in a world where political correctness rules the day. As a result, people today seem more easily offended and believe they are justified in demanding only experiences of affirmation, acceptance, and success. The world has become less rather than more civil. Expecting the world to cure our identity problems is a little like thinking a street-corner drug dealer can help take away our craving for drugs. In the end, we feel the need for even more of the deadly substance and may justify nearly any sort of behavior to get it.

FIND THE ONLY WAY OUT

The world and the Evil One will never offer us a genuine solution to the problem of self-image. The only way out comes through the truth of God's Word. Jesus says in John 8:32, "Then you will know the truth, and the truth will set you free." But the truth we must know goes deeper and well beyond simply acknowledging the precious truth that God has made a way for us to spend eternity in heaven through the blood of Jesus Christ. As John Eldredge has said:

> A man who calls himself a Christian, attends church, and has some hope of heaven when he dies has *not* received the lion's share of what God intended him to receive through the work of Christ. He will find himself living still very much alone, stuck in his journey, wondering why he cannot become the man he longs to be.
>
> He has not come into sonship.[5]

John 1:12 tells us, "But to all who believed him [Jesus] and accepted him, he gave the right to become children of God" (NLT). Rights are a wonderful blessing, but they are useless if not acted upon. We may have the right to vote and to worship freely, but if we don't exercise these rights, we gain no benefit from them. It's the same as having no right to them at all. God has given us the right to become his beloved children, to enter into an intimate, family relationship with himself. He has exposed our sin of looking to the world for our identity. We need his forgiveness, and he has offered it to us. He has given us the right to turn away from viewing ourselves in the broken and distorted mirror of the world and to see who we are as reflected by his face and revealed in his Word. No longer are we rejected, worthless, unloved, and alone based on our failure to measure up to expectations. Instead, by faith we are chosen, made holy, and are dearly loved children of God (Eph. 1:4).

> Many of us say we believe that salvation brings a "new birth," a new identity, but the way we view ourselves betrays our words; we don't believe its reality in us for a second. Instead we think we must keep striving to become someone who will be better. And all along we deny the mind-boggling truth that we have already become that someone.
>
> BILL THRALL, BRUCE MCNICOL, JOHN LYNCH, *TrueFaced*

I have learned so much about becoming a child of God by observing families who have adopted children. Some have traveled to far-flung corners of the world and at great expense have rescued children from poverty, disease, and death. They have brought these children into their homes and lives, and have given them all the benefits and privileges of a biological child. They have sacrificed, struggled, and fought to help these children know how deeply loved and wanted they are. Yet as deep as the love of these adoptive parents is, it still pales in comparison to God's love and sacrifice to give us the right to call ourselves his dearly loved children. None of these adoptive parents have ever had to allow one of their biological children to be put to death to pay the price for them to adopt the child of another. If this were the price, adoption would be unheard of. Yet this is the price that God the Father paid to bring us not just eternal life but full intimate relationship with himself. To fail to take on and live according to the identity of God's dearly beloved children, to fail to live in intimate relationship with the Father, is to fail to appreciate the cross of Christ and all that has been done for us.

IT REQUIRES HUMILITY

The great gift of our new identity in Christ is one that can only be received as we humble ourselves. Of all the things that keep us from accepting the truth of who we are in Christ, pride is probably the most tenacious. Our arrogant, fallen nature wants to *earn* our way into sonship. Our pride resists coming to the Father just as we are, with all of our weakness, failure, and sin. It hinders our ability to trust in his delight and full acceptance of us.

We stay dressed in the rags of our old identity, attempting to smooth out some of the wrinkles and brush off some of the dirt. We don't realize that no matter how hard we try, our rags will still be rags. God doesn't want us to clean up the old rags; he wants to give us a whole new wardrobe (Gal. 3:26–27 NLT). The story of the Prodigal Son is not just a picture of salvation but also a story of entering into sonship and coming into intimate relationship with the Father. When we come to God, admitting our sin, admitting the best we have is filthy rags, it's a humbling experience. But it's in that moment that the Father pulls out the finest robe and declares us a member of the family!

IT BRINGS FREEDOM

Jesus said, "I tell you the truth, everyone who sins is a slave of sin. A slave is not a permanent member of the family, but a son is part of the family forever.

So if the Son sets you free, you are truly free" (John 8:34–36 NLT). Through Jesus' sacrifice, God has made us members of the family and has set us free from our old identity. We are no longer obligated to do, or not do, what our old identity dictated was necessary for us in order to have the sense of value and worth that we long for. As we trust in the truth that we are loved and accepted and valued by God, we are set free from the need to manage and manipulate the world around us. We are set free from the need to get the people around us to affirm and appreciate us. We are set free from the need to impress others with what we have, what we can do, or what we look like. We are set free from the world's way of thinking and what it values. We are liberated to think of the needs of others.

One of the ways I've found freedom in accepting the gift of my identity as God's dearly loved daughter is in the area of facing my failure. When I'm operating by my old identity of *undesirable*, it's very difficult for me to hear criticism or to admit I'm wrong when confronted. Having my failure, sin, or incompetency exposed creates a lot of shame. I used to react in defensive anger or drown in self-contempt. While it's still not easy or comfortable to have my sin and failures exposed, I've grown in putting on my new identity in Christ, and I find that I'm much more able to hear and receive negative feedback without going to anger or wallowing in shame. When I focus on the fact that I'm God's dearly loved daughter who is valued and accepted by God, then I am able to relax, accept myself, and admit the truth of my flaws both to him and to others. I am free to be honest, authentic. No longer needing to defend myself, I am able to hear how I may be negatively impacting others and let them know that how they feel matters to me. I am open to seeking God's help to change where it is needed. I am being set free to love.

There are many ways that receiving the gift of who we are in Christ sets us free from self-centeredness to love. When we know we are God's dearly loved sons and daughters and when we trust in the heart of our heavenly Father toward us, then we know that he will generously provide for all that we really need. Paul wrote, "Since he did not spare even his own Son but gave him up for us all [our greatest need met!], won't he also give us everything else?" (Rom. 8:32 NLT). Further, we can trust in his evaluation of what we really need, rather than in our own (Matt. 6:8; 7:9–11), so we are set free from anxiety, worry, demanding, striving, and controlling. We no longer have to compare ourselves to others; we are set free from jealousy and envy. Others are no longer the competition, vying for the love, respect, attention, and esteem that we crave; we are liberated to be genuinely happy for those who have certain blessings that have not come our way. We can be content with God and what he chooses to provide for us at any given moment.

When we know who we are in Christ, we are set free to interpret all that comes to us in life, both the good and the bad, as filtered through the hands of a loving heavenly Father. Only when we know who we truly are does the command in James 1:2 make any sense at all: "When troubles come your way, consider it an opportunity for great joy" (NLT). The groaning that comes to us is no longer some random event or simply the result of someone else's failure. It's part of God's well-planned journey designed to bring us into conformity with the image and likeness of Christ. We are set free from the victim mentality that focuses only on how we have been harmed and fosters resentment, bitterness, and a spirit of revenge. Instead, we can see the bigger picture of what God is up to in our lives. He's not seeking to hurt us but to grow us into becoming like his Son (Rom. 8:28–29). Often this training is difficult and painful, but as we trust in and submit to the heart of God, our lives will yield the fruit of his training (Heb. 12:7–11).

When we are set free from the victim mentality, we are also set free to forgive those who have victimized us. Not long ago I was working for an organization that took a really big hit when a major player suddenly chose to leave and start a competing organization. This action felt like betrayal to those of us who really loved and supported this individual. Months later, as a result of the impact of this person's choices, some of us lost our jobs at a time when the American economy was in crisis and jobs were scarce. Through no fault of my own, major groaning had intruded on my life. At first, I struggled with going south in anger toward this person, but gradually as I came to God with this circumstance, I was reminded of the truth of his love and his sovereignty over every detail of my life. I was reminded of the bigger picture. My heavenly Father is in control, and I am his dearly loved daughter. This circumstance didn't happen apart from God's loving plan for my life. I don't need to hang on to bitterness toward this person who harmed me. I can forgive, pray for, and honestly desire God's best for this person. Even though I am still experiencing the consequences of this person's choices, I can trust that God is in it both for my good and for his glory.

Set free from a victim mentality, we are freed from some of the destructive force that wounds can bring. While others can still hurt us by their failure and sin, their ultimate power to define and destroy us has been neutralized by faith in God's ultimate, providential love.

ENGAGE IN THE BATTLE

Freedom never comes without a fight. Satan's lies will triumph in our lives if we do nothing to expose and stop them. "For we are not fighting against flesh-and-blood enemies, but against evil rulers and authorities of the unseen world, against mighty powers in this dark world, and against evil spirits in the heavenly places" (Eph. 6:12 NLT). God's truth will always trump Satan's lies, but we must engage daily in the battle for truth to be the controlling factor in our hearts and minds.

A CONSCIOUS CHOICE

One of the first and most significant steps toward winning the battle to go north in the groaning of life is to consciously choose to repent from the sin of receiving our identity from this world and instead receive the great gift of our new identity in Christ. Of course, in our weakness, even this is not something we can do on our own. Like Bob Wylie, we'll never convince ourselves of the truth of who we are in Christ by simply repeating it to ourselves as a mantra. But as we cry out to the Father, he comes to us and, through the power of the Holy Spirit, enables us to receive the truth of his love for us. He dresses us in his righteousness and quiets us with his love. We are enabled to cease striving and to relax in his love and wise provision for all of our needs. As our friend Craig put it, "I finally just let God love me." In doing so, Craig was receiving and beginning to live out his true identity as a dearly loved son of God.

In John 15:9, Jesus instructed his disciples, "I have loved you even as the Father has loved me. Remain in my love" (NLT). It is only as we remain in God's love, as we continue to see ourselves as holy and dearly loved children of God, that our lives will bear any fruit for the kingdom of God (John 15:4). We cease to bear fruit, cease to go north, when we lose sight of the truth of God's love, acceptance, and provision for our needs. Therefore, it's imperative that we choose daily to put on the new clothes of who we are in Christ by spending time in prayer and meditating on the Word of God. As we meet with the Father in personal, intimate time, asking him to speak to our hearts and reveal his truth to us, we are entering into the battle against the lies of the Enemy. Just as we do not neglect to put on our physical clothing to meet the challenges of the day, we mustn't neglect to put on our spiritual clothing, our true identity in Christ. In this way we can be in the world, but not of it.

THE NEW HEART

Jesus came to destroy the work of the Devil (1 John 3:8). He did this by paying the price to make us holy and by giving us a place in God's family as dearly loved children. We are set free from lies and the destruction they bring. As we embrace this identity, an exciting truth comes to light: not only are we accepted by God, holy and completely loved just as we are, but we have also been enabled to share in his divine nature (2 Peter 1:4). We have been given a new heart!

Before Christ came, God's people were under the law, the old covenant. God's commandments were written down on tablets of stone, and keeping them was the condition for God's blessing. But there was a major problem: no one could keep the law. Our hearts were cold and hard. We were slaves to sin. We would not and could not obey our way into relationship with God. So God, in his love for his wayward people, instituted a new covenant. "I will give you a new heart," God tells us, "and put a new spirit in you; I will remove from you your heart of stone and give you a heart of flesh. And I will put my Spirit in you and move you to follow my decrees and be careful to keep my laws" (Ezek. 36:26–27). Jesus put this new covenant into effect through his death on the cross. Those of us who have received Christ and our new identity in him have also received this new heart.

Our new heart is a heart that actually wants to obey God. At our deepest core we now want to love God and others. As the apostle Paul wrote, "My old self [old identity with the old heart] has been crucified with Christ. It is no longer I who live, but Christ lives in me" (Gal. 2:20 NLT). Through the Holy Spirit, the heart of Christ dwells in each child of God. Paul continued to explain, "And the Spirit gives us desires that are the opposite of what the sinful nature desires" (Gal. 5:17 NLT). When the groaning of life comes, the sinful nature wants to go south, but our new heart wants to go north.

Often, however, we find ourselves wrestling like the apostle Paul in Romans

7:15: "I don't really understand myself, for I want to do what is right, but I don't do it. Instead, I do what I hate" (NLT). But Paul, as we should, comes to a wonderful conclusion: "But if I do what I don't want to do, I am not really the one doing wrong; it is sin living in me that does it" (v. 20 NLT). Paul concludes that this tendency to sin is no longer *who he is*, part of his deepest identity, but rather a power within that he must contend with (v. 23). The battle is in his mind, in the realm of thinking and belief. The Enemy is still there—always wanting to drag us back into slavery to sin by tempting us to believe and act on his lies. But Christ has set us free from the obligation to believe those lies. We no longer have to allow our old way of thinking to dominate our minds and our choices. We can now let the Spirit control our minds, which will result in life and peace (Rom. 8:6). We are free now to do not just what we "should" do but what we "want" to do. When as redeemed, loved children of God we do what we want to do, we are being led by his Spirit, and our lives will produce the fruit of his Spirit.

WHEN WE FAIL

Of course, in this life, there will be times when we fail. Like Paul, we'll want to go north, but we'll end up going south and doing the very thing we hate. At times like this, the Enemy comes with his lies to tell us that we're not who we thought we were after all. He uses our failure as an opportunity to get us back on the performance treadmill and away from the Father's heart. He tempts us to hide, to distance ourselves from God and other believers. At this point, it's vital to remember the truth of who we are and once again receive the Father's forgiveness and grace. We must get back up and choose to believe we're wearing the clothing of our new identity as dearly loved children of God. God is with us and for us. We have a Father who has promised never to condemn us but rather to help us with our weaknesses so that we might bring him glory. He lives within us; we are never alone.

QUESTIONS FOR SELF-EXAMINATION AND DISCUSSION

1. What events, wounds, failures, or circumstances have had the biggest impact on the way you view yourself? What has been communicated to you about your identity through those wounds, failures, and circumstances?

2. How has that shameful or negative self-image influenced the way you
    respond in life and relationships? How does it encourage you to go
    south when you face groaning?
3. How does that negative self-image impact the way you view and inter-
    pret the actions of others?
4. If you truly embraced your identity as God's dearly loved son/daughter,
    how would you respond differently to the groaning of life?
5. As a new creature in Christ, you also have a new heart that wants to
    obey God. What will help you put that new heart into action?

8

GRATITUDE

THE RESPONSE TO GOD'S LOVE

GARY

God is most glorified in us when we are most satisfied in him.
John Piper, *Desiring God*

In the face of God's lavish generosity, the Serpent cultivated discontent and coveting in Eve's heart. He drew her attention to the one thing she couldn't have, causing her to want it more than God and all he provided. The Evil One fostered a spirit of rebellion within her heart. The Enemy seeks to breed the same spirit in you and me. And our culture, which is under Satan's dominion, constantly tells us we deserve to have a newer and bigger truck, a better body, name brand clothes, and the latest and greatest electronic gadget. We need the widest cellular coverage or sharpest and biggest HDTV. We live in constant tension between the Spirit and our fallen nature, with truth and lies. We live in a world system that works to breed discontent and coveting instead of thankfulness to our Creator. Francis Schaeffer put it this way:

> The beginning of men's rebellion against God was, and is, the lack of a thankful heart. . . . The rebellion is a deliberate refusal to be the creature before the Creator, to the extent of being thankful. Love must carry with it a "Thank you," not in a superficial or "official"

way, but in being thankful and saying in the mind or with the voice, "Thank you" to God.[1]

Gratitude is the first evidence of a humble and surrendered heart. It's one of the hallmarks of living north as we embrace God's grace and our true identity in Christ. The heart of a surrendered life knows a core peace and contentment in God and whatever he chooses to provide, even if the storms of life continue.

I once heard a friend say that when we sin, God invites us to sing of his forgiveness. When we love sacrificially, we can celebrate his gracious enablement. When people wound, overlook, or abandon us, we can celebrate God's presence. As the prophet Jeremiah wrote, "The 'worst' is never the worst. Why? Because the Master won't ever walk out and fail to return. . . . His stockpiles of loyal love are immense" (Lam. 3:30–32 MSG). He's always with us. He's always for us. He's gloriously enough to sustain us in the groaning of life. When we walk with God, there's always a reason to be grateful. Ellen Vaughn said:

> The small, compliant human action of saying "thank you" constantly links us to the awesome Creator of the universe. In the practice of perceiving every part of every day as a gift from Him, we stay connected to Christ. . . . The conversations of a continually grateful heart become a way of life, a fountain flowing in us, the means by which we acknowledge our dependence on Christ.[2]

Just as grumbling is a signal telling us we believe lies, gratitude is a signal. It emerges as we believe the truth about the supremacy and sufficiency of Christ. Gratitude grows as we choose north by trusting in God's grace, as we surrender control, as we continue to entrust our soul's deepest longings to God alone, making Jesus the treasure and center of our lives. Our thankful spirit will be demonstrated when we, like the psalmist, can say, "Because your love is better than life, my lips will glorify you. I will praise you as long as I live" (Ps. 63:3–4).

MY PAINFUL JOURNEY

I had high hopes in the early days of my counseling career. With God's help and with my counseling abilities, I dreamed of how it would all turn

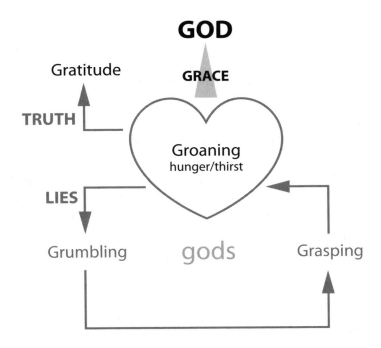

out: people would change, and I'd be a successful, well-known counselor in my Christian community. I'd have a nice house, a nice car, and a nice office to showcase my success. God, of course, would get the glory. I think God was laughing. He dreamed different dreams for me.

The first years of my counseling practice went well. I had a full counseling load with a sizeable waiting list of people who wanted to see me. But as years rolled on and I continued to enter the brokenness of people's lives and marriages, I became discouraged. Christians I worked with struggled significantly—affairs, addictions, domestic violence, childhood sexual abuse, out-of-control spending, divorce, attempted suicide. Such brokenness was not confined to my counseling office. At every church and every small group Lisa and I attended, we saw a plethora of grasping behaviors: eating disorders, marital conflict, depression. . . . These were good, evangelical churches mind you. I was not naive. I knew we all had problems, but I hadn't yet realized that my sense of worth was dependent on my ability to get people to change. God would use failure to bring my lie to the surface so I could worship him.

During the ten years of my private practice, many people repented from going south, turned to God, and genuinely changed. They became humble, grateful, and giving people. I often sang when God allowed me to be a part of such life change. I still do. But many people I worked with refused to walk the painful path of repentance. When that happened, feelings of failure and inadequacy crippled me. I recall the discouragement I felt when one counselee said, "My husband and I have decided to change counselors." That statement held the power to take me deep south for days. Those words brought back my shame of childhood wounds and lies that told me I was and always would be a strikeout. I was choked by weighty feelings of worthlessness, failure, and self-contempt because I wasn't getting affirmation and a sense of significance from the people I foolishly depended on.

During those years, I came to the painful but vital realization that I cannot make people change. Only God has the power to change people, including my own arrogant and idolatrous heart. As anger and self-contempt smoldered within me, I saw how broken and self-centered I was. That's when I came to see that my emotions were signals telling me I believed lies about who could satisfy my longing to feel competent. I saw that I was grasping for significance by getting people to change and to affirm me by saying, "You have what it takes!" I was covetous for power and control instead of surrendering to God's. Though I loved God deeply, I was blind to how I was giving people more power to define my identity than Jesus Christ. It took a long time for me to be able to put these words to my inner struggle. Through the process, I was disillusioned with God, people, and myself. Yet God was ruthlessly and graciously thwarting my false gods. He was a jealous lover fighting for my heart's affections.

I was on the verge of burnout because I was trying and failing to be God. One day in my office, I screamed at God, "Why don't you do more to change people? Why do you just stand there and watch all this moral carnage? Are you happy with the mess down here? Don't you care? Why don't you do more to help me help others turn to you and grow?" Habakkuk's lament was my own:

> How long, O LORD, must I call for help?
>   But you do not listen! . . .
> Must I forever see these evil deeds?
>   Why must I watch all this misery?

Wherever I look,
> I see destruction and violence.
I am surrounded by people
> who love to argue and fight.
The law has become paralyzed. (Hab. 1:2–4 NLT)

I felt powerless, paralyzed by fear of failure, and God seemed to just watch as my "wish dreams" of success crumbled.[3] That was fifteen years ago.

As I grieved and continue to grieve the thousands of ways I and other Christians grasp for life in the false gods of the world, I've been stunned and silenced by God's grace and kindness toward me. As God has helped me see my life through the paradigm of this book, I've come to truly believe that my identity is in Jesus Christ instead of in being good at what I do. Rather than raising my fist at God and asking why he doesn't do more, I'm asking questions like, "God, why do you do *anything* to help me? Why don't you destroy me and be done with the mess I've made of your world?" Instead of grumbling at God for not doing enough, I'm growing in gratitude for his patience and kindness for me and for every other broken person I have the privilege to work with. And I'm singing of the miracle of the new covenant heart within God's people who want God enough to humbly face the truth about themselves.

Of course the pull to go south is there every day, and I still go there. But something is growing in my soul. God shattered my worldly songs, and from the rubble of my false dreams, he is tuning my heart to sing a new song, the song of his unfailing love. God doesn't destroy us because he's in love with us. He tells me again and again I'm his beloved son. His names for me are *Mighty Warrior* and *Field Commander*. By his grace and enablement, I am not a strike-out. Songs of gratitude well up in my heart as I think of Jesus. He's the lover and treasure of my soul.

GROWING IN GRATITUDE

There are thousands of reasons to say thank you to God—good health, a kind word, someone's thoughtful deed, a warm bed, a good job, a good marriage, a trustworthy friend. . . . God enjoys blessing us with good things. It's his nature to give. And when we remember that every good thing comes from

God (James 1:17), good things point us back to him. No gift is small if it comes from God.

Growing in gratitude requires new eyes. We must learn to see that God's good gifts surround us every day. For example, Jesus saw his Father's goodness in the littlest, most natural events of life. Jesus said, "Look at the birds of the air; they do not sow or reap or store away in barns, and yet your heavenly Father feeds them" (Matt. 6:26).

Every day we experience hundreds of ordinary examples of God's grace without noticing. In the rush of our busy schedules, how many of his gifts do we fail to see or enjoy? If we want to cultivate a heart of gratitude for the goodness and greatness of God, we must learn to develop what John Ortberg has called, "the discipline of noticing":

> To notice something—to truly pay attention—is a powerful thing. Children demand it. Spouses feel hurt without it. . . .
>
> The practice of noticing is a skill. It involves learning to pay attention to gifts that we otherwise take for granted. Stop for a moment and try it. The breath you just took, the way your eyes are reading these words, the working of your mind to understand and learn—*notice them*. They are not accidents. Nor are they entitlements. They are gracious gifts. And what's even more amazing is that their Giver is lovingly present with you even as you are experiencing them.
>
> The sight of a garden blooming in a riot of color, a cold glass of water on a hot afternoon, an encouraging word from a coworker, a warm blanket on a chilly night, the taste of your favorite food, a long conversation with a good friend. All ordinary, but all grace nonetheless. Train yourself to notice, to pay attention, to become absorbed in the grace of your Shepherd.[4]

NATURAL GRATITUDE AND GRACIOUS GRATITUDE

In *Religious Affections*, Jonathan Edwards described two types of gratitude: *natural gratitude* and *gracious gratitude*.[5] As the terms imply, natural gratitude is that which we may "naturally" feel and express as a result of a good, pleasant experience; gracious gratitude is rooted in our experience of God's grace, independent of externals. It's important to know the difference between the two or we'll likely become disillusioned with God.

The material world is good. God created all good things for us to enjoy (1 Tim. 6:17). We glorify God when we gratefully enjoy and acknowledge these things as his undeserved gifts. But we must guard our hearts. Yes, material things are good, but they're a limited good. Richard Foster has well said that "to deny the goodness of the created order is to be an ascetic. To deny the limitation of the created order is to be a materialist."[6] Learn to enjoy God's gifts while holding them loosely because natural blessings can be lost. The loss of a job, the betrayal of a friend, a harsh word, an impatient person, a cancerous tumor, or a natural disaster—none of these are far from any of us. Such things will cause us to go south if we're holding onto natural blessings for our core sense of contentment. *Natural gratitude* will not keep us faithful in the groaning of life, especially when our dreams shatter.

When thanks to God comes only in good circumstances, our faith stands on thin ice. It's not a matter of *if* but *when* it will break. When we make created things our god, grasping for our security and significance from them, we'll live in fear of them being taken away. "The greatest enemy of joy is fear," wrote Mike Mason. "Nothing can be deeply enjoyed for fear it will soon be gone."[7] And we'll grumble when they're taken away. C. S. Lewis said that beauty, or life, comes through created things, but it is not *in* them. What comes through them is a longing—ultimately—for God. But when we set our hearts upon those *things*, they become dumb idols that break our hearts.[8]

Toward the end of Jesus' earthly life, he called his disciples *friends*—a tender and intimate word. "I no longer call you servants. . . . Instead, I have called you friends, for everything that I learned from my Father I have made known to you" (John 15:15). Jesus opened his heart to his disciples, disclosing the most intimate truths his Father had shared with him. And on the night Jesus was betrayed, he told his disciples, "I have eagerly desired to eat this Passover with you before I suffer" (Luke 22:15). Jesus eagerly desired to be with his friends that night. Why? "You are those who have stood by me in my trials" (Luke 22:28). Jesus was grateful for his friends. Yet he knew Judas would betray him and Peter would succumb to the fear of man and swear he never knew Christ. Jesus knew all his disciples would forsake him. But he wasn't shaken by their weakness and failure. "You will leave me all alone," he told them. "Yet I am not alone, for my Father is with me" (John 16:32). Therefore, "he loved them [his disciples] to the very end" (John 13:1 NLT). Jesus experienced the natural gratitude of friendship, but when friends failed, he remained true to them because he knew his Father's sustaining power from which *gracious gratitude* flows.

Edwards said the truest and deepest form of gratitude gives thanks for who God is and for all he's done: "Love is . . . the fountain of all the affections," and from it springs, "gratitude to God for his goodness."[9] We naturally praise what we most deeply value. If the supreme value of our hearts' affections is on one thing—God—our lives will spill over in gratitude and praise. It is right to seek and find our deepest contentment, joy, and personal satisfaction *in God.*

In the face of suffering and life's unfairness, Asaph experienced such gratitude:

> Whom have I in heaven but you?
>> And earth has nothing I desire besides you.
> My flesh and my heart may fail,
>> but God is the strength of my heart
>> and my portion forever. . . .
> But as for me, it is good to be near God. (Ps. 73:25–26, 28)

No suffering can destroy gracious gratitude:

> It is the real evidence of the Holy Spirit in a person's life. Gracious gratitude can grow in the midst of pain, trouble, and distress. We hear it in the intimate whispers of the psalmist who longs to know God more deeply even as enemies surround him. We see it in the otherwise inexplicable surety of Job: "Though You slay me, yet will I trust in You." We feel it in the apostle Paul's contentment regardless of his circumstances. If threatened with death, he says: "Fine. To die is gain!" If kept alive, fine again: "For me to live is Christ!" He was unstoppable, unquenchable, full of thanks and peace and joy, not because of what he had, but Who he knew. . . .
>
> Though our world may shatter, we are secure in Him.[10]

Gracious gratitude grows as we hone the affections of our hearts down to treasuring Jesus. That's simplicity of heart—finding our significance and security in Christ *and nothing else.* A. W. Tozer explained the evil of seeking *"God-and"*:

> In the *and* lies our great woe. If we omit the *and* we shall soon find God, and in Him we shall find that for which we have all our lives been secretly longing. . . .
>
> The man who has God for his treasure has all things in One. Many ordinary treasures may be denied him, or if he is allowed to have them, the enjoyment of them will be so tempered that they will never be necessary to his happiness . . . for having the Source of all things he has in One all satisfaction, all pleasure, all delight. Whatever he may lose he has actually lost nothing, for he now has it all in One, and he has it purely, legitimately and forever.[11]

TAKE THIS TEST

We may say we seek Christ alone, yet we're often blind to the ways we covet something in addition to him. How can we discern if we're coveting something in God's place? The Ten Commandments provide the context for a test we can take every day, all day.

The first of the Ten Commandments says, "You shall have no other gods before me" (Exod. 20:3). The last commandment declares, "You shall not covet" (Exod. 20:17). The bottom line is this: You have God, so be content. *Contentment in God that results in gratitude for God is the result of making God our only God.* Therefore, whatever breaks our contentment in God tells us we are coveting something in place of him. We are breaking the first and last commandments.

> I think there are two practical tests as to when we are coveting against God or men; first, I am to love God enough to be contented; second, I am to love men enough not to envy. . . . A quiet disposition and a heart giving thanks at any given moment is the real test of the extent to which we love God at that moment.
>
> FRANCIS SCHAEFFER, *True Spirituality*

Grumbling is a signal that tells us our contentment in God has been broken. Believing the truth of Christ's sufficiency means we will have a core contentment in God that frees us from the enslavement of demanding or coveting *anything* from people or circumstances. We may have many deep desires, and we may hurt deeply if those desires are denied us, but when we believe the truth of Christ's incomprehensible worth, his unfailing love, and our true identity as his dearly loved children, we will be able to stay centered on Jesus in the groaning of life. We do not have to go south and sin. "Give thanks in all circumstances," the Bible tells us, "for this is God's will for you in Christ Jesus" (1 Thess. 5:18).

We need not pretend to be thankful *for* tragic circumstances. God certainly cares about our suffering (2 Cor. 1:3–6), and there is a place for grieving and lament, but we can be thankful for the good he is working in us through those circumstances. The good is always God. What more can we *need* if the transcendent, living God is always with us, for us, and in us? This is the secret that Paul *learned* (yes, it is a process) when he said, "I have learned the secret of being content in any and every situation. . . . I can do everything through him who gives me strength" (Phil. 4:12–13). This isn't easy; it requires intentionality to flesh this out in our daily lives (Phil. 2:12–13).

CONTENTMENT CENTERED IN GOD

Our pastor once invited our church to share how God had helped us grow. One Sunday morning while I was sharing with our congregation how I was learning to make Jesus the treasure and core contentment of my soul, God opened the heart of a sixteen-year-old girl named Emily. She later shared with our church how God helped her find her contentment in him:

> When in public situations, women have a tendency to scan the area for the boys they like. If they are spotted, we proceed to "arrange" ourselves in such a way that they take notice of us. . . . This has been a pattern for me because I feel sick with the weight of loneliness that attacks me daily. For so long, I have spent irreplaceable time wishing to have a boyfriend and making every effort to be as attractive as possible to ensnare one. I did this because I knew I must be affirmed by someone. I need to be loved, treasured, and desired because that is the way God created me. . . .

Today while I was listening to Mr. Heim talk about his struggle to be content, it hit me like a five-ton elephant. God created me. Hah! He created me to be fulfilled. But here's the thing that I didn't comprehend and that was clearly waiting to make itself known to me; he created me to be fulfilled by . . . himself! I am not made to be fulfilled by humans but by *him*. Him. *Him!!!* I could have sung! What a beautiful thing to be hit by. Much pleasanter than being hit by an elephant, but with a similar effect. I don't think I can be or act the same way anymore.

You never really see your own folly until you see it in writing. When I think about it, the affirmation that can be received by a boy is irrelevant compared to the affirmation gained when God, who created everything in existence, chose to love me.

I hope this enthusiasm will last, but I am reminded of what Aslan said to Jill in the *Silver Chair:* "Here on the mountain I have spoken to you clearly: I will not often do so in Narnia. Here on the mountain, the air is clear and your mind is clear; as you drop down into Narnia, the air will thicken."[12] I am so thankful that God has spoken to me clearly today. I guess the real next step I need to take is to remember how incredible God is. I choose to be content every day with his love and promise to try to seek acceptance and fulfillment only in him.

Like all of us, Emily struggles to maintain her contentment in God. But she understands the daily battle for her heart and God is helping her win the war. Whoever marries Emily will be one lucky man.

Schaeffer's contentment test leaves us no room to justify our sin of going south into coveting and grumbling. While sorrow and righteous anger may be legitimate responses to certain circumstances, when we return evil for evil, our contentment in God has been broken and we have gone south. God graciously invites us to come to him, face the darkness, grieve our pain, face the lie, and repent. At times, my contentment in God can be shaken by something as simple as misplaced car keys, by an unexpected bill that comes in the mail, or a harsh word from a friend. My immaturity saddens me, but my security in Jesus is growing and I'm grateful.

> I know of no other way to triumph over sin long-term,
> than to gain a distaste for it, because of a superior
> satisfaction in God.
>
> JOHN PIPER, *Desiring God*

We either believe in Christ's sufficiency and the fullness of his love, which leads to a core contentment and gratitude in God, or we'll live for ourselves, covet something in this world, and grumble and grasp. Will we worship God or gods? That's the battle. When we see life through the test of the Ten Commandments, we understand how utterly dependent we are on God's forgiving grace and enabling power every day. As we live by his grace and forgiveness, we worship him. Growing our gratitude in God grows our ability to resist the pull to go south.

THE JOURNEY CONTINUES

Experiencing gracious gratitude and contentment in God doesn't happen with a single choice to believe God is enough, though each choice matters. It grows over a process of years and decades that involve failure, repentance, brokenness, and abandoning ourselves to God again and again. We learn to walk with God as he uses the dance of sorrow and joy throughout our lives. Dan Allender commented:

> Aging is inevitable, while becoming mature is uncertain. . . .
>
> Growing up, as opposed to merely growing old, compels us to embrace both joy and sorrow. To mature we must learn to suffer and not yield or turn hard. To mature we must also learn to engage joy and not demand that it hang around, nor fabricate a counterfeit when it departs. There are many other ways to measure maturity, perhaps, but they all dance to the music of sorrow and joy.
>
> How we embrace—or refuse to hold—sorrow and joy will define our lives. If we capitulate to sorrow, we will become cowards. If we allow sorrow to make us hard, then we will grow cold and eventually cruel. If we demand that joy remain constant, we will become self-consumed. And if we create a counterfeit joy, our lives will be riddled with impulsivity and addictions. Life demands that we either grow or stagnate.[13]

During a time of significant struggles in my counseling career, an additional season of sorrow crashed over me by way of an unexpected lawsuit. Depositions, meetings with attorneys, and the uncertainty of the outcome haunted me for well over two years. I didn't know if the outcome of the suit would leave me poor and indebted. During this dark night of my soul, I would turn to God and entrust myself to him no matter what, but then I'd lose sight of him and go south into unbelief, fear, and anger. I went through this cycle many times. Early one morning as I was driving to one of my counseling offices in Muskegon, the words of Habakkuk spoke deeply to me. That morning I worshipped God in a way I never had worshipped him before. In the face of possibly losing everything, God became my everything. From a place deep within, I confessed that even if I ended up on the street, I could be joyful in God my Savior. He was enough to sustain me. It was an experience of holy abandonment. The words of Habbakuk were life-giving truth:

> Though the fig tree does not bud
>   and there are no grapes on the vines,
> though the olive crop fails
>   and the fields produce no food,
> though there are no sheep in the pen
>   and no cattle in the stalls,
> yet I will rejoice in the LORD,
>   I will be joyful in God my Savior. (Hab. 3:17–18)

I thank God for Frederick Buechner. God used his story to help me surrender to God as I read *A Room Called Remember*. Buechner helped me understand Habakkuk in fresh ways as I walked with God in the wilderness of unknowing. There I learned to sing the greatest love song I can ever sing. This is the heart of gracious gratitude:

> To be commanded to love God . . . in the wilderness, is like being commanded to be well when we are sick, to sing for joy when we are dying of thirst, to run when our legs are broken. But this is the first and great commandment nonetheless. Even in the wilderness— especially in the wilderness—you shall love him.

We know that wilderness well, . . . there isn't one of us who hasn't wandered there, lost, and who will not wander there again before our time is done. Let me speak for a moment of once when I wandered there myself. The wilderness was a strange city three thousand miles from home. In a hospital in that city there was somebody I loved as much as I have ever loved anybody, and she was in danger of dying. . . .

I had passed beyond grief, beyond terror, all but beyond hope, and it was there, in that wilderness, that for the first time in my life I caught sight of something of what it must be like to love God truly. It was only a glimpse, but it was like stumbling on fresh water in the desert, like remembering something so huge and extraordinary that my memory had been unable to contain it. Though God was nowhere to be clearly seen, nowhere to be clearly heard, I had to be near him. . . . I loved him because there was nothing else left. . . . I loved him not so much in spite of there being nothing in it for me but almost because there was nothing in it for me. For the first time in my life, there in that wilderness, I caught a glimpse of what it must be like to love God truly, for his own sake, to love him no matter what. . . .

"My God, my God, why hast thou forsaken me?" As Christ speaks those words, he too is in the wilderness. . . . He speaks them when there is nothing even he can hear except for . . . his own voice and when as far as even he can see there is no God to hear him. And in a way his words are a love song, the greatest love song of them all. In a way his words are the words we all of us must speak before we know what it means to love God as we are commanded to love him.[14]

FEELING AND REJOICING IN GOD'S LOVE

Our healing will never be complete on this side of glory. Until we see Jesus' face, hear his voice, and feel his embrace, we'll never be satisfied. But our healing on this side of glory can be substantial enough for us to experience contentment and gratitude in God in the face of hardship and daily groaning. And God wants us to feel the peace and joy that comes from being content in his love. Such experiences of joy and happiness are not a consistently felt reality. We get tastes, but those tastes stir our heart's desire for more of God.

Yet many good Christians admit they have never felt God's love. While it's important to choose to believe we are secure in God's love whether we *experience* it or not, I believe God wants us to feel his love. No good husband should be satisfied to hear his wife say, "I believe you love me, but I've never felt your love." Or what good parent would be content if his child said, "I believe you love me, but I've never felt close to you." If good husbands and parents want their loved ones to feel their love, I believe God does too. And lest we be overly pious by saying, "We shouldn't care about feelings; just be obedient," remember that the fruit of the Spirit—the fruit of abiding in Jesus—is, in part, joy and peace (Gal. 5:22). Jesus said, "Ask, and you will receive, that your joy may be full" (John 16:24 ESV). And the psalmist humbly prays, "Satisfy us in the morning with your steadfast love, that we may rejoice and be glad all our days" (Ps. 90:14 ESV).

> "I want to be happy" may be Christian shorthand for "I want to know the One, and the only One, who is in himself all I have ever longed for in all my desires to be happy."
>
> JOHN PIPER, *When I Don't Desire God*

Yet we must take caution. We cannot seek or demand experiences and feelings from God. To demand anything from God is to stop being submissive to him. What then can we do? First and foremost, we must choose to believe God loves us even when we don't feel his love and when life experiences seem to tell us God has abandoned us. We must allow truth to define experience, rather than allowing experience to define truth. Truth keeps us faithful, not experience. The Bible says God loves us. The cross proves it. That settles it. That's the first and most important step toward embracing God's love and growing in gracious gratitude. Until we firmly make that choice, we'll habitually go south when we face pain and difficulty.

Years ago, Lisa and I attended a communion service where the pastor asked everyone to raise their hand if God had met them in some special way that year. Lisa's hand went up. While driving home I asked her why she raised her hand; how had God met her in a special way? Lisa told me she had made a deliberate decision to believe God loved her even though she had never felt his love. She said she was tired of doubting God's love when life didn't go well. This was a major turning point for her. Today, Lisa's decision to trust in God's love continues to bear spiritual fruit in her life. *Choosing* to believe God loves us is the bottom line. But what will help us *feel* God's love?

We must take risks with God. David Benner has well said that, "It is not the fact of being loved unconditionally that is life-changing. It is the risky experience of *allowing myself* to be loved unconditionally."[15] Truth transforms us when it's received in vulnerability. That is, truth transforms us when we trust in God's love enough to take the risk of being fully honest and emotionally naked with him; letting him see all our brokenness, sin, and failure. We must linger with him in prayer and confession, allowing him to look deep into our eyes. We must not pull back in shame or try harder to shape up in order to earn his love. In those vulnerable and intimate moments, we have the opportunity to receive and experience God's love. When Israel's rebellion was at its worst, God disciplined her. At the same time, the word of the Lord came to her, saying, "The Lord your God is with you, he is mighty to save. He will take great delight in you, he will quiet you with his love, he will rejoice over you with singing" (Zeph. 3:17). When Israel was at her worst, God still delighted in her and sang over her. When we're at our worst, God sings over us too! When we trust that is true, we experience the joy of being loved by him. And we please God when we trust that he loves us and sings over us even in all our brokenness. There is no condemnation to anyone who is in Christ (Rom. 8:1). None. We're a mess, and he's crazy about us. We can't earn his love; we can only surrender to his love. That's life changing. That brings repentance and gratitude. We want to obey God. Coming to this place requires time in the Word of God, asking the Holy Spirit to speak to us and to tell us what Jesus thinks of us. It means waiting and listening for his response. It will come to us in God's time and way. He will quiet us in his love.

Taking the risk of being loved unconditionally by God requires the risk of being vulnerable with others by confessing our sin and brokenness to trusted friends. This often feels riskier than confessing to God; therefore, many do not experience God's love in this way because they hold back. Such confession is a risk because our friends may not respond in loving ways. They may think less of us, scold us, or try to fix us by giving quick advice. That hurts. *But as we entrust ourselves to God alone for our security and significance, we can take risks to open ourselves to others.* Dan Lokers, Ron Underwood, and Tim Hoyt are three good men who know everything about me. I've taken many risks in letting them know my struggles and failures. And I know everything about them. We want God enough to confess our sins to one another and pray for each other so we can be healed (James 5:16). Hearing God say through them, "Thank you, Gary, for trusting us enough to tell us your sin. We *know* your sin doesn't define you. Christ in you defines you. We're grateful that you open your heart to us like this" is life-giving. Christ comes to us through the love and acceptance of one another. Love opens the heart. Truth transforms it. Being fully known and fully accepted is life changing.

As Dan, Ron, Tim, Lisa, and others in my life reflect the heart of God to me and I to them, we feel God's love, and in turn, our love for him is stirred. Our passion for God is deepened.

Moreover, trusting in God's love enables us to take risks in loving others. Truly trusting our needs for security and significance to God alone must translate into taking risks in loving others. There is no greater joy than pointing people to God. Loving others can be risky, though. We can experience rejection and failure. But in light of who God is and all he's done, the risk is worth taking.

> Be kind to each other, tenderhearted, forgiving one another, just as God through Christ has forgiven you. Imitate God, therefore, in everything you do, because you are his dear children. Live a life filled with love, following the example of Christ. He loved us and offered himself as a sacrifice for us, a pleasing aroma to God. (Eph. 4:32–5:2 NLT)

Gratitude comes when we receive God's gifts. *Joy* comes when we give his gifts to others.

QUESTIONS FOR SELF-EXAMINATION AND DISCUSSION

1. How would your life be different if you practiced "the discipline of noticing"—seeing and thanking God for all his ordinary gifts each day? Make a list of those gifts.
2. Do you typically depend on natural gratitude or gracious gratitude for your sense of well-being? Why do you think that is true? What are the consequences of depending on one or the other?

3. If a quiet disposition and a heart giving thanks at any given moment is the true test of your dependence on God, what does that test reveal about you? Are you typically living north or south?

4. Is your life characterized by gratitude that comes from contentment in Jesus or by grumbling that covets something in his place? Why is that true? What will help you experience the gracious gratitude that comes from depending on Christ alone for your longings, for your security and significance?

5. Recall the Piper quotation on page 168. What sin would God want you to triumph over by gaining a distaste for it because of superior satisfaction in God? What will help you gain that superior satisfaction in God?

6. Has there ever been a time in your life when you sang "the greatest love song" of loving God when everything seemed lost? What happened? How did you come to that place of surrender?

7. In what ways have you experienced God's love and acceptance? If you have never experienced God's love, which risk or risks might you be avoiding—confession to God, confession to others, loving others— and why?

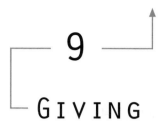

9

GIVING

THE FRUIT OF A GRATEFUL HEART

LISA

The only thing that counts is faith expressing itself through love.

Galatians 5:6

I love sweets. I love candy, pie, brownies, ice cream, and cookies—especially cookies. Warm peanut butter cookies with a big chocolate kiss in the middle, shortbread cookies layered with chocolate, homemade chocolate chip cookies with pecans, oatmeal cookies with raisins, and buttery sugar cookies are all foretastes of heaven if you ask me. We can't keep them in the house; the temptation is just too much. Gary, on the other hand, is a meat man. If he doesn't have meat at a meal, he thinks he hasn't eaten. He's happy when he finds beef jerky in his Christmas stocking. He's been known to cook a chicken at midnight just for a snack.

We've all tasted things in life that are so good they make us want more and more. To the forgiven sinner-turned-saint, there's nothing sweeter than the taste of God's generous and unfailing love. And the more we find our deepest satisfaction at the table of his love, the less we'll approach the world and relationships as hungry takers, motivated to fill our own growling stomachs. But it's not enough to sit endlessly at the Lord's table, gorging ourselves on his goodness. As our own needs, by faith, are met in Christ, we are freed from demanding that people meet our needs, and we are called to begin to offer tastes of God to a hungry and thirsty world. God made us for a mission.

> Some people are always greedy for more,
> but the godly love to give!
> PROVERBS 21:26 NLT

Gary mentioned in an earlier chapter that around our church we have a saying: the greatest day in your life is the day you face yourself. Though I was unaware of it, by that standard I was about to have a fantastic day on the day a friend and mentor invited Gary and me to lunch. It started innocently enough with casual conversation that drifted to a discussion about the church small group that we all attended. "Lisa," our friend said, "tell me why you come to the group. What keeps you going back?"

Like an unwitting mouse, oblivious to the trap set for me, I took the bait and answered honestly. "Well, I just enjoy being with that group. I find the discussions helpful. I guess I get a lot out of being with those people."

My friend sat back in his chair, was quiet for a moment, then leaned forward and looked me in the eye. Without a hint of harshness or condemnation, he asked another question. "Lisa, when do you come to the group thinking about what you could do to encourage Bob and Mary, or what you could give to Tammy?" Though the confrontation was delivered with gentleness, the question hit me like a ton of bricks. Suddenly no longer hungry, I pushed my half-eaten lunch aside to eat the humble pie I had just been served. We both knew the answer was *never*. I never came to the group with the clear thought or intention of giving, blessing, or encouraging someone there. Oh, I may have blessed someone there from time to time, but it was never by thoughtful intent. The truth was, I was happy, and I continued in the group mostly because I was a satisfied taker. Through the power of the Holy Spirit, my friend's question had exposed my self-centeredness, and I'm grateful for that. In my heart of hearts, I truly don't want to be a self-centered person. The Spirit, working through my friend, enabled me to face something about myself that day and set me on a course of repentance.

My journey from self-centeredness (going south) to other-centeredness (going north) is an ongoing excursion that has had to be revisited many, many times since that transformational lunch with my friend. I think that many Christians, like me, struggle with a consumer approach to life. That is, we evaluate the quality of our churches, small groups, friendships, jobs, and marriages based on what we get from them instead of what we give to them. As a result we focus on how these relationships are meeting our needs more than on what impact we can have on them for the good.

Our culture reinforces the idea that things and people that don't meet our needs can and should be discarded for something or someone else that promises to do so. A consumer is most happy when his world is meeting his needs, but he is extremely prone to going south when faced with disappointment. While there is a time and place for evaluating whether or not it's right to stay with a particular church, small group, relationship, or job, sometimes we trade these as easily as we trade our automobiles. But as the Spirit helps each of us have our "greatest day" by opening our eyes to our own self-centered and consumerist approach to life and relationships, we find not condemnation but grace. We receive help to move from being grasping consumers to grateful givers for the sake of others who groan.

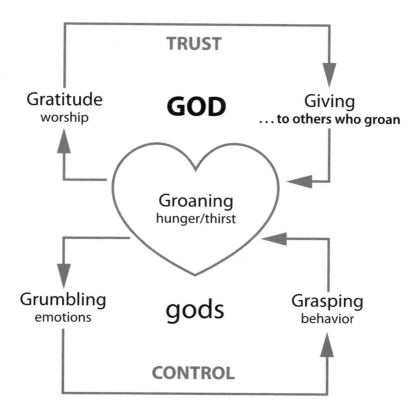

GIVING FLOWS FROM GRATITUDE

The woman could not stop kissing those feet, those beautiful feet that had brought her the good news of her forgiveness and acceptance before God. Luke 7:36–50 tells us the story of this woman, whose well-known reputation for immorality preceded her. She wept as she washed and anointed the feet of Jesus in the presence of those who obviously held contempt in their hearts for both of them. Simon the Pharisee, the pious spiritual leader, had neglected to greet Jesus with a kiss or to even give the common courtesy of water to wash the dust from his feet. This woman, however, even in the presence of those who would shame and mock her, could not keep from giving. Forgiven and set free from her sin, no longer bound to draw her identity from those who would call her a worthless prostitute, she found a way to express her gratitude to the only one whose opinion of her mattered. With strength and dignity, her love overflowed and beautifully exposed the shame of those who sought to shame her. Unlike this woman, they had earned their righteousness, or so they thought, by following the law. But earned righteousness is always a thin and filthy rag that can never cover the sin of a self-centered life. The self-righteous are always exposed by their lack of love. As Jesus told Simon, the one who is forgiven little, loves little; the one who is forgiven much, loves much (Luke 7:47).

Only when we are truly stunned by our self-centeredness, as I was that day at lunch with my friend, do we begin to see how much we need to be forgiven. Sometimes it's harder for folks like me who grew up being "good," who have not lived lives of obvious sin, to understand this. But as we look deeper into our own heart's motivations to see the many subtle ways we habitually go south into grumbling and grasping for control over life and as we refuse to justify our actions before a holy God, we can begin to see our desperate need. When we find ourselves caught in our sinful responses, helpless to do any better, we also find that Jesus is there offering us his hand of forgiveness and help. Humbled and thankful, we begin to see that we have more in common with this former prostitute than we do with the Pharisees. And that's a good thing. We begin to respond more like her and less like them. Our gratitude begins to overflow into joyful giving. While giving can be wrongly motivated by many things, including pressure, guilt, the desire to look good, tradition, or obligation, the kind of giving that delights God is the free, cheerful giving that flows from the gratitude of forgiven sinners (2 Cor. 9:5–9). It is the desire to bless others with a taste of the God that we have tasted.

GIVING BEGINS WITH PRAYER

In John 15:1–8, Jesus tells his disciples that our lives bring great glory to the Father when they bear much fruit. It is through bearing fruit that we give back to God and pass on his nourishing love to others. As we stay connected to Jesus, the life-giving Vine—through time in the Word and the intimate conversation of prayer—and find our needs met in him, we're enabled to become life givers. It's in this context of bearing fruit that Jesus informs us that we may come to him and ask for anything we want and it will be granted! It is his will that our lives produce lasting fruit. He's ready and willing to supply anything we need for that to happen.

When we come to God in prayer with the heart and mind-set of bearing fruit for his kingdom and of being a giver, he will immediately begin to show us areas of life where we can give. Beginning with those closest to us, he'll show us people he wants us to touch with words, acts of kindness, patience, gentleness, support, and generosity. As we bring our family members, friends, church, country, and the world before the throne of grace, not only are we asking God to meet their needs, but we're also asking God what they most need from us. What would it look like for us to intentionally build redemptive relationships with others by offering them "cups of cold water" as they daily face a world of groaning? What would it look like for us to respond redemptively to those around us who are going south in grumbling and grasping? As we bring these questions to our heavenly Father in prayer and listen for the Spirit's direction, we will find all that we need to be wise, Spirit-led, intentional givers. Our lives will bear fruit for the kingdom of God.

LOOKING OUT ANOTHER'S WINDOW

One of the things that can help us begin to be people who give cups of cold water and respond redemptively to others is what we call learning to look out the other person's window. We are indebted for this image to psychologist Irvin Yalom, who illustrates this idea through the story of a cancer patient:

Decades ago I saw a patient with breast cancer, who had, throughout adolescence, been locked in a long, bitter struggle with her naysaying father. Yearning for some form of reconciliation, for a new, fresh beginning to their relationship, she looked forward to her father's driving her to college—a time when she would be alone with him for several hours. But the long-anticipated trip proved a disaster: her father behaved true to form by grousing at length about the ugly, garbage-littered creek by the side of the road. She, on the other hand, saw no litter whatsoever in the beautiful, rustic, unspoiled stream. She could find no way to respond and eventually, lapsing into silence, they spent the remainder of the trip looking away from each other.

Later, she made the same trip alone and was astounded to note that there were *two* streams—one on each side of the road. "This time I was the driver," she said sadly, "and the stream I saw through my window on the driver's side was just as ugly and polluted as my father had described it." But by the time she had learned to look out her father's window, it was too late—her father was dead and buried.[1]

Learning to look out the other person's window enables us to understand, or at least imagine, the groaning that may be part of their life experience. It draws us to empathy. Justified self-centeredness is the hallmark of those who take little time to think about another person's pain. Even though the other may be going south and reacting sinfully in their groaning, our compassion for their pain will allow them to experience us as someone who genuinely cares.

Years ago Gary and I were traveling home from a conference with a good friend and mentor. Facing a two-hour layover before our connecting flight, we decided to pass the time in the airport coffee shop. Sliding into a booth, we chatted while waiting for the waitress to arrive. After several minutes passed, we began to try to get the waitress's attention. Though she certainly saw us, the desire for service on our part created no apparent urgency on hers. Eventually she made her way to our table and greeted us with all the enthusiasm of a soggy doughnut. Our requests for coffee and apple pie were met with an irritated sigh, and, "I'll have to check what we got." As she walked away, Gary and I exchanged a look of frustration and grumbled about the poor service. Our friend, on the other hand, took a totally different tack. "I wonder if her husband drinks up the check every week," he said. "I wonder if she had a lot of other dreams for her life that just haven't panned out, and here she is stuck working in this lousy coffee shop." Instead of joining in our grumbling about the poor service, he shifted our attention away from ourselves and onto her world. Humbled, we began to imagine what her story might be and the groaning that she may be facing. Our friend had helped us to look out her window. As a result, we found a feeling of compassion and a desire to somehow be a blessing to this woman. We delighted in making attempts to chat with her when she returned with our order and leaving her a generous tip that day—not because she deserved it but because we wanted to be a taste of Jesus to her obviously weary soul.

All around us people are hurting more than we know. The people we come into contact with on a daily basis—whether spouse, friend, cashier, custodian, pastor, or prima donna—have a story, a window through which they view and respond to life. Often we find ourselves simply reacting to the ways in which they hurt, offend, or inconvenience us without considering what might be at the heart of their behavior. While pain never excuses sin, it's often behind it because in a fallen world, everyone's story involves groaning of some kind.

Though there are times that we need to confront and hold others accountable for their sin, when we allow ourselves to imagine the world from their perspective, we are much less apt to be harsh and judgmental and more prone to be compassionate and tenderhearted. While it is not possible for us to know the individual story of every person we meet, we can to some degree assume that they too hunger and thirst to know that they are valued, loved, and respected.

Furthermore, they have probably been deeply impacted by relationships and circumstances that have communicated something to the contrary. They too have a fallen nature and are predisposed to live according to lies. When we go north in response to them and offer them a taste of God's kindness and strength, we invite them to go north to him as well. Keeping these things in mind throughout the day helps us to maintain an other-centered focus and helps us to be intentional as a conduit of Christ's love to everyone we come in contact with.

Of course, the better we know another person and their story, the clearer we can see out their window and the more specifically we can respond to their needs with love and truth. There should be at least a few people in our lives whose stories we have taken the time to know in depth—our spouses, children, close friends, and small-group members. What people or events have impacted their lives the most deeply for ill or for good? What lies are they tempted to believe about God, themselves, and others? What helps them to believe God's truth? How can we best be used of God to communicate that truth to them?

Learning to ask good questions about such matters should not be left to the counselors and therapists among us but should be the practice of every truly giving person. Asking questions communicates interest and a desire to listen to and learn about the other person's world.[2] When others sense our interest, understanding, and acceptance, trust is built. As trust is built, we have the opportunity to go deeper in offering the truth, help, and encouragement that they may need to get on and stay on the path of righteousness. The better we know another person, the more specifically we can pray for wisdom and discernment about how to love them well.

GIVING CALLS FOR LOVE

In Ephesians 5:1–2, Paul calls us to be imitators of God and to live a life of love. And how does God love? Not just when we are dressed in our Sunday best, doing well, on top of life, and being good. No. He loves us when we're a ragged, failing, miserable, ugly, selfish mess. At our worst moment, when we're going south as an enemy of God, he sent his Son to die for us. Likewise, we are called to love as we have been loved and to give as we have been given to. The giving that sets Christians apart from the world is the willingness to love others—not just those who are good to us but also those who have opposed, betrayed, hurt, used, and abused us. We are called to love our enemies and do good to them (Matt. 5:44). It's then that we best display the character and heart of our God and act most like his dearly loved children. We reflect God when we offer forgiveness, which then opens the door to many other good gifts of love.

A superb taste of God was offered to the world in March of 2003 when the story of Vickie Prantle was featured on the front page of the *Grand Rapids Press*:

Vickie Prantle is not bitter or filled with hate, but she wants the teenagers accused of disfiguring her face to see the photograph taken of her at the hospital. In the picture that will be used as evidence by the Kent Country sheriff's department, her face is unrecognizable—her nose and right eye and upper lip laid open by the brown brick dropped randomly onto her Chevrolet Blazer from a highway overpass. . . .

Her husband said he believes his wife's attitude has helped her focus on healing, but he's amazed at how quickly she could forgive. "The part that people don't understand is this forgiveness is not something that comes from us," he said. "It comes from God."

He and his wife believe the brick had a purpose. It is the only way they can explain the randomness. . . . Vickie Prantle is shy, working behind the scenes at Smyrna Bible Church. The incident has provided her with a chance to show her faith in God, she said.

"He was in control of this, just like He's in control of everything," her husband said. "The bigger the thing that happens to you, the bigger the things that will come out of it. . . . When would Vickie Prantle be able to tell people how she feels about God?"[3]

The brick that was dropped through Vickie's windshield broke nearly every bone in her face and completely destroyed her right eye. Years later she was still undergoing painful reconstructive surgery to put her face back together. Yet Vickie was never just a victim of some random act of evil. Follow-up stories featured her ongoing battles with pain, but also the positive impact of her forgiveness on one of the young men who caused it. Though she held him accountable for his actions, her kindness and forgiveness toward the one who caused her irreparable harm humbled the young man and helped set his life on a new course. Vickie gave as it was given to her. It was a taste of God that left us hungering for more of him and inspired us to be more like him.

While few of us may have to forgive in such dramatic and public situations, in a fallen world, we all have to forgive. Daily we must forgive the ways that others fail to love us well—the spouse who makes a disrespectful comment; the coworker who takes credit for your work; the child who disobeys; the neighbor whose dog digs holes in your yard; and the mother-in-law who, for the four-hundredth time, offers advice you've not asked for. But only those who have been humbled by coming face-to-face with their own failure and need for forgiveness can truly forgive. As we recognize the ways we have dishonored God and hurt people by blindly grasping for control to fill the hunger and thirst of our hearts, we can begin to identify with those who sin against us. We know that we are no better than they are and that we have needed God's help and kindness to find repentance and forgiveness.

Also, only those who are not bound by lies can forgive. We know the Bible's command to forgive those who sin against us, but often we struggle to really do so. Instead, we stuff our anger and try to be nice. Though well intended, this shallow form of forgiveness bypasses our heart and often ends in failure. True forgiveness comes as we trace our anger to our heart belief. Usually our block to forgiveness is the belief that this person has done something to us or has taken something from us that is essential to our well-being. As long as we believe that lie, bitterness will remain. While others do have the power to hurt us and to deprive us of our desires, they do not have the power to deprive us of our deepest personal needs of significance and security. Regardless of their actions, we are still secure in the Father's love (Rom. 8:31–39). Our lives still have meaning and purpose.

Because of this fact, true forgiveness is possible. We may have to grieve the loss of something we held dear such as a job, marriage, or friendship. And we may have to deal with the ongoing, painful consequences of another's actions, but we need not be held hostage to anger and bitterness. As we let go of the lies and embrace the truth, we are freed to overcome any evil with good (Rom. 12:19–21).

Forgiveness moves us past reacting to the sin of another to seeing their deepest need and responding to it from our hearts. Forgiveness enables us to have compassion for people who are lost in their own self-centered worlds, going south, grumbling and grasping to make a life for themselves. When we live a life of grasping, we simply cannot give to others. We cannot even see their needs because we're so bent on getting them to fill our needs. But as we turn away from grasping to a life of giving, we can begin to see the thirst in their hearts that they're seeking to fill from the polluted, stinking stream that can never quench it. In our hearts we find a longing for them to taste the clear, cool, satisfying water of an intimate relationship with Christ that sets them free to love.

This is what Jesus wanted for us as we nailed him to the cross. He gave his life that we might find the spring of Living Water. With our forgiveness, we can now draw others there as well. In Christ, we find the strength and power to choose to go with them the second mile and to continue giving even when our face has been slapped. We can bless when we are cursed, and we can give when no one gives back. Our love is no longer dependent upon the person involved or their response to us but upon the Lord who enables us to give a cup of cool water—a taste of himself.

GIVING INVOLVES RISK

By nature I'm a very cautious person. I like to play it safe, think things through, make no sudden moves. My family makes fun of the way I drive with both hands on the wheel at all times and the way I will go two blocks out of my way just to avoid having to make a left-hand turn across more than one lane of traffic without a stoplight. They once talked me into going on a roller coaster at an amusement park. It was a horrifying experience that, once they pried my white-knuckled hands from the coaster car, I vowed would never be repeated. Though some people thrive on thrills, I enjoy safety and security.

While at times my caution can be wise and helpful, I must relinquish my self-preserving ways when it comes to living a life of love. Growing in other-centered giving often means moving away from what is safe, easy, and comfortable. Just as grasping involves attempting to control another person or circumstance to minimize our groaning, giving often involves letting go of those same people and circumstances and trusting in God's control, provision, and timing. While giving doesn't always have to be a white-knuckled roller-coaster ride, true repentant giving often leaves us feeling vulnerable to the groaning that we most deeply fear. If we take the risk to give our money, we may come up short for things we want. If we risk giving our time or our talents, we may experience criticism or feel unappreciated. If we risk letting go of control, we may be hurt or disappointed. If we risk giving our love, we may be misunderstood, rejected, or taken advantage of. People may take what we give and never reciprocate. Our efforts to lead for the sake of others may lead to failure. Love involves risk.

Two of the biggest obstacles to giving are our feelings of inadequacy and our fear of what others may think of us. In Exodus 2:24–25, we are told that God heard the groaning of his people under slavery in Egypt and decided it was time to act. He chose Moses to be his instrument to bring deliverance to the people of Israel. Moses, however, responded in protest, "Who am I to lead the people of Israel out of Egypt?" (Exod. 3:11 NLT). In other words, "God, I don't have what it takes. Go find somebody else. There's a lot of potential for things to go wrong if I try this, and I really don't want to take that chance." Even though God reassured Moses of his presence and help, Moses continued to throw all the what-if and I'm-not-good-at-this arguments back in God's face. But God would not accept Moses' personal fear of failure as an excuse for him to neglect the groaning of the people in Egypt. Though he did have to face a lot of obstacles and resistance, both from Pharaoh and the people he was seeking to deliver, Moses also saw the great power of God move in ways he never would have had he remained an obscure shepherd in the wilderness (Exod. 3–12).

Many years later the Lord called Jeremiah to speak truth to the nation of Israel. Like Moses, he initially responded with arguments of inadequacy, saying, ""Hold it, Master God! Look at me. I don't know anything. I'm only a boy!" (Jer. 1:6 MSG). Called to bring an unpopular message, fearful Jeremiah wanted out of the assignment. He knew that what God wanted him to give would not be well received. In fact, he was to *expect* opposition, but he was to give anyway.

God refused to accept Jeremiah's arguments: "Don't say, 'I'm only a boy.' I'll tell you where to go and you'll go there. I'll tell you what to say and you'll say it. Don't be afraid of a soul. I'll be right there, looking after you" (Jer. 1:7–8 MSG).

In the same way, we're often called to take the risk of giving for the sake of others even when we doubt our own abilities and see the possibility of failure and rejection. John Ortberg, in his book *If You Want to Walk on Water, You've Got to Get Out of the Boat*, poses the question, "What am I doing that I could not do apart from the power of God?"[4] We naturally want to limit our giving to that which we are certain we can do in our own power. We gravitate toward a giving that allows us to feel safe, well liked, and in control. But Spirit-led giving often brings us to a place where we must enter unknown territory, where trusting in the power of God is essential.

For Patti, repentant giving meant beginning to be more honest with others about her desires, feelings, failures, and limitations. Most of her life had been spent seeking to meet her own needs for security by pleasing and coming through for others. The thought of telling certain people in her life no, or of asking for help with projects and responsibilities caused her anxiety. She felt vulnerable and weak when she let others know her needs, but she was overwhelmed with trying to meet the expectations of those around her, and she was secretly resentful of anyone who would ask for more. As she grew in her relationship with Christ, Patti came to see the idolatry behind her determination to have the approval of certain people, which led her to constantly work herself to a frazzle in order to please them. As she shifted her dependence for her ultimate need for approval to the Lord, she was able to risk the disapproval and rejection of those who had come to expect constant compliance to their wishes. Surprisingly, as Patti found freedom to say no, she also found freedom to say yes in a new way. Though on the surface it looked like she was giving less, in reality she was giving more. Now what she gave was given freely and cheerfully, not under compulsion or out of guilt or fear. Her giving began to be giving that brought glory to God. Her courage to say no when it was called for drew others to respect her, and enabled them to see her as a person they could trust to give an honest answer.

For Greg, Spirit-led giving meant becoming a servant leader to his family. Like Moses, he wanted God to send somebody else, but he, like all husbands and fathers, was the chosen man for the job. Though he had always been competent and well respected in his work life, his pattern of passivity and avoidance at home had created a lot of pain, frustration, and loneliness for his wife and had helped foster a spirit of rebellion in his children. For Greg to begin moving north in repentance meant risking failure and rejection as he stepped into the lives of his family members with greater involvement and direction. This led to, among other things, taking greater responsibility for the family finances and being willing to discipline the children. It meant leading in prayer and getting the family up for church instead of sleeping in. The shift was difficult for the whole family at first, but over time they began to experience the fruit of Greg's giving as he became the leader of the household. His children began to have greater respect for him as their father, and as a family they were able to climb out of debt. This only happened as Greg was willing to start depending upon the power of God by stepping out into an arena of life where he felt neither competent nor confident. He did it for the sake of his love for God and love for others.

Spirit-led giving will always include some element of risk because we are addressing the needs of others while learning to trust God with our own. Often God calls us to giving even when we think we have nothing to give. The widow at Zarephath was called by God to give food to Elijah when she seemed least able to do so. Resigned to certain death from starvation during a time of drought in Israel, she was out gathering fuel to prepare a final meal for herself and her son when Elijah asked her for bread. In fear, she balked at his request, unwilling to part with what little she had left. Faced with her own groaning, her knee-jerk response was to go south and maintain control over what little resources she had. But Elijah encouraged her to go against her fear and obey the Lord by feeding him first. He assured her that in doing so her needs would be met until the crops were once again plentiful in the land (1 Kings 17:9–16). Had she chosen to give way to fear and stay in control, she may have indeed had her final meal and then died. But miraculously, she experienced God's power to provide for her in ways she probably never imagined. Like her, we also put ourselves in a position to see God provide for our needs when we risk giving what we have for the sake of others.

GIVING REQUIRES BOTH TRUTH AND LOVE

Psalm 62:11–12 describes God as both strong and loving. The passage goes on to say that God rewards each person according to what he or she has done. God relates to each of us based on what is most needed from him. At times we experience more of his strength and discipline in our lives, and at other times we experience his great tenderness and compassion. Jesus himself is described as being "full of grace and truth" (John 1:14). Those two qualities defined his style of relating, but were tailored to the person and the need of the moment. For the woman caught in adultery, Jesus led with grace and offered truth. For the Pharisees, he led with truth so that they might find grace. Jesus did what he saw his Father doing.

For us to be imitators of God, who give and love as Jesus did, we too need to be people of both strength/truth and love/grace. Unfortunately, our self-centered patterns of reacting to the groaning of life usually draw us toward being seriously out of balance on one side or the other. Because our fallen nature has only our own needs in mind, we give only the side that we believe will serve us well and get the response that we're looking for. But truth and strength, without a heart of grace and love, result only in harshness, condemnation, and shame. Grace and love, without truth and strength, result in weakness, indulgence, and license. The reality is that when we're out of balance with truth and love, our truth isn't truth and our love isn't love at all. Instead, they become tools for self-centered manipulation and control, and essentially harm others. Anyone can give with just truth or just love. It takes dependence on God and the power of the Holy Spirit to give with a proper balance, tailored to the need of the moment.

DOMINANTS: TRUTH WITHOUT LOVE

As we face ourselves and the ways we have grasped for control and begin to surrender to God, we can also begin to see what others need most from us. Those of us who have been more dominant in our approach have been heavy on the side of truth and strength. Pete was this kind of man. Considering himself a man's man, he had little time for those who struggled with pulling their own weight. He was quick to confront, correct, and advise. He liked to take charge and sometimes take over if things weren't being done the way he believed they should be. Though Pete was usually right in his evaluation of things, he was crushing the spirits of people around him. He led his family in marine-sergeant fashion. With the help and honest feedback of a courageous friend in their small group, Pete came to see the effect his heavy-handed strength and truth were having. He began to see that his wife and children needed not only his willingness to speak the truth but also his kindness, compassion, and patience. As he became slower to speak and quicker to listen and respond with encouragement and kindness, he found that his family relationships took on a new tone. Instead of always resisting his ideas, direction, and leadership, they seemed more cooperative and willing to work together. Pete was becoming a giver, and his family was reaping the rewards.

DOORMATS: LOVE WITHOUT TRUTH

Those of us who have been more fearful and people-pleasing in our approach are usually heavily out of balance, tipping to the side of love and grace. That is, we have been accommodating, compliant, kind, and patient, but at the expense of truth. In fear of losing relationships or the approval of others, we have failed to take the risk of being appropriately honest and forthright. Pete's

wife, Julie, had been this kind of woman (opposites attract and then attack).
She had been a doormat, allowing herself and others to be treated with disre-
spect, as she grasped for acceptance. Growth for her required entrusting her
need for acceptance to God alone as she developed increased courage and willingness to speak honestly with Pete about her feelings. In addition, she started
to offer him truth about the way his leadership style was impacting her and
the children. As she took the risk to give the truth in love regardless of the cost
to herself, others began to experience her as stronger and more confident. Her
husband, though at first threatened by her courage to speak honestly, grew to
enjoy her strength. For the first time in their marriage, he was getting his real
wife. Though she remained kind and compassionate, in strength she was able
to apply boundaries for the sake of others. They began to live with love and
respect.

Dr. Henry Cloud has written that the elements that bring about change in
a person's life are grace and truth combined with time.[5] Certainly, those of us
who are seeking to turn north to God can testify to the important part that
both truth and grace have played in our journey. In turn, we are called to give
both grace and truth, over time and according to the need of the moment, so
that others might turn north as well. The more our relating is flavored with
both, the more we reflect an accurate picture of Jesus to a world in need.

GIVING PRODUCES JOY

Gratitude comes when we receive God's gifts. Joy comes when we give his
gifts to others. There are many wonderful, giving people in our church body—
many who freely and sacrificially give their money, their time, their talents,
and their very lives out of love for God and love for others. Two such people
are Joel and Lois, who, after having three biological children, decided to open
their hearts and their home to five more children who lacked the love and security that every child needs. The latest to join them, eleven-year-old Jael, came
to them especially discouraged and pessimistic. In her world, good things just
didn't happen. She had learned not to hope, not to dream. She couldn't grasp
the love of God or understand the hope and joy of heaven. So Lois hatched a
plan. A few years earlier, they had seen another one of their children, Lydia,
come alive as a result of a family trip to Disney World. Somehow experiencing
the Magic Kingdom had opened the heart of this young girl to the wonder of

God's goodness and the delight of being a little princess, his little princess—something far, far from the world she had known before coming to live with this loving family. Lois's hope was that a similar trip might help Jael open up to the possibility of love as well. Thus, the planning began. Now Joel and Lois are not wealthy people, and they choose not to depend on credits cards, but they were very determined. Their tax refund—plus a 40 percent off deal—covered Disney tickets and hotel rooms. For eight months Lois carefully saved for their travel expenses. The family van needed new tires before they could safely take it on the thirteen-hundred-mile trip. But when Joel took the van in, they learned that tires weren't the only problem. The alignment was off, and the shocks and struts were shot. Every dime that Lois had saved for the trip, plus more, had to be handed over for the repairs. Now they had a reliable vehicle, but no money for gas or food.

Heartbroken, Lois lamented to her Facebook friends that this looked like the death of the Disney trip. Her own dream of doing something special for Jael to help her see that good things do happen seemed lost. She was tempted to stop dreaming herself. Just then something wonderful happened. Though Lois didn't ask for this, and never would have, one of her Facebook friends threw out a bold challenge. "Why don't we help this family? They have given and helped all of us so much. If we each give a small amount, together we can make this happen. Who's willing to help out?"

Immediately, members of the body of Christ began to step up, responding with excitement over the opportunity to bless this dear family. Beginning the following day, money began to come in. Someone handed Joel money at work, and Lois cried. That Sunday at church, numerous friends handed Lois envelopes and checks. Lois cried some more. Love in the form of dollar bills came in the mail every day that week. Anonymous gifts of one hundred dollars and then two hundred dollars came in. By the end of the week, nearly all the money they had spent repairing the van had been replaced. The trip was back on. And Jael, the girl who didn't believe that good things could happen to her, who was afraid to hope, was watching all this. This goes far beyond just a special family vacation for some good people. This is a story of God using his people to rescue a young girl's heart, to help her see love is real.

Lois and Joel cried many tears of joy as they saw God work through his people, but the greatest joy that week wasn't theirs. The greatest joy belonged to those who gave. No one gave because they had to, but rather freely, cheerfully, they gave out of the sheer joy of being part of a plan to love a family and a young girl who had known so little love in life. As Jesus told us, it's truly more blessed to give than to receive (Acts 20:35).

When we care only for our own groaning and we seek to grasp joy by controlling people and circumstances, joy will elude us. But when we tune to the groaning of others and give what we long to receive, we find that joy comes to us. Jesus' command in Matthew 7:12, "Do to others what you would have them do to you," is not just a command to be unselfish; it is the route to life and joy. When we give, we receive.

GIVING AS BOND SERVANTS AND STEWARDS

For us to move north toward God in the groaning of life, we must embrace the truth of who we are as God's dearly loved children. With this truth firmly at our core, we receive and enjoy the reality of his intimate involvement in our lives and the promises of his protection and provision for our needs. But there's another aspect to our identity that must be embraced if we're to see ourselves with accuracy. Not only are we beloved children, but we're also God's servants. As children we receive his love; as servants we have responsibility to give his love away. Jesus himself was God's one and only Son, who knew all the joy of love and fellowship with the Father. Yet he also took on the nature of a servant in order to give to us what he enjoyed.

Something in us recoils at the thought of being someone's slave. But in the days of the Old Testament, some people fell upon such hard times that they were left with no alternative but to sell themselves into slavery in order to receive food, shelter, and wages for their work.[6] In the book of Exodus, God provided laws of protection for those who fell into such troubled times. The law of Moses said if a man bought a Hebrew servant, he was to serve for six years. But in the seventh year, he was to be set free. The servant was to pay nothing for his freedom. If after living and working for his master, however, the servant said, "I love my master, . . . I do not want to go free," then the master was to bring his servant before the judges. At the doorpost he was to pierce his servant's ear with an awl. The servant would then become his master's bond servant forever (Exod. 21:1–6).

When we experience the goodness of our master, we too want to become his bond servant. We want him to pierce our ear. We *want* to live for God and do his will. We *want* to love and serve others just as God lavishly loves and serves us. Every day, all day, God calls us into a life-giving adventure of walking with him as we serve others. This is true security, significance, and meaning in life. After Paul wrote eleven chapters to explain what God has done for us, he said, "And so, dear brothers and sisters, I plead with you to give your bodies to God because of all he has done for you. Let them be a living and holy sacrifice—the kind he will find acceptable. This is truly the way to worship him" (Rom. 12:1 NLT).

When we see ourselves as God's grateful, willing servants, we come to understand that we're also stewards of all that we have and all that we are. In biblical times, it was common for a master who had to travel to a distant place to leave the management of his entire estate in the hands of trusted servants. Even though they did not own the property, they were responsible to see that it flourished and prospered in the master's absence. We have been entrusted with our lives, time, talents, abilities, and money to be managed for the Master and for the sake of his kingdom. *Everything* we have is really God's. Because of the Master's love for us, we voluntarily surrender our freedom to use these gifts for our own prosperity and pleasure, and instead use them to build up the church and bring the message of Christ's love to a dying world.

I once heard Don Cousins comment that while many organizations in the world have volunteers, the church has servants.[7] The difference has tremendous implications for the way we view ourselves and our giving. While volunteers may give their time and resources to support an organization, servants serve a master—a person. We give and serve to please our Lord and to bring him joy. Motivated by love for the Master, we seek to bring him honor by our humble service, knowing that we have already received far more than we could ever repay. We choose to delay our immediate gratification in order to live for the day of glory when we will hear the words, "Well done, my good and faithful servant" (Matt. 25:21 NLT). Though the world typically doesn't value servants, in the kingdom of heaven they are the true VIPs and will be invited to enter into the joy of the Master. It's in receiving our identity as dearly loved daughters and sons that we find our security, and it is in living out our identity as bond servants who produce fruit for the Master that we find our eternal significance.

When we're grumbling and grasping, our own needs, desires, fears, and worries are the focus of our lives. Giving requires shifting our focus from our own concerns to those around us. We're called to build God's kingdom, not our own. This is dying to self. Sometimes our giving can result in immediate joy as we see the impact that we're having for good in the lives of others. At other times, like Jesus, when we give, we'll experience rejection, heartbreak, persecution, and suffering at the hands of those we may be truly seeking to help and love well. Giving to others in the name of Jesus is a risk in terms of earthly responses and outcomes; yet we can be sure that it's a safe investment in God's kingdom. Even if our attempts to give and love well end in groaning for us, we can be assured that we are participating in the suffering of Christ and these troubles are producing for us a glory that vastly outweighs them (2 Cor. 4:17). Our giving will always lead to joy—either in this world or in the world to come. As the martyred missionary Jim Elliot once said, "He is no fool who gives what he cannot keep to gain what he cannot lose."[8]

QUESTIONS FOR SELF-EXAMINATION AND DISCUSSION

1. Do you approach your church, small group, job, marriage, friendships, or other relationships primarily as a giver or as a taker (grasper)? How do you handle things when you don't get what you want from those groups or relationships? Rate yourself on a scale of one to ten. If ten means, "I'm a living sacrifice," and one means, "It's all about my comfort," what number would you say best describes the way you live?

2. Whose "windows" do you need to learn to look out more often? How will learning to see life from their perspective aid you in giving to them?

3. Is there anyone you need to forgive so that you can begin to give to them? What do you think giving to this person might look like? Do they need more grace or truth or both? Why?

4. Where do you think God might be calling you to take more risks in giving in order to love him and others? Describe a moderate risk, a big risk. What fears might be holding you back from taking these risks?

5. Share a time when you experienced joy as the result of giving. How did your giving impact others as well as yourself?

PART FOUR

YOU-TURN

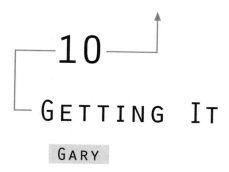

—10—

GETTING IT

GARY

Whenever the Spirit of God is involved we can expect that the focus will be on Christ—in community, on Christ being formed in us individually and together.
Julie Gorman, *Community That Is Christian*

"Getting it" means we begin to see and understand how we specifically forsake God and go south when we experience groaning. We begin to "get it" when we put words to our specific lies that take us south and when we recognize the specific ways we grasp for control. We start to get it when we begin to repent from those lies and choose to believe that Jesus Christ alone, and whatever he chooses to provide, is enough to sustain us in the groaning of life. We understand that making Jesus Christ the center of our affections is the central purpose for being alive. And we get it when we begin to gratefully love others because we know we're all loved by God. We'll stumble, fall, and fail many times. But getting it means we're learning to make this our new way of life: we're choosing to trust God with our needs and bless others instead of going south. When we get it, we realize we can't do this on our own. We need God, his Spirit, and his people relating together in spiritual community.

One of the first steps to getting it involves being known.

BEING KNOWN

On September 11, 2001, evil showed its face when two airliners slammed into the World Trade Center. New York City was rocked to its foundations as

197

the Twin Towers came crashing down. As tragic as that day was in American history, 9/11 was not the worst terrorist attack against humanity. The most tragic attack came by way of a simple, theological question asked in the quiet of a garden. The Serpent asked, "Can God be trusted?" Adam and Eve said no, and they, along with the entire human race, came crashing down (Gen. 3:1–7).

Prior to this spiritual 9/11, the sound of God's footsteps filled Adam and Eve with joy. But after that day, something changed. Genesis says the "the LORD God called to the man, 'Where are you?' [Adam] answered, 'I heard you in the garden, and I was afraid because I was naked; so I hid'" (Gen. 3:9–10). Instead of running toward God, Adam and Eve fled in terror. They cowered; they hid in shame.

That's the legacy of the Fall. We live with a terror of being known because we fear that the shame of our inner nakedness will be seen. We know something's wrong with us. We hide from God, and we hide from each other. We grasp for safety in thousands of overt and subtle ways: being passive, passing the blame, staying busy, being tough, being shy . . . My friend Ron has said that, by default, we're committed to our own safety. Left to ourselves, we survive by faking it. We pretend we've got it together. We work to manage and control people by keeping them at a distance. In one way or another, everybody lives like Adam and Eve. Three dynamics describe how fallen people relate: We're *afraid*. Why? Because we're *naked*. Therefore, we *hide*.

But God comes looking for us. He seeks us out just as he sought Adam: "Adam, where are you?" God knows everything. He asks the question for Adam's sake. For our sake, God asks, "Gary, where are you? Will you trust me? Will you come out and be known? My heart overflows with love for you. I've come to help you not harm you." But like Adam, we reflexively, foolishly, and stubbornly believe our life depends on hiding instead of trusting God's grace. John Ortberg has said, "Our tendency since the Fall is to hide as if our life depended on it. This is exactly wrong. Our life depends on getting found. *There is no healing in hiding.*"[1] God's help comes by way of being known. So he continually invites us to come to him by asking, "Where are you?"

BEING KNOWN SINNERS

In the last chapter, Lisa referred to a woman in the Bible who had a reputation for being a prostitute. She was a known "sinner." Jesus knew everything about her. And she knew he had forgiven her. She knew he loved her. The affections of her heart spilled over in extravagant, gift-giving gratitude.

We must become known sinners if we want to worship God like that dear lady. We've all prostituted ourselves with the world. When we're fully known and we know we're forgiven and loved with all our failures and faults, we'll worship Jesus. Obeying Jesus will be a *get to*—not a *have to*. Being known means we come out of hiding and open our lives up to God. That happens by way of letting trusted people know our struggles, wounds, lies, and secrets. It means trusting each other enough to stop pretending we have it together. We must become the fellowship of the broken. True community is a place of safety where our walls come down; where our lies, sins, weaknesses, and inabilities are disclosed; and where we are fully accepted. This is where life in Christ can flourish. It doesn't matter how smart and talented we are, how ugly or good looking we are, how popular or unwanted we are, or how much money we have or don't have. We must become known sinners together.

> The irony of the masks is that although we wear them to make other people think well of us, they are drawn to us only when we take them off.
>
> JOHN ORTBERG, *Everybody's Normal till You Get to Know Them*

We're all haunted by disappointments, wounds, and desperate longings to be loved. We want to belong, to know we're not alone in our brokenness and shame. In true, spiritual community, people see the mess, but they see something more. They see and celebrate the life of Christ that stirs beneath—no matter how big the mess may be. The gospel is all about acceptance and delight. When the prodigal came home, his father partied. He danced and sang (Luke 15:11–32). We need to see the Father dance for us. We need to hear him sing over us when we "come home" by way of humble honesty and confession. That's, in part, the power of life-changing community, as Larry Crabb explained:

> In a spiritual community, people reach deep places in each other's hearts that are not often or easily reached. . . . They openly express love and reveal fear, even though they *feel* so unaccustomed to that level of intimacy.

When members of a spiritual community reach a sacred place of vulnerability and authenticity, something is released. . . . An appetite for holy things is stirred. For just a moment, the longing to know God becomes intense, stronger than all other passions, worth whatever price must be paid for it. . . . *Togetherness* in Christ encourages *movement* toward Christ.[2]

BEING KNOWN IS NOT OPTIONAL

If we want to make Jesus Christ the treasure and ruling passion of our lives, we must have a safe place where we can talk about anything and everything that gets in the way of our wholehearted devotion to him. We can't become wholehearted followers of Jesus while hiding secrets and cowering in fear or shame. "Confess your sins to each other," James tells us, "that you may be healed" (James 5:16). Secrets haunt us. They drain our heart's passion. Hiding breeds loneliness and shame. Our Enemy hammers us with accusations such as, "If you tell anyone this secret, you'll be condemned. People will be so hurt and disappointed in you. Hide. Take it to your grave." Our loneliness begs for relief, making us vulnerable to further temptation. Our own fallen nature, our Enemy, and our culture offer a warehouse of immoral options: have an affair, click on a porn site, masturbate to a fantasy, eat a couple more doughnuts and loath yourself in the mirror, have a couple more drinks, yell at your loved one, buy one more toy you can't afford to impress people you don't care about. It's insanity. Our lusts rise to a fever pitch. Our sense of emptiness and despair deepens. We become like wretched Gollum in *The Lord of the Rings* trilogy, hating yet clinging to our "precious" that is destroying our life.[3]

> He who is alone with his sin is utterly alone.
>
> DIETRICH BONHOEFFER, *Life Together*

Perhaps you don't harbor secrets such as sexual perversion, looking at porn, having had an abortion or an affair, but we all struggle with failure and sin. We're all in the same boat. And we can only be loved to the extent we are known. When we keep our struggles or secrets to ourselves, our self-talk sounds something like this: "Yeah. You say you like me, but if you really knew me, you'd reject me." Having secrets and hiding from others destroy intimacy with God and with each other, driving a wedge of fear and shame between a husband and wife, friends, or small-group members. We can never be one with God and others till we take off our masks. We'll only do that when we get sick and tired of our dark, inner world. We must be so desperate for God that we take the risk of being known no matter how people may respond. Until then, we'll never know God deeply. We'll never be the man or woman God dreams for us to be.

Grant's a good friend. One day he sat in my office telling me about a one-night stand he once had with a woman while he was on a business trip. "I told myself I'd take this secret to my grave," he said. That day, Grant was set free from prison. No more hiding. Through a journey of confession, grieving, counseling, and spiritual friendships, Grant's marriage has been restored. Grant and his wife help others in our church and community find healing from the pain and bondage of sexual struggle and sin. God uses honest, broken people like Grant and his wife to heal broken people. Servants of Christ lead from their brokenness. That's God's way. Henry Cloud explained how the honesty and brokenness of their group leader helped him open up and grow during his college years:

> The group was an informal combination of Bible study, discussion, and life sharing. . . . Dan, the facilitator, was a warm, personable student a couple of years older than the rest of us. I was drawn by his attitude and maturity. One night, however, he started the group by saying, "Hey, I am really struggling with lust and sexual temptation, and I need to let you guys know what is going on so you can help me and pray for me." As he talked about the struggle, a chain reaction occurred; the rest of us started chiming in about how tough the sexual purity battle was for us, too.
>
> This may be normal for your group, but for me it was world shattering. It was my first experience of sane, healthy, open discussion with other guys about sex . . . that night Dan helped us open up our lives, hearts, and emotions. I came away pretty shaken up inside, but in a good way. I felt connected to the other guys in a way I had never experienced before. It was as if deeper parts of me had a place to go, where we were all the same.

... The people and what happened there became more important to me. Something changed within me. Though I still got . . . spiritual growth, learning, friendship—I began receiving another spiritual benefit I hadn't signed up for. That surprising benefit was the possibility of being connected, heart and soul, to God and others without having to edit, pretend, or hold back.[4]

I'm grateful for my church. It's a place where people experience this kind of safe and honest community. People can be fully known without fear of condemnation. One of the most common comments we hear from new attendees is how honest and authentic people are about their life struggles. Newcomers typically experience this honesty as refreshing, validating, and life changing as truth is spoken into real-life problems. For the first time, they realize they're not alone; they're not the only ones who struggle with anger, lust, greed, shame, failure, inadequacy, or depression. We're a fellowship of broken, fallen people who struggle together. We disclose secrets, failures, and sins for one clear purpose—to help one another become wholehearted followers of Jesus. We invite each other to talk about whatever gets in the way of loving God and loving others.

FINDING AUTHENTIC COMMUNITY

At our church, small groups have been the primary venues for fostering safe and authentic relationships. But what if you don't have such a safe place in your church? What if you would be condemned if you admitted you struggled with rage, lust, or jealousy or that you had an affair or an abortion? The church is meant to be a hospital for the sick, wounded, and suffering. It's meant to be a place where known sinners can find acceptance, forgiveness, truth, and love. I'm sad that many churches are not that way. But there's hope for you to have authentic community no matter where you are.

Begin with prayer. Talk honestly with God about your longing for safe relationships where you can know and be known for the sake of knowing God. God wants this for you. Prayerfully consider one or two people whom you believe share a similar hunger for God. They may be people in your church, your workplace, or your neighborhood. (Women should seek out women and men should seek out men. Most men and women will not be fully honest about their struggles in mixed company. And the details of certain struggles shouldn't be shared in mixed company.)

After prayerfully selecting one, two, or more people, ask them to read this book so you can discuss it together. Take risks to be honest as you review the questions after each chapter. Building trust takes time.[5] While no one should be pressured to share more than they're ready to tell, it's important to remember that real growth requires risk.

Many people are hungry for this kind of authentic Christianity. But if at first no one will meet with you, ask God to help you resist going south into discouragement. Don't take it personally. This idea of being known for the purpose of knowing God is foreign to many Christians. It will provoke fear for many, and some will choose to stay hidden. People need to be desperate for God before they'll take the risk of stepping out of their comfort zone. Trust God to provide for you in his time and way. Continue to pray and ask.

After reading and discussing this book with the trusted friends who join you, the next step in being known involves sharing your life stories together.

THE PURPOSE FOR TELLING OUR LIFE STORIES

Through history, God is telling his story of redemption. He tells part of his story through *your* life. God loves stories. Seventy-three percent of the Bible is written in story rather than proposition. Stories touch our souls in ways that principles cannot. God shows us how to walk with him through the real-life dramas of men and women who struggled with fear, failure, doubt, faith, love, and courage just like you and me. Moreover, stories in the Bible show us God's faithfulness throughout redemptive history. The apostle John tells why he shares his story, "We proclaim to you what we have seen and heard, so that you also may have fellowship with us. And our fellowship is with the Father and with his Son, Jesus Christ. We write this to make our joy complete" (1 John 1:3–4). In the same way, we write and share our stories to proclaim what we have seen and heard about God's faithfulness and redemption in our lives. Many fear their story is boring. Truth is, we all have unique journeys that show how Jesus is personally pursuing and redeeming us. Your story was meant to be told.

As we build authentic Christian relationships, we share our stories because we need to know how to help each other grow toward full devotion in Jesus.

Inviting one another into fellowship with the Father, with his Son, and with the Holy Spirit makes our joy complete; our lives have true significance. To serve one another in this way requires that we know where we struggle, what lies we believe, and how they take us south. Thus, we can know how to pray and speak truth in love, encouraging one another to go north. Instead of just praying for Aunt Lucy's foot surgery, or for traveling mercies on our vacation (these prayers matter), we can go deeper and let one another know how we're being tempted to go south and grasp for relief. We're at war between good and evil. We either believe the truth or lies about where our security and significance are found. We either go to God or gods. Every day all day, we choose north or south. Let's not fight this battle alone!

WRITING YOUR LIFE STORY[6]

Begin your story by thinking back over some of the disappointments and wounds you've experienced in your life. We've all been frustrated, disappointed, hurt, or wounded by someone's words or actions. Last night the news reported on a high school girl who hung herself. She had been teased and mocked for months by her classmates.

When I was a kid, I joined Cub Scouts. Gordon was in my pack. He was overweight, so I nicknamed him "Fatso." I thought I was being funny. One afternoon in Gordon's backyard, he and his mom and I were inside a tent with others in our pack. I looked at Gordon and warmly said, "Hi, Fatso." I clearly remember his wounded look as he turned to his mom and, nearly in tears, pleaded, "Mom, please help me." Even now I feel sad for the pain and shame I caused him. Gordon's mom, our den mother, appropriately spoke up for her son with gentle firmness. "Gary, Gordon is my son, and I love him. I don't want you to call him that name anymore." I was stunned. Unbelievably, it wasn't until she confronted me that I realized my teasing was hurting my friend.

Childhood hurts and wounds run deep. No little kid thinks, "I feel so alone and unwanted, but I'm turning to you, Jesus. You are my refuge and strength!" Proverbs tells us that "foolishness [living as if there is no God] is bound up in the heart of a child" (Prov. 22:15 NASB). We didn't turn to God. We faced our childhood disappointments, hurts, and wounds alone. Most of us didn't have the words or ability to talk about them with our parents or teachers, and most of those adults—preoccupied with their own wounds and lies—never thought to ask. But in the fires of childhood rejection, abuse, and failure, we make life-changing decisions. Without realizing it, we decide what kind of person we have to become in order to make life work. We pretend and pose. We grasp for acceptance. We work to avoid rejection. We fear people more than God. No one's exempt. We go toward being aggressive, tough, and angry, or passive, needy, and fearful. Tough and aggressive men and women usually grew up in relationally cold or distant homes. Those characterized by neediness were most often overindulged.

This is not about blaming others or avoiding responsibility for our actions or choices in life. But if we don't face our disappointments and wounds and the lies they've fostered, they will influence the way we see God, ourselves, and others. We will sin by going south into self-protective behavior. Our insecurities will take us south into grasping for control of situations that feel similar and threaten to expose or reject us. We'll live for something other than loving God and loving others.

For example, due to multiple ear infections, I missed nearly half of the third grade. My teacher counseled my parents to hold me back. I was devastated. I worked hard to hide the shame of that "failure" for many years. This painful event was one of many events in my life story that "named me," telling me I was a stupid failure. Other wounds and lies have also shaped my personality. When I played softball at recess, I usually struck out. I was always picked last. Team captains fought over me.

"You can have Heim."

"Nope. I don't need him. I've got the guys I want. He's yours." The message was clear: no one wants a strikeout. And so the shame of striking out and being picked last fostered and fueled a lie in me. Without realizing it, I began to define *life* as getting people to pick me. I defined *death* as having others see my inadequacies and reject me. People's approval based on my performance became the false god I worshipped and served. I succumbed to the daily pressure of performance and the daily terror of shame and failure. In those days I had no category for understanding how Jesus' love could be my security. I needed to please and impress people if I had any chance of being anyone to anybody.

Moreover, because I believed "stupid failure" and "strikeout" were my names or true identity, I made a vow without even realizing it. I determined to avoid anything that could make me feel like a stupid failure or strikeout again. Instead of dealing with problems, I avoided them through passivity; I pursued what I was good at and avoided whatever threatened to expose my inadequacies. I was committed to my own safety and survival. I was living a self-centered life.

Wounds, failures, and disappointments come in all shapes and sizes. Maybe you were hurt by something someone said to you on the playground at recess like Lisa was: "Are those corrective shoes?" It was not only the words that hurt but the mocking laughter Lisa heard as the girls ran away. Maybe it was when someone you trusted betrayed your trust by sexually abusing you. Maybe it was when your father or mother walked out on your family. A church leader I looked up to once yelled at me, saying, "You're the most worthless hunk of humanity I've ever met!"

STEP ONE IN WRITING YOUR LIFE STORY: FACE THE WOUNDS AND LIES

Take some time and reflect on one of the first disappointing or wounding events you can remember in your life. Complete the following statement: "A painful event in my life story is . . ." As you reflect on that snapshot in time, what do you think you felt? What did you believe about yourself as a result of that experience?

Reflect again on two or three other wounding events in your life. Write them down along with the one above. What did you feel and come to believe about yourself as a result of those failures, hurts, or wounds?

If you took all the disappointments, hurts, or wounds you've written down, along with others you can remember, and boiled them down to a word or phrase about how you see yourself, what would that word or phrase be? Some people have said things like: *Unlovable. Unwanted. Failure. Loser. Idiot. I'm on my own. I'll always screw it up. I'll never be good enough. Never chosen.*

One woman I worked with had been sexually abused as a child. As we talked through her life story, she came to realize that she lived with the false identity of thinking she was *Pond Scum.* Anytime a man smiled at her or was kind to her, she instantly assumed he was seeing her as easy. She instantly felt shame and contempt for herself and the man.

As you boil down your wounding events to a word or phrase, what would you say your false name or identity is? Write it down. Look at it. Give yourself permission to grieve the pain and the weight of all the sorrow that lie has brought you. Talk honestly with God about those painful memories. It's not selfish to feel and lament the sorrow of this fallen world. It's not wrong to experience the ache of unmet longings. It's in those deep and tender places of our hearts that God longs to speak to us and meet with us. It's there he longs to be our God. He longs to be a Father to the fatherless, a husband to the widow. Ask the Holy Spirit to speak to you. He is the Comforter. Listen for his still, small, and gentle voice.

As we experience the pain of life, our Enemy comes to us in order to twist the knife. He accuses us and tries to name us. He says, "You're such a loser! You're all alone. You'll never succeed at anything. You're just an idiot. You gave in again! You lost control *again*? God could never delight in someone like you!" Sadly, we choose to believe these lies and hide from God and each other instead of embracing the truth of God's unwavering and unconditional love for us. When we believe the lies about our false identity, they will influence the way we relate to God and others. Finish the following statements:

The lie (false name/identity) tells me I must *always* _____
if I am to be wanted, loved, or seen as competent and respectable.

The lie tells me I must *never* _____ if I am to avoid
rejection or the shame of failure and incompetence.

My false name or identity as a "stupid failure" and a "strikeout" tells me I have to impress people if I'm to be wanted, loved, or seen as competent and respectable. That lie breeds a lot of fear of failure and a lot of pressure to perform. The lie also tells me that I must be better than anyone else if I'm to be noticed and wanted. I must never be less than someone else if I'm to avoid rejection or the shame of failure and incompetence. Those are devilish lies. These falsehoods have stirred up a lot of jealousy and envy toward others more gifted than me. I have been like King Saul and have feared and hated all the Davids in my life (1 Sam. 18:6–11). I've harbored anger and resentment toward others who are chosen and who are better than I am at what they do.

When Lisa and others have not affirmed me or when they have treated me in ways that have caused me to feel like a strikeout, I've either lashed out in anger or withdrawn into self-pitying silence.

When you believe the lies, how does your style of relating impact the people you love? Consider how those lies take you south and keep you in bondage to self-centeredness, hiding, and grasping for life. Put yourself in the shoes of those you hurt. What's it like for them to be around you when you're choosing to believe the lies and grasp for control? How often do you think about that? How often do you consider what they long for from you? What might their false name or identify be?

STEP TWO IN WRITING YOUR LIFE STORY: EMBRACING THE TRUTH

"It's in Christ that we find out who we are and what we are living for" (Eph. 1:11 MSG). The truth sets us free to be who we were meant to be. Entering our wounds and facing our lies allows us to turn from them and embrace the truth about who God is and how he sees us. This is important because we must adopt God's image of us as our true self-image.

Michael Jordan was a gifted basketball player, and he knew it. But imagine Jordan forgot who he was. Suppose he believed he wasn't good at basketball. Would that impact his performance on the court? Would Jordan's doubts cause him to play differently? Of course. He wouldn't be so eager to get into the game.

If deep down I believe I'm a strikeout, that will influence the way I relate to Lisa, my kids, and others. I won't be so eager to take risks in living for God and others. I'll be tempted to play it safe. It will influence the direction I'll choose when I face groaning and hardship. If I don't believe I have what it takes, I'll go south. I'll feel threatened and either react in anger or passively retreat into silence when I fail or when others treat me disrespectfully. If I truly believe I'm a beloved son of God, known and kept by him, I have a good chance of choosing north in the groaning of life as I interact with people, disappointment, and pain. It doesn't mean it will be easy or that I'll never fail, but I can make a choice to give life to others instead of taking it from them if I remember who defines me: God, not people.

Revisiting our life story will help us define how frustrations, disappointments, and wounds have shaped and fueled the lies we believe. More importantly, knowing our stories can help us embrace the truth about who we really are in Christ. This is foundational to helping us on our journey of becoming grateful, giving children of God. That's the life Jesus came to give us. My friend Andrea wrote me one day to tell how God is using her story for his good purposes.

Dear Gary,

I have been meaning to e-mail you about a conversation I had with my mom over Thanksgiving. We were in the kitchen, cleaning up after a meal and talking about our relationships with our spouses, and I began sharing more of the material you had taught me. Mom is somewhat familiar with it because of my time counseling with you, but every so often I relate to her how I process life using your paradigm. Most of what I referred to was going "north" to Christ instead of "south" to our husbands to get our needs met, how we can truly give to them once we are abiding in Christ, and turning to the Lord for our strength instead of grasping for strength and security from our husbands. All of a sudden she got tears in her eyes. . . . She said to me: "Andrea, you are so strong." I answered gently, "The Lord is my strength and my song." I wanted her to know that I don't consider myself strong, I have just improved at turning to him for strength. She continued saying, "I always thought you were so weak; I don't know if it's because you were born early and had to be in an incubator, but I've always thought of you as 'my little Andrea' and that I needed to take care of you." I then shared with her that her view of me was the way I had seen myself my whole life, that I am incapable of doing much on my own and that I am helpless and feel the need to be rescued, very much that "little girl" mentality. To have her verbalize a comprehensive statement of my most significant "wound" was incredibly freeing, to have my own remembrance of my childhood confirmed. I then told her the "new name" God had given me from the passage in Psalm 34:5, "Those who look to him are *radiant*; their faces are never covered with shame." My dad came into the kitchen while I was saying this verse. I went on to explain how much God has used my new name (Radiant) to speak quietly to me when I feel tempted to sin and go down into self-contempt and self-pity. He has spoken my new name to me several times, reminding me that my worth and position before him is not dependent on my performance but on the performance of his Son.

Hallelujah! My dad was sitting on a stool in front of where I stood, and he was *beaming* with happiness for me in what I have been learning. My mom was happy too. I just hugged my dad and said tearfully, "I love the Lord Jesus."

I am so encouraged even as I write this and remember the conversation I had with my parents that I am a daughter of the *King* and he has claimed me as his own. This security in his love is something that has taken me so long to understand and accept, but I think I'm finally getting it. Even more exciting is how God is using my understanding of him to reach my parents with Truth.

What do you believe Jesus would say to you right now if you could hear him speak to you? Most Christians assume they would hear some kind of advice, correction, or rebuke instead of tenderness and delight. We assume Jesus is focused on our failures. But he isn't. Listen to God's heart for his people (and for you and me) even when their sin and failure has been overwhelming: "'Oh! Ephraim [Israel] is my dear, dear son, my child in whom I take pleasure! Every time I mention his name, my heart bursts with longing for him! Everything in me cries out for him. Softly and tenderly I wait for him.' God's Decree" (Jer. 31:20 MSG).

We are God's dearly loved children (Eph. 5:1). The Bible says there is no condemnation for anyone who is in Christ (Rom. 8:1). None. Let that sink in. God never has a condemning thought toward you. As we've said before, *grace* means "unmerited favor." If you're in Christ, God favors you. He loves you. His heart is moved with compassion for you and your struggles. Read and reflect on Luke 15:3–24 to understand how God feels about you. Consider what the good shepherd, the woman, and the father feel in these stories. They feel deep concern and love for that which is lost. Here are a few more examples of the truth about how God thinks and feels about you.

THE LIE	THE TRUTH
I'm unloved and rejected.	I am a beloved child of God: 1 John 3:1; 4:10
I am unacceptable due to my performance.	I am accepted and loved because of Jesus' performance: Romans 3:21–24; 15:7; Titus 3:4–5
I am ugly, undesirable, too sinful.	In Christ, you have a new heart. You are a new creation: 2 Corinthians 5:17
I am unwanted and alone.	You are chosen: Ephesians 1:4–5, 11
I am unusable. I've blown it too badly.	You are called by God for his eternal purposes: Matthew 9:9–12; Luke 15:7; 2 Timothy 1:9–10
I'm just one of the crowd.	He knows every detail about your life. His thoughts about you are more than all the sand on the seashores. He goes before you and behind you. Psalm 139:1–6

The Bible is clear. You and I are not merely forgiven sinners, we are saints. That word *saint* has twisted meaning in our culture. People say things like, "Old Aunt Bertha sure was a saint. She never said an unkind word." Or we think of very special people, like Saint Francis of Assisi, who live such miraculous lives that they're called saints. That isn't the true meaning of the word *saint*. To be a saint means to be holy. *Holy* means set apart. Everyone in Christ is a saint. God has chosen us and set us apart for himself. We are his. We literally have Christ living, breathing, speaking, and moving within us. The term *in Christ* is used eighty-two times in the apostle Paul's letters: "If anyone is in Christ, he is a new creation; the old has gone, the new has come!" (2 Cor. 5:17). "This is the secret: Christ lives in you" (Col. 1:27 NLT). This truth is the bedrock of Paul's theology. "I have been crucified with Christ and I no longer live, but Christ lives in me" (Gal. 2:20). "Do you not know that your body is a temple of the Holy Spirit, who is in you, whom you have received from God?" (1 Cor. 6:19). Paul doesn't talk to the Corinthians as sinners who need to try harder to get it right. He speaks to them as saints who need to remember their true identity.

> Being the Beloved expresses the core truth of our existence.
>
> HENRI NOUWEN, *Life of the Beloved*

God's Spirit dwells in our hearts! Therefore, deep down, in our redeemed hearts, we want to love God. Through the miracle of our new covenant heart, our hearts are now inclined toward God—not away from him (Rom. 6). We want to love God and others because that's what Jesus, who lives in our hearts, always wants to do! Sadly, too many Christians have been taught that they are forgiven and covered by the blood but that their hearts are still utterly sinful. No. There is gold inside every believer. We are no longer sinners by definition. By definition, we are saints who struggle with sin. That's the truth.

You and I are not just forgiven sinners; we are new creations in Christ. While sin exists in our fallen nature, our fallen nature no longer defines who we are. We are alive to God (Rom. 6). Our sin is the tarnish that hides the gold. But the gold defines who we are. Sin is not our master. I know it often feels like it is but we must believe the truth. Christ in us is our truest and deepest identity! Jesus lives in our hearts! Therefore, our hearts are good. Ask God to help you embrace who you really are in Christ. Ask God to help you believe the truth about your true name and identity. He created you. He saved you. He alone has the authority to tell you who you are.

Many people ask about Jeremiah 17:9, which says, "The heart is deceitful above all things and beyond cure." How can our hearts be good if Jeremiah says they're deceitful and beyond cure? When Jeremiah wrote chapter 17, Israel's heart was so corrupt they were beyond cure. There was no hope. As a result, they needed a new heart. Israel needed a heart transplant. Therefore, Jeremiah foretold that the new covenant was coming (Jer. 31:31–33). You and I are living in the time of the new covenant. Through Christ, we've received the heart transplant. The double transfer has taken place: our sins have been transferred to Jesus and the righteousness of Jesus has been transferred to us. This isn't just theology. Christ actually lives in our hearts! Our hearts are good. That's the biblical doctrine of Christ's imputed righteousness. It's real and alive! Jesus lives, breathes, and speaks from within our hearts.

As you reflect on these truths, continue to think on your life story. Write down ways God has spoken into your life. Think about the significant people who have believed in you and mentored you in ways that have helped you believe the truth about God and his love. How did they help you come to believe that Jesus is for you? If memories like that don't come to mind, write about the other ways you have seen the faithfulness of God in your life.

In light of what God says and feels about you, what would you say is your true identity—the identity bestowed upon you by God's kind and loving heart? Write it down. My true identity in Christ is _____.

We all share a glorious identity in Christ. We are God's dearly loved children. We are his new creations. Andrea embraced her identity in Christ as *Radiant*. During a men's backpacking trip in the Manistee Forest, we all gave feedback to one another about how we see Christ in each other. My friend Chris said, "Field Commander" came to his mind when he saw me leading other men toward Christ. I've also been told the name "Gary" means "Mighty Warrior." Those names have a common theme. In Christ, I'm not a strikeout. I'm a warrior and field commander of the King, who fights for the hearts of others.

Reflect on the following questions as you finish writing your story:

- If you believed the truth of who you are in Christ, how would that influence the way you relate to others?
- How would you see others differently if you saw their true identity? How would you treat them differently?
- What will help you live from your new covenant heart?
- What will help you hear and believe the truth about who you are in Christ as you greet your spouse, children, boss, coworkers, friends, and enemies?

- Write down Bible passages that you can take with you through the day to help you believe the truth when you face the groaning of life. Those passages can help you hear God's voice, urging you to turn north to him and to be thankful, knowing you're secure in Jesus.

Now, share your stories with your trusted friends so God can use each of you to help one another believe the truth about who you are in Christ. And have fun embracing your security in God as you take risks in loving others.

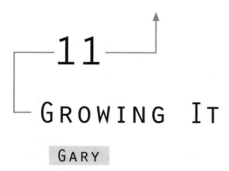

11
GROWING IT

GARY

"Let all my words sink deep into your own heart first. . . ."
Ezekiel 3:10 NLT

Yesterday I talked with a man who's beginning to get it. He feels hope. "I've always depended on God to help me make decisions in life," he said, "but until now I never understood that I'm supposed to depend on God for my emotional needs too. This is big. I'm seeing how wrong I am for demanding and pressuring my wife and kids to meet those needs." He's turning to God instead of going south. He's beginning to give to his family instead of grasping for life from them. His wife affirms it's true. It's a miracle. No one turns to God and gives to others without the work of the Holy Spirit.

My friend is getting it. How can he keep growing it? Remember, getting it and growing it ultimately mean one thing: we're living as grateful, giving children of God because we're learning to make Jesus Christ the center and treasure of our heart's affections. Growing it requires radical assumptions that we must stake our lives upon.

God can be known in personal experience. And this *knowing* is the deepest dream we could ever dream. That's the first assumption we must stake our lives upon. Nothing this world offers can compare to the wonder and ecstasy of knowing God. The Bible has different meanings for the word *know*. It sometimes means sexual intercourse. In the beginning, "Adam *knew* Eve his wife; and she conceived, and bore Cain" (Gen. 4:1 NKJV, emphasis added).

Likewise, in obedience to God, Jesus' earthly father, Joseph, "did not *know her [Mary]* till she had brought forth her firstborn Son" (Matt.1:25 NKJV, emphasis added). God uses this same word to describe the intimate relationship he had with his chosen people Israel. "You only have I *known* of all the families of the earth" (Amos 3:2 NKJV, emphasis added). God unashamedly uses sexual language and imagery to describe the relationship he has or longs to have with his covenant people (Ezek. 16; Hos. 2). God uses the thrill and passion of human sexuality to help us imagine the exceedingly greater joy of knowing him.

> God created human beings in his image—"male and female he created them" (Gen. 1:27)—with capacities for intense sexual pleasure. . . . And his goal in creating human beings with personhood and passion was to make sure that there would be sexual language and sexual images that would point to the promises and the pleasures of God's relationship to his people and our relationship to him.[1]

God is always inviting, working, and waiting for us to seek him and press in to know him because to know God is to know "eternal life" (John 17:3).

We must shift our focus from the seen to the unseen world. *Faith brings us into God's presence*—it's the key that enables us to enter, see, and experience God. This is the second assumption we must stake our lives upon. "He who comes to God must believe that He is and that He is a rewarder of those who seek Him" (Heb. 11:6 NKJV). As fish are unaware of the water they breathe, we're often unaware of God's presence. Just as Jacob confessed, "Surely the LORD is in this place, and I was not aware of it" (Gen. 28:16). We're often unmindful of the truth that we live and move and have our being in God's very presence (Acts 17:28).

Why do some people have a living faith and growing personal experience of knowing God while others are content with less? Tozer identified what people who *know* God have in common:

> The one vital quality which they had in common was spiritual receptivity. Something in them was open to heaven, something which urged them Godward . . . they went on to cultivate it until it became the biggest thing in their lives. They differed from the average person

in that when they felt the inward longing they *did something about it.*
They acquired the lifelong habit of spiritual response. . . . As David
put it neatly, "When thou saidst, Seek ye my face; my heart said unto
thee, Thy face, Lord, will I seek" (Ps. 27:8).[2]

"Spiritual receptivity" is cultivated as we pursue God through the Word
of God, the Spirit of God, and the people of God. We'll consider one at a
time.

CONNECTING WITH GOD THROUGH THE WORD OF GOD[3]

God longs for us to experience him. In the Garden, Adam and Eve walked
and talked with God. Put yourself in the Garden. Would God want to walk
and talk with you too? Yes! That has been his purpose throughout redemptive
history. The Bible begins in the Garden with God dwelling on earth with his
people. After our banishment from the Garden, the tabernacle and then the
temple in Jerusalem became God's dwelling place among his people throughout the Old Testament. At the beginning of the New Testament, Jesus became
a human being. He "made his home among us" (John 1:14 NLT). His name
was *Emanuel,* which means "God with us." God's Son walked and talked with
his people on earth. And now God dwells in the temple of our hearts, living
and speaking within. God's story in the Bible ends with him dwelling on earth
among his people again (Rev. 21–22). Can it be clearer? It's God's dream to
dwell with us. He longs to intimately relate to you and me. He wants to walk
and talk with you personally.

Be careful. Something in us may counter these thoughts by saying, "That
will never be my experience. It may be for others, but it won't happen to me."
Resist any thoughts that contradict the truth. God deeply desires to meet with
you, speak to you, and dwell with you. God has clearly said that he wants you
to know him *personally.* The greatest fact of the Old Testament tabernacle
was that God was there, waiting for his people to meet with him. Similarly,
the presence of God is the greatest and most central fact of Christianity.[4]
Meditating on the Word of God is one primary way to be in the presence of
God and personally connect with him. Meditation on God's Word must not
be regarded as a mere duty; it's a lifeline to the heart and voice of God. We

cannot go north without personally connecting with Jesus through his Word. Through faith, God wants to speak to us heart to heart. And Jesus gives us a promise: if we will remain in him and his *words* remain in us, our lives will bear spiritual fruit (John 15:7). Fruitfulness glorifies God. This brings great joy to us and to our Father (John 15:8).

YOU WILL BE OPPOSED

Many believers do not experience personal connection with God through their devotional time in the Word. Why are personal devotions such a struggle? Our amazing God loves us, and in the core of our being—our redeemed heart—we long for him too. So this should be easy. Right? It's not that simple. Spiritual warfare is going on. We are opposed. The Enemy does not want us to personally connect with God through his Word. Satan cannot stop what God can do in us and through us when we meditate on the Word of God. The Enemy will throw every discouragement and distraction our way to keep us from personally connecting with Jesus. Richard Foster wrote:

> In contemporary society our Adversary majors in three things: noise, hurry, and crowds. If he can keep us engaged in "muchness" and "manyness," he will rest satisfied. . . .
>
> If we hope to move beyond the superficialities of our culture, including our religious culture, we must be willing to go down into the recreating silences.[5]

And Proverbs 4:23 says, "Above all else, guard your heart, for it is the wellspring of life." Can you imagine not setting a guard before your most treasured possession? We're not careless with our kids. Nor do we leave the keys in our car. So why be careless with our hearts? Meditation on the Word of God is perhaps the most important way to guard the heart (Ps. 119:11).

REFLECTING THOUGHTFULLY ON GOD'S WORD

Meditating on the word involves more than just reading words with our intellect. It's like a cow chewing its cud. We roll the words around in our minds, so to speak, pondering, chewing, and savoring what is read so the truths become life-giving food for our souls.

George Mueller was a man of faith who depended on God to feed hundreds of orphans in his care. He saw God provide in miraculous ways. Mueller commented on the vital role meditation played in his life:

> My practice had been . . . for ten years . . . to give myself to prayer . . . in the morning. *Now* I saw, that the most important thing I had to do was to give myself to the reading of the Word of God and to meditation on it, that thus my heart might be comforted, encouraged, warned, reproved, instructed; and that thus, whilst meditating, my heart might be brought into experimental, communion with the Lord. I began therefore, to meditate on the New Testament, from the beginning, early in the morning.
>
> The first thing I did . . . was to begin to meditate on the Word of God; searching, as it were, into every verse, to get blessing out of it . . . for the sake of obtaining food for my own soul. . . .
>
> . . . Now what is the food for the inner man: not *prayer*, but the *Word of God:* and here again not the simple reading of the Word of God, so that it only passes through our minds, just as water runs through a pipe, but considering what we read, pondering over it, and applying it to our hearts. . . .
>
> I dwell so particularly on this point because of the immense spiritual profit and refreshment I am conscious of having derived from it myself, and I affectionately and solemnly beseech all . . . to ponder this. . . . How different when the soul is refreshed and made happy early in the morning.[6]

My times of meditation naturally flow into reflective and responsive prayer. These times can be rich and particularly meaningful conversations with God.

The Bible uses the word *meditation* fifty-eight times. It means listening to God's Word, reflecting on God's works, rehearsing God's deeds, ruminating on God's law. The psalmists wrote:

> I lie awake thinking of you,
> meditating on you through the night. (Ps. 63:6 NLT)

Blessed is the man [whose] . . . delight is in the law of the LORD,
   and on his law he meditates day and night.
He is like a tree planted by streams of water. (Ps. 1:1–3)

Jesus himself often withdrew to lonely places to be alone with God (Mark 1:32–39; 6:46; 14:32). He listened to his Father and communed with him. Christ invites us to follow his example.

Practical ways to meditate. Meditation is simple. It's for everyone, not just the religious few. Read a passage of Scripture slowly and thoughtfully. Read it again. Make mental notes of words or phrases that stir your soul or catch your attention. The Holy Spirit may be bringing those particular words or thoughts to your mind. Pause and reflect on them. Ponder what is read and apply it to your heart. What might God be saying to you? For example, I recently came upon the story of the rich young ruler during my devotional time (Mark 10:17–24). The story struck me in fresh ways. I pondered the story verse by verse as if reading it for the first time. I wrote some thoughts in my journal:

February 1, 2010
   Jesus was on his way to Jerusalem. He knew the religious leaders would kill him there. *Nothing* deterred Jesus from doing his Father's will. While on his way, a rich young man came to Jesus and fell to the ground asking what he had to do to inherit eternal life. Seems the young man knew something was missing in his life. In a nutshell, Jesus told him to obey the Law (Mark 10:19). Seemingly blind to his sin and the utter impossibility of ever keeping the Law (love God and others perfectly all the time. If you fail once, you fail all!), the young man told Jesus he had kept the Law since he was a little boy (Mark 10:20). I too can be so blind to my sin. When I measure my life against the Law, I'm hopeless without grace. The text says Jesus looked at the young man and loved him (Mark 10:21). Mmmm. I'm so drawn to the heart of Jesus. Dear God, even when I'm blind and arrogant, you look at me with love.
   Jesus saw the young man's problem: covetousness. He was break-ing the last commandment and, therefore, the first one too. With one

sentence Jesus got to the heart of the issue. He told the young man, "Go, sell everything you have and give to the poor, and you will have treasure in heaven. Then come, follow me" (Mark 10:21). I just realized that these two sentences summarize the Christian life: First, sell everything you have. Second, give to the poor. Third, follow Jesus. Jesus invited the man to know true wealth. But the young man "went away sad" (Mark 10:22). He treasured worldly wealth more than following Jesus. How tragic.

My false "riches" will always turn me away from the one true Treasure. They will leave me sad even though they hold the illusion of life. What lies and illusions do I believe will make me rich apart from following Jesus wholeheartedly? What "treasure" am I tempted to value more than knowing and following God? A few things quickly come to mind: I'm still tempted to covet people's approval and applause instead of resting in God's. I tend to believe I must impress people in order to be significant. Fear of man vs. fear of God. That's my false wealth. I so want to completely sell those lies and false riches so I can give life to people instead of grasp for it from them. More than anything, I want to follow Jesus with my whole heart. What will help me put my lies in their place as I follow Jesus? Listening to him speak to me like he is speaking right now is one way. . . .

Get all the meaning from the text you can before moving on to the next phrase. Less is more. Reflect on one chapter or one story or just a few verses again and again. Put yourself in the story. What did the people want, think, feel, do, and why? What was God up to? Take your time. Prayerfully listen. The Spirit of God within you resonates with the Word of God you're reading. Let the words you're reading sink deep into your own heart. What might they be saying to you right now in your current life circumstances?

Kathryn is a dear lady in our church. She loves God. She shares a wonderful example of how God spoke specifically to her as she meditated on God's Word. She courageously agreed to let me share it with you:

About a week ago in my devotions, I was reading Isaiah 49. Verse 9 stood out to me. I couldn't quite move past it. It says, "I will keep you and will make you to be a covenant for the people . . . *to say to the captives, 'Come out.' And to those in darkness, 'Be free!'"* I kept rolling it around in my head. I wasn't exactly sure what God was trying to say to me through that verse, but I knew there was something there. I thought about the fact that God says, "Come out," before he says, "Be free." There's a reason for that. Because we have to come out of hiding before we can be free.

My husband, Matt, has often told his story of when he was bound in sin through pornography. By the loving pursuit of our small-group leader, Geoff, Matt says Christ opened the door to his jail cell. Geoff continually and lovingly invited him to "come out" and be known. But for a long time, Matt refused to come out. The door was open, but he wouldn't go through it because he really believed that he belonged in the cell.

Matt had to take a risk. He had to step out of the prison of his secrecy before he could be free. The day came when he did that through confession. Through confession he experienced the miracle of God's forgiveness. It makes me think of Joshua 1:3: "I will give you every place where you set your foot." Notice Joshua had to first plant his foot before God gave it to him. He had to step out in faith.

God spoke to *me* this morning. I was praying about my weight struggle. He said, "You need to move." We've had this conversation before. He keeps telling me the same thing. For some reason, I want to hear something else. Maybe fifty pounds falling off me in the middle of the night? So I said, "Okay, God. I will start walking." I've been here so many times. I've made promises to God. I've tried to be faithful. I usually lose about twenty pounds. Then I flip out and gain it all back. Why, you ask? Fear, plain and simple. Let's just call it what it really is—fear.

I have been wounded by men, and I am afraid of them. The extra weight makes me feel safe. I won't go into all the details, but the lie is, "You turn good men bad." God has spoken powerfully to this lie. He has placed many very good men in my life. Men I can trust. And if you're receiving this letter, then yes you are one of them, and I want to say thank you. But the lie has a serious hold, and I keep clinging to it.

It wasn't until I actually was out walking today that I realized all these things are connected. (Notice I had to plant my foot out in faith before God revealed this to me.) I have placed myself in my own jail cell. I wear it with me everywhere I go. Christ has opened the door, but I won't walk through it. Sometimes I kinda peek my head out and look around a bit. Then in terror I run back in, curl up in a corner, and stay there for a couple of months. I'm sorry, Lord. I really truly am.

Why am I telling you all this? Partly because I'm afraid to and I'm tired of being afraid. But mostly because I so desperately want to be different! I want out of this stinking jail cell! I have been hiding my whole life, and I don't want to do that anymore. That is my flesh, my old self. I am not that person anymore. I am now Redeemed Kathryn, Warrior-Princess Kathryn, Delightful Kathryn, Engraved-in-God's-Hand Kathryn.

So I guess this is me planting my foot out in faith. There is part of me that is terrified. I'm afraid that I've poured my heart out to you and in a year, nothing will have changed. I will still be in this jail cell. So I guess that is what accountability is all about, huh? But there is another part of me that's screaming out, "Yes! Satan, take that!" That sounds more like the Warrior-Princess Kathryn.

I want to end this by asking you to pray for me. Satan has a powerful hold on me in this area, and the only way I will be set free is to humble myself and say I need help. So I'm saying it. I need help.

Thank you for being a friend I can trust! I thank God for our church family every day and will continue to do so. You are "Christ with skin on" to me.

Kathryn

Common difficulties in meditating. I know many good Christians who find it difficult to meditate on God's Word. I personally struggle with distracting thoughts. Henri Nouwen likened his distracting thoughts to monkeys jumping around in a banana tree.[7] It often takes time to quiet our thoughts and focus on the text. Some mornings, I never get there. When my distracting thoughts are motivated by worry, I sometimes acknowledge those worries and bring them to God as I prepare to read. Through meditation God clearly speaks to me. A few times a year, he speaks profoundly. Other mornings nothing special seems to happen. I've learned to be okay with that. Just being with God is good.

Many of us carry unhealed wounds from our life's journey. Take for example an abusive or critical father or mother who never connected with you in a loving way. Those wounds can result in a significant and discouraging struggle to connect with God. Please consider talking about those wounds with your small group or with one or two trusted friends who can be the heart and voice of Jesus to you. Let Jesus come and speak to you through them and through listening prayer and meditation in his Word. This healing journey can sometimes be a long and difficult path, but with trusted spiritual friends you can make progress. If you don't have such community, consider talking with your pastor, elder, or a well-recommended Christian counselor.

Another difficulty people often encounter with having devotions is finding quality time. This is especially true for mothers with little children. We must fight for this. Meditating on God's Word is as important as eating our natural food. No, it's more important. As Jesus quotes from Deuteronomy, "Man does not live on bread alone, but on every word that comes from the mouth of God" (Matt. 4:4).

It's important to understand that the pursuit of God requires a pattern of being with him. Like any good relationship, fostering a personal connection with God grows over years of consistent time together, through all the ups and downs of life. Some days are better than others. If there's a dry season, it doesn't mean you should give up on talking and relating. We must keep presenting ourselves to God. As one friend puts it, all we can do is put up our sail. The Spirit of God has to blow on it.

While this journey of knowing God through mediation in his Word cannot be quickened by our American impatience, don't think you can't connect with God just because you don't have a lot of time to spend with him. God meets us where we are—not where we "should" be. Start with a small step. Begin by meditating in God's Word for ten or fifteen minutes a day. Take one key verse from your devotional time into the day. Chew on it. Pray over it. Draw strength from it. Use a verse like "My soul finds rest in God alone" (Ps. 62:1). Or "I will never leave you nor forsake you" (Josh. 1:5). Ask God to give you such a longing to meet with him that you'll want to get up a little earlier or stay up later in order to have more time together. It's not about time, it's about quality. But quality takes time. I know one man who says mornings or evenings are not an option for quality time with God. He meets with God in his truck during his lunch hour.

Once you begin to taste and see the Lord is good, you'll want more (1 Peter 2:2–3). Please don't give in to guilt or discouragement. Take one step at a time. Be patient with yourself. The book entitled *When I Don't Desire God* by John Piper is the best book I've read on the why and how of meditating on the Word of God. Whether you're struggling or not, I highly recommend reading that book.

My friend Dan once struggled with devotions that resulted in many occasions of discouragement. He would conclude his devotion time for the morning and not feel anything. He was carving out consistent quality time to be alone with God for years, but many times an experience of emotion was absent. This drove him to discouragement and sometimes anger at himself or at God: "God, why do you make this so hard? Why can't you move more when I seek your face? I must be doing something wrong. My pursuit must be tainted or it isn't earnest enough."

Desiring a rich experience with God is good, but Dan came to see that he was making his emotions a litmus test for whether he was or wasn't doing something right. He felt his time with God was null and void if he didn't experience something. He came to realize this was a serious error. Just like human relationships are not always on an emotional high, he stopped demanding or expecting that his relationship with God would always be so.

God helped Dan with this discouragement through Hebrews 10:19–23. The writer speaks of God's invitation to come boldly, to come with confidence, and to come by faith into the Holy of Holies. We are to come to God in the Holy of Holies through the doorway of the sprinkled blood of Christ. He came to see how important it was for him to live by faith in this area. Now when he spends time with God in his devotions, Dan declares that he is in God's presence—accepted and clean because of the blood of Jesus. He believes this and hangs tightly to it even if his time is void of emotional experience or if it's marked by wandering thoughts.

Now Dan often tells God how grateful he is that God is with him no matter what he feels. He claims this by faith. He thanks God for his guarantee in Hebrews 10. He always tries to think of himself as the tree planted by the rivers of water in Psalm 1:3. Dan says a tree by a river does not appear to be emotional, yet those roots are going deep into the soil and are actively being nourished. He tries to be content with quiet nourishment in God's Word, all the while acknowledging an honest desire for a passionate connection of heart and mind with God. This desire is healthy when it is not a demand and when it no longer serves as a litmus test for God's presence or as proof of a proper pursuit of God.

Last of all, some people avoid reading the Bible because they don't know a lot about it. They've never been to seminary. They've never had in-depth Bible teaching. For some, this creates a sense of inadequacy, so they avoid reading it altogether. I strongly encourage the in-depth study of God's Word. I urge you to be a student of the Bible. There are many good books to help us understand the Bible.[8] But having such knowledge is not necessary to begin to meditate in God's Word. The smallest child can hear from God through his Word.

God is not coming to beat you up or put pressure and guilt on you to be somewhere you are not. He's inviting you to his heart. He wants you to begin where you are. Take one step at a time. Put the oars in the water and reach for him. Don't float downstream in discouragement.

THREE THEMES

There are many themes in the Bible, but God commonly speaks about three: who he is, who we are, and our idolatry. Through these themes, God invites us to turn north to him.

The Word reveals who God is. When King David faced difficult times, he gazed upon the beauty of the Lord by meditating in his temple (Ps. 27:4). He was strengthened by two truths about God:

> One thing God has spoken,
>   two things have I heard:
>   that you, O God, are *strong*,
> and that you, O Lord, are *loving*. (Ps. 62:11–12, emphasis added)

We cultivate spiritual receptivity when we learn to continuously gaze upon the greatness (sovereignty/strength) and goodness (love/faithfulness) of God.

Every moment, every detail—everything good and bad—in our daily lives is filtered through the sovereign greatness and loving goodness of God (Rom. 8:28). Security in God's character is the foundation for living north. It's the source from which our contentment, inner rest, gracious gratitude, and sacrificial giving grow.

Mary, the mother of Jesus, burst into songs of gratitude as she mused upon the character of God:

> "My soul glorifies the Lord
>   and my spirit rejoices in God my Savior. . . .
>   for the *Mighty One* has done great things for me—
>   *holy* is his name.
> His *mercy* extends to those who fear him,
>   from generation to generation."
>   (Luke 1:46–47, 49–50, emphasis added)

To live north we must remember who God is. We must continuously gaze upon the Sovereign Lord. If there is anything God does in response to all our needs and struggles in life, he shows us and gives us more of his Son. Therefore, when David faced daily groaning, his soul reflexively sought God. "My heart says of you, 'Seek his face!' Your face, Lord, I will seek" (Ps. 27:8; see also Pss. 4:6; 63:2–7).

Seeing the glory of God's character can be dangerous. When Isaiah, the prophet, caught a glimpse of the holiness of God, he cried out in horror, "Woe to me! . . . I am ruined! For I am a man of unclean lips, and I live among a people of unclean lips, and my eyes have seen the King, the LORD Almighty" (Isa. 6:5). And when the apostle John—exiled on the Island of Patmos because he witnessed about Jesus—turned to see the one who spoke to him, he saw the glorified Son of God whose head and hair were white like wool. His eyes were as flames of fire, and out from his mouth came a sharp, two-edged sword. John was so shaken, so filled with terror, that he fell on his face as a dead man (Rev. 1:12–17). When we get a glimpse of the greatness of God, our sin will be exposed. We'll be shaken, humbled, and undone. Yet being captivated by God's transcendence is vital in our battle against sin. John Piper wrote:

My conviction is that one of the main reasons the world and the church are awash in lust and pornography (by both men and women— 30 percent of Internet pornography is now viewed by women) is that our lives are intellectually and emotionally disconnected from the infinite, soul-staggering grandeur for which we were made. . . .

Therefore, the deepest cure to our pitiful addictions is not any mental strategies—though I believe in them and have my own. . . . The deepest cure is to be intellectually and emotionally staggered by the infinite, everlasting, unchanging supremacy of Christ in all things.[9]

God is humble, tenderhearted, slow to anger, and abounding in mercy. God is also sovereign, holy, and just. He will judge every man and woman for every deed we have done. Living in the tension of God's goodness and greatness is to live in the fear of the Lord. The fear of the Lord means there are certain things we don't do (gossip, for example) and certain things we will do (such as forgive as we've been forgiven).

Such a God leads, shepherds, protects, and sustains you in this dark and dangerous world. But if we lose sight of God's greatness or his goodness, we will lose heart.[10] We'll go south and grasp for comfort and relief. We'll try to make this world home.

The Word reveals who we are. Life is difficult. It beats us up. We fail and get discouraged. Some days the crushing weight of life, discouragement, and loneliness seem too much for me. I cry out to God. Many times he kindly speaks to me and encourages me by reminding me of who I am. We are God's sons and daughters, his servants, and his soldiers.[11] The order and balance are important. If we switch the first two around and think of ourselves first as servants and then as sons or daughters, we'll work to earn God's love instead of working because we are loved.

We are God's sons and daughters. Through the Word of God, God reminds me again and again that I am his dearly loved son. I find new courage to keep going. In spite of my failure, he loves me. He's for me. Last year I talked with a young woman who struggled to believe God loved her. She grew up with a distant, alcoholic father. After a fight with her husband one night, she felt desperately alone. She asked God if he loved her. She asked if he would somehow speak to her. She longed to know what he thought of her. She happened to notice her daughter's *Adventure Bible* sitting nearby. She opened it up. and on the page was a question and an answer: "Does God love you? Yes. More than you know." She wept with gratitude. Embracing our identity as God's sons and daughters is foundational to our sense of security. "May you experience the love of Christ, though it is too great to understand fully. Then you will be made complete with all the fullness of life and power that comes from God" (Eph. 3:19 NLT). Listen for God's still small voice to whisper to you. You are his dearly loved son or daughter. That is *first*.

Secondly, we are God's servants. God's Word reveals our purpose in life. We are bond servants of Jesus Christ. Jesus said, "The Son of Man did not come to be served, but to serve, and to give his life as a ransom for many" (Mark 10:45). Amazing. God is a servant! We are not better than our Master. We too were made for a mission. Until our gratitude for being God's sons and daughters translates into heartfelt, sacrificial giving to others, we do not understand Christianity (Gal. 5:13–14). We do not have a biblical worldview. Every day, all day, God invites us into the adventure of joining him in living out the double-love command by serving others.

Finally, the Bible tells us we are soldiers. We face hardship. We groan in this fallen world. Remember, there is always purpose—both God's and Satan's—to our pain. Learning to suffer well is essential to learning to live north. Having a theology of suffering (such as this book provides) gives us biblical categories and practical tools for processing daily struggles, enabling us to "endure hardship . . . like a good soldier of Christ Jesus" (2 Tim. 2:3).

The Word reveals our idolatry. We need to face the ways we forsake God by going south. To help us do that, we need biblical categories for understanding people. Study and apply the categories within this book to the stories of people in the Bible. Ask what was going on inside their hearts and minds as they struggled with problems:

- How were they groaning?
- How and why did they go south into unbelief, grumbling, and grasping?
- What helped them turn north to God?

- How did God reveal himself to them?
- How was God reminding them of who they were as his covenant people?

Ask yourself how you are like those people in the Bible. What can you personally learn from their examples? How is God calling you, through their stories, to deeper levels of repentance so you can know him better?

Don't read the Bible to merely gain knowledge. Read it to know God. Read it to know yourself and others. It's a painful, yet wonderful thing to be exposed, humbled, and drawn back to Jesus. The Spirit of God makes this happen. He exposes our hearts and points us back to God.

CONNECTING WITH GOD THROUGH THE SPIRIT OF GOD

The Holy Spirit is a living person who indwells every believer. He plays such a vital role in our walk with God that it's impossible to even mention everything he does for us. The result of the Holy Spirit's work in our lives is manifested by love, joy, peace, patience, kindness, goodness, faithfulness, gentleness, and self-control (Gal. 5:22–23 NLT). The Holy Spirit teaches, enlightens, intercedes, empowers, cleanses, transforms, and leads us. The Spirit of God comforts us in our trials. He guides us in our daily life. Prayerfully ask him for wisdom when you face problems and frustrations. Don't just go south into worry, panic, or anger. Stop! Ask God to help you turn north and quiet your soul. Listen for his still, small voice within. Listen to his promptings. The Holy Spirit will help you respond to life's difficulties in redemptive ways.

The Holy Spirit convicts us by exposing our sin (John 16:8–11). David prayed, "Search me, O God, and know my heart. . . . See if there is any offensive way in me" (Ps. 139:23–24). The convicting work of the Holy Spirit is a gift. When we go south, he convicts us and invites us to turn back to God, our heart's true treasure.

But what keeps us from experiencing the convicting work of the Holy Spirit? Too often we focus on the sin of others instead of facing the ways we sin or sinfully react to other's sin. God cares about our pain when we're sinned against. He longs for us to turn to him in our groaning. The Holy Spirit will comfort us if we do. Yet we so naturally and stubbornly justify our sinful responses when we're mistreated. We quench the Spirit's voice. We call our grumbling "righteous anger" as we verbally attack or emotionally withdraw from the one who hurt us. Cultivating spiritual receptivity to the Holy Spirit requires us to humble ourselves and come to the Word of God, asking the Spirit of God to expose the sin of our self-centeredness so we can receive God's grace and help to go north. The following is written by a man in our church who wished to remain anonymous to protect his wife and children. He is a good friend and a good man. I'm thankful for his spiritual receptivity to the Holy Spirit's conviction!

This past year presented a significant challenge in my marriage of thirteen-plus years. I never realized until the last six months how much I have sinned against my wife. I had always equated a good marriage with uninhibited and frequent sex. However, what I did not realize is that whenever I felt insignificant or discouraged by life, sexual relations with my wife was my way to get relief from the emotional pain. In other words, I was going south by trying to find life in this world. If my wife ever refused to have sex with me, I would punish her by pouting, withdrawing, ignoring, and pouring guilt on her by telling her she was not doing her part as a wife.

This was a form of idolatry, but I was calling it a physical need. I believed a godly woman must not deny her husband. Now I know that this is a huge sin. I was forsaking God and putting immense pressure on my wife to come through for me. This negatively affected the oneness in our marriage. Each time my wife said no to my demands, I would resent her more and more. In my view, she was withholding love from me. This made me feel unattractive and unwanted so I enjoyed it when other women said flattering things to me or looked at me. It fed my sinful self, which drew me further away from my wife. The more she turned me down sexually, the more I chose to avoid her. I did this so she would know I was not dependent on her. Ultimately I did not want anyone to have the control of withholding "life" from me. This was a vicious and destructive cycle.

During a two-week holiday, I wanted to pursue my wife sexually a dozen times or more. However, I knew this was getting out of control and God had been working in my life, helping me see that I needed to turn to him for my emotional needs instead of pressuring my wife for relief. Each time I felt like pursuing my wife, I chose instead to spend time with God alone, praying and reading his Word. This decision did not feel natural. What I found happening, however, which to me is nothing short of a miracle, is that the emotional needs that I was trying to fill through sexual experiences with my wife were being more deeply satisfied, in the short and long term, by pursuing and developing a closer relationship with my Creator. Even writing this sounds unbelievable and I wonder if I would believe it if I heard another man say this. But God is becoming more real to me. Instead of pressuring and hurting my wife, God is helping me love her.

Connecting with God through the people of God

God has graciously given us the people of God with whom we can further cultivate spiritual receptivity. Friendship is no small thing. We long for safe friends who are not demanding. We long for friendships where we share deep belly laughs around good food at our favorite restaurant. We yearn for good people with whom we can be ourselves, having no need to pretend.

But it's easy to have friends who are just fun, convenient, and comfortable. That poses a problem. There's no risk and little chance of growth. People who are hungry for God long for something more than safety and good times.

Hebrews 10:24 says, "Let us consider how to stir up one another to love and good works" (esv). The word *consider* means to think deeply. The words *stir up* mean to inflame or create fever. I think of a poker, stirring up hot coals. The coals burst into flame creating warmth. I meet regularly with several men. Lisa meets with a group of four ladies. We "stir up" one another. Together, we think deeply about our lives. We have fun and do ministry while speaking words that challenge and stir our hearts' affections for Jesus. We experience the life-changing power of authentic friendship.

Some years ago I was building a new friendship with Mark. We drove a couple of hours to Cabela's. I wanted to buy some backpacking gear and a fly rod for steelhead fishing. Mark was looking for a 12-gauge shotgun. As we drove to the store, our conversation moved from lighthearted conversation to questions about how we were doing in life, work, and our marriages. We both shared how our self-centeredness could get in the way of loving our wives well. As we opened up and talked honestly about our struggles, God spoke through us and helped us want to be better men. We wanted to be the shelter for our wives instead of being or adding to their storms in life. We were encouraged. Through honest sharing and acceptance of one another, we took a big step in fostering genuine, life-changing friendship.

During a lull in our conversation, Mark smiled as he said, "Gary, what's wrong with this picture? Here we are, two *men* talking about *relationships* as we're on our way to go *shopping* for the day." We roared with laughter. It was a day I won't forget.

PURSUE ONE ANOTHER

Be curious about people. I call it "redemptive curiosity." What are the dreams, wounds, fears, struggles, and strengths of people you want friendship with? Learn to ask good questions that invite others to open up without pressuring them to do so: What frustrations are you facing in life? What do you believe you *need* when you go south? When you don't get what you want, how do you grasp for control? What helps you turn to God and seek him in those moments of struggle? Good questions are open-ended and personal, and there's no right or wrong answer. They invite the person to talk about themselves.

The more you process your lives together through the categories offered in this book, the more you'll think of good questions to ask others that invite them to talk about what takes them north or south. Learning to pursue others with good questions is more of an art than a science. The art of loving requires first knowledge, then experience, and finally intuition. Just as a heart surgeon needs to know about human anatomy before he or she picks up a scalpel, you should study the Bible and other good books to understand yourself and others. And as an effective surgeon needs experience to become competent, you need experience added to your knowledge in order to learn how to love and pursue others well. You have to get in there and care enough about people to take the risk of "opening them up" by asking them good and penetrating questions as you also share your struggles with them. At times it won't work.

You'll get resistance, but don't quit. It takes years. A master surgeon didn't get there overnight. Learn to grow from your mistakes. Trust the Holy Spirit to help and guide you. Get back up and keep trying. Nothing is more important than learning how to love.

No textbook addresses every situation a surgeon faces. His or her knowledge and experience will, over time, cultivate intuition. Similarly, as you grow in knowledge and experience and prayerfully depend on the Spirit of God to guide you, your intuition will grow. Your best form of knowledge, experience, and intuition will come by facing the log in your own eye. The process works humility and compassion in us. The process will help us see clearly how to take the speck out of our brother's eye (Matt. 7:1–3).

Be aware that there is always mystery to life. Pursuing and entering people's hearts and real-life struggles is often messy and confusing, and for good reason. We need to depend on the Word of God and the Spirit of God to guide us. We'll make plenty of mistakes, but we'll never love well without taking risks and learning from our failures. We grow in the art of loving others as we are broken by our sin, renewed in his grace, walking humbly with God, and offering mercy and truth to those who struggle. The joy of helping others treasure Jesus is worth it. It's the life we were made to live whether we're a plumber, pastor, or parent.

CELEBRATE THE NEW COVENANT HEART IN ONE ANOTHER

Because of the miracle of the new covenant heart that we referred to in chapters 7 and 10—the miracle of Christ living inside us—our hearts are inclined toward God rather than away from him. Therefore, when God looks at his redeemed children, he smiles with delight. When we meet with our small group, family, or friends, we need to remember that they have a new covenant heart if they're in Christ. Having such a view of people will help us believe in them and like them even when they're annoying.

This has helped me relax as I relate to others. A close friend confessed he had looked at pornography *again*. He was so discouraged he couldn't look us in the face. Knowing my friend had a new heart, I prayerfully asked God to help me see it. I quietly listened to my heart as I listened for the Holy Spirit's voice within. An idea came to me, and I spoke into my friend's life. "Do you realize that I'm drawn to God right now as I see how troubled you are by your sin? It makes me worship God. You're troubled by your sin because looking at pornography is not who you really are. It's not what you most deeply want. Deep down, you want God. The fact that you're so troubled by your sin says the Holy Spirit is working in your redeemed heart. What most defines you is a man who deeply wants God."

My friend's eyes glistened with hope. My words resonated with his redeemed heart, and he knew I believed in him. He was fully known, yet fully loved. Moreover, I saw the gold beneath the tarnish of his sin. His new heart had been seen and celebrated. His shame was transformed into gratitude.

Our calling isn't primarily to pressure one another into going God's way. It's to help one another see that that's what we most deeply want to do. Christ lives in us. True community and spiritual friends believe this about one another even when it's hard to see, even when conflict and difficulty arise. They prayerfully look for its evidence and speak authentic words that fan it into flame.

Imagine how we would treat one another if we really believed this truth. We treat things we value much differently than those things we believe have little or no worth. I once heard Bill Hybels say that "vision is a picture of the future that produces passion."[12] See people for who they could be, for who is already powerfully alive inside them, even though it may be hidden by their ugly grumbling and grasping. How would your attitude be different toward your friends, family, kids, and small-group members if you saw them this way? Imagine how safe we would feel together if we all knew that we believed this about each other no matter how we struggled with our fallen natures.

Within every believer lies something deeper than greed, lust, jealousy, anger, arrogance, and insecurity. Stir it into flame and celebrate it when you see it. Here's an example: "Jane, as you share your struggles with depression, I thank God for you. You've trusted us with that, and that is a gift. Thank you! I think you took that risk because deep in your heart, you want God. That makes me worship Jesus!"

SPEAK THE TRUTH IN LOVE TO ONE ANOTHER

Have fun. Share your life stories. Pray. Study God's Word. Pursue one another with good and probing questions because you care about one another. See and celebrate the new heart as people step into the light and are known.

Realize that there will be times when we need to take the risk to give and receive hard feedback to and from one another. Real friends take the risk to speak truth when love calls for it. You may have to say something like, "Mike, as you talk about your wife, you seem cold and uncaring about her struggles. Are you aware of that?"

Our new heart defines us, but we don't always see how we violate the double-love command as we relate to others. While love covers a multitude of sins, there will be times when it calls us to speak the truth in love. Ask permission before you speak. "Ruth, would it be okay if I shared some of my concerns about your new relationship with Bill?" This communicates respect because giving advice that isn't asked for is a form of rejection.

In the early days of being self-employed as a counselor, I worried. The phone wasn't ringing, and I was concerned about our finances. One night as Lisa and I sat on our porch, I voiced my worries with a grumbling, self-pitying tone of voice. Lisa gave me time to share, and then softly but clearly, said, "I know you're going through a lot right now and it isn't easy. . . . But I long to see a faith in you that says, 'God will get me through this.'"

Lisa's words provoked anger in me. I wanted affirmation not confrontation. But I sat quietly and pondered her words. I asked myself why I felt anger. I realized that what I really felt beneath my anger was shame. I loved God. I was a man of faith. Yet my wife saw something different as I spoke that day. That saddened me. Instead of defending myself, I thought and prayed about Lisa's feedback for a whole week. God helped me see something about myself: when I faced hardship, I tended to live as if there was no God. My worry came from believing that it was all up to me to make life work. I didn't think I had what it took so I felt despairing. Seeing this about myself was a turning point in my faith and walk with God. I thank God for Lisa's courage to take the risk to speak the truth in love to me.

Speaking truth can be risky. It can make or break a friendship. We are not responsible for how someone responds, but we are responsible to take the risk to speak when love calls for it and to speak in love for the good of the other (Eph. 4:29).

When we get it and learn to grow it, we'll *want* to give it away to others. We'll want to help others treasure Jesus and make him the blazing center of their lives.

QUESTIONS FOR SELF-EXAMINATION AND DISCUSSION

1. How convinced are you that God wants to speak to you and connect with you *personally*? What will help you take your next step in believing this is true?

2. Do you have any secrets you are keeping from your spouse or trusted friends? Will you take the risk to be fully known with someone? This is a crucial step toward wholehearted devotion to God.

3. How has God spoken to you through this chapter about the importance of meditation in his Word?

4. Are there any changes you want/need to make in giving greater priority to connecting with God through meditation in his Word (i.e., less TV, get up fifteen minutes earlier, etc.)?

5. Are you connected with good, spiritual friends on a regular basis—friends who know each other well enough to speak the truth in love to one another? If not, will you prayerfully take the risk of asking some people to meet with you for that purpose?

6. As you've read the last two chapters, "Getting It" and "Growing It," what might God be asking you to do to continue to grow?

12

GIVING IT AWAY

MENTORING OTHERS

The most profoundly good effect of a parent on a child comes . . .
from the parent's unrelenting pursuit of God, a pursuit that
continues through every setback of life.
Larry Crabb Jr. and Larry Crabb Sr., *God of My Father*

If there is any focus that the Christian leader of the future will need,
it is the discipline of dwelling in the presence of the One who keeps
asking us, "Do you love me? Do you love me? Do you love me?"
Henri Nouwen, *In the Name of Jesus*

Do you want to be a wise person? The answer seems obvious. Who in their right mind wants to be a fool? But what does it take to be wise? The Bible says,

> A wise person thinks a lot about death,
>   while a fool thinks only about having a good time now.
> (Eccl. 7:4 NLT)

Sounds a bit morbid and depressing, don't you think? The Bible tells us how to live life well. So why does it tell us to think a lot about death? Because this is certain: we're all going to die. And if we never slow down long enough to think about our death, we may never stop to think about why we're living. What are *you* living for? When you get down to the heart of it all, what's your ruling passion in life? What will your family and friends say about you when they show up at your funeral to say their last goodbyes? What would their epitaph on your tombstone say? I can't think of anything more important in life than to live with divine purpose. Jesus told a story about a man who lived to have a good time now (Luke 12:16–21). The guy stored up a lot of stuff and told himself to eat, drink, and be merry. He became so self-absorbed he decided to tear down his barns and build bigger ones so he could store more stuff. Then God spoke to him, "'You fool! You will die this very night. Then who will get everything you worked for?' Yes, a person is a fool to store up earthly wealth but not have a rich relationship with God" (Luke 12:20–21 NLT). What could be more tragic than to wake up one day and realize you wasted your life?

I know a spiritual leader who has talked and prayed with inmates on death row. As they face their death and reflect on their lives, they don't wish they had made more money or gotten a bigger house or a nicer car. They don't wish they had spent more time climbing the corporate ladder. No. When people face their death, they wish they had cared more about the people they loved.

Life is about relationships, first with God and then with others. Deep things like that matter to all of us. But what matters most often gets pushed aside for lesser things: painting the bedroom, getting the lawn just right, shooting a bigger deer, buying a another dress, reading another book. Those may be good and important things, but they're not the main thing. Too often we let our children, our husbands and wives, brothers and sisters, friends and neighbors walk past us day after day without letting them know how much we love them, how much they matter to us.

As I mentioned in chapter 5, Nicholas Wolterstorff's son was killed in a mountain-climbing accident. When grieving the loss of his son, Nicholas realized how much he had taken him for granted. Then it was too late.

> We took him too much for granted. Perhaps we all take each other too much for granted. The routines of life distract us; our own pursuits make us oblivious; our anxieties and sorrows, unmindful. . . . We do not treasure each other enough. He was a gift to us for twenty-five years. When the gift was finally snatched away, I realized how great it was. Then I could not tell him.[1]

And so the book of Ecclesiastes warns us:

> Better to spend your time at funerals than at parties.
> After all, everyone dies—
> so the living should take this to heart. (Eccl. 7:2 NLT)

Why should we take this to heart? To make sure our lives count for what really matters. The greatest joy in life comes by giving to others what God has given to us. It means letting God use all our struggles of life to grow us up so we can become spiritual friends, guides, and mentors for others. When I think of mentors like that, I think of Gandalf, the beloved wizard of Middle-earth in Tolkien's trilogy, *The Lord of the Rings*. I'm drawn into the part of the story when Frodo falls into despair and Gandalf speaks profound truth into his life.

"We now have but one choice," Gandalf says with grave concern. "We must face the long dark of Moria. . . . Be on your guard. There are *older* and *fouler* things than Orcs in the deep places of the world." Gandalf must lead the other eight members of the Fellowship of the Ring through the deep, dark, goblin-infested Mines of Moria. "Quietly now . . . ," he warns. "Let us hope that our presence may go unnoticed." They have a four-day journey to the other side.

Three days pass as they journey through Moria. Their path leads to three doorways. Gandalf cannot remember which they should take. While waiting for Gandalf to decide, Frodo, a small hobbit among the Fellowship, is terrified when he sees Gollum—a wretched, beastly creature who is stalking them from a distance. He tells Gandalf what he has seen.

"He's been following us for three days," Gandalf tells Frodo. Gollum wants the ring. Frodo has the ring. He alone has been given the mission of carrying the ring to Mount Doom, where it must be destroyed. If he fails to carry out his mission, Middle-earth will be overcome by evil. Frodo is overcome with fear: They are lost in the dark mines. Wretched Gollum stalks him. Evil surrounds them.

Frodo falls into despair. Lamenting all that's happening to him, he breaks down and says, "I wish the ring had never come to me. I wish none of this had happened." Gandalf is not shaken by Frodo's confession. Gandalf trusts in Frodo's heart. Gandalf speaks life words into Frodo's despair, "So do all who live to see such times, but that is not for them to decide. All we have to decide is what to do with the time that is given to us."[2] Days later the Fellowship escapes from Moria, but after a fierce battle, Frodo is all alone. Gandalf is thought to have been killed, evil Orcs have captured Frodo's dearest friends, and one of the Fellowship has been killed in battle. Frodo must make a decision: Will he live for himself and flee to the safety of his home in the Shire? Or will he choose to stay faithful to his mission? He is the only one who can carry the evil ring and destroy it in the fires of Mount Doom. But there Frodo will likely be captured and tortured to death. Frodo's decision holds staggering consequences for everything he holds dear. In that moment of decision, Frodo remembers his beloved Gandalf's words: "All we have to decide is what to do with the time that is given to us." Frodo chooses faithfulness. He finds courage to reject passivity. He moves into the face of fear.

Oh to have a Gandalf in our lives when all seems lost, when hardship takes us south into despair. I thank God for the men and women who stay faithful in the refining fires of life, who do not capitulate to immorality but emerge from their dark nights of the soul with compassion, courage, wisdom, power, and ability to speak life words to the next generation. I do not know where I would be today in my spiritual journey without such mentors. Larry Crabb, Dan Allender, Kevin Huggins, Ed Lewis, and Wilbur Wanner have been Gandalfs for me. And through all the years and hardships of the winding trails and trials of life, God has used adversity to grow me and shape me so I, too, can be a Gandalf for others. More than anything, I want God to continue to grow me and use me to help others get it, grow it, and give it away. I know no greater joy in life than pointing people to God. Maturity in Christ brings us to the place where we live for the purpose of giving life to others.

THE MAKING OF A MENTOR

Moses was a Gandalf for Israel. He led God's people out of Egypt, through the long dark of wilderness, and to the glories of the Promised Land. But Moses had to experience his own dark wilderness training before he could lead Israel through theirs.

"Everybody—at least everybody who has anything to do with God—spends time in the wilderness."[3] Moses fled into the wilderness for forty years (Exod. 2:11–23). Israel wandered there for forty years (Num. 14:26–35). David was chased into the wilderness (1 Sam. 20–27). Jesus was driven there by the Spirit

(Matt. 4:1). John the Baptist lived there (Matt. 3:1–4). Yep. Whether it's for two days, two weeks, two months, or many years, anybody who's anybody in God's kingdom will spend time in the wilderness. Our first inclination is to escape, but we must learn to embrace it. It's a vital part of our biblical training. As Eugene Peterson wrote, it's how we learn to discern. Are we going north to God or south to gods?

> In the Moses wilderness story the people of Israel were trained to discern between idols and the living God, taught to worship; through their wilderness experience they were prepared to live totally before God. In the Jesus wilderness story our Lord learned to discern between religion that uses God and spirituality that enters into what God does, and he was thereby prepared to be our Savior. . . . In the David wilderness story we see a young man hated and hunted like an animal, his very humanity profaned, forced to decide between a life of blasphemy and a life of prayer. . . . In choosing prayer he entered into the practice of holiness.[4]

BROKEN AND DEPENDENT

Moses was a natural leader. He was trained by the best in Egypt. Moses thought his training and giftedness qualified him to lead Israel. His first attempt to lead failed miserably. He fled into the wilderness to escape Pharaoh's wrath (Exod. 2:11–15). Forty years passed. Then God called to Moses from a burning bush. God told him to go speak to Pharaoh and lead his people from their bondage into the Promised Land (Exod. 3:4–22). The wilderness experience had done its work. Moses was not the same; his self-confidence had been broken. Moses told God he couldn't even speak (Exod. 4:10). How could he stand before Pharaoh? When Moses thought he was ready to lead, God said, "No, you're not." When Moses said he wasn't ready, God said, "Now I can use you."

We tend toward two extremes when it comes to ministry. We're either too self-confident or too self-loathing. Self-confidence thinks our giftedness and training are enough to make things happen. But if we're fortunate, the time will come when we'll see they are not. On the other hand, self-loathing tries to excuse ourselves from God's call. God will not accept either extreme. A godly leader must be *broken* and *dependent*.

Moses was broken. We know the story. He eventually obeyed God and went to Pharaoh (Exod. 5). He was also dependent. The Bible says he was the most humble man on the face of the earth (Num. 12:3). God forged within Moses a heart of a mentor. Moses got it, he grew it, and he lived to give it away. He lived to lead others to God's best. That's our calling too.

ZEALOUS AND PASSIONATE

A true mentor is zealous for God. Moses' one burning passion was the Lord. One day God was furious with Israel's stubbornness of heart. He told Moses he would send his angel to lead them to the Promised Land but he would not go with them. Moses would have none of it. He fought with God, saying, "Don't take us there [Promised Land] unless you go with us" (Exod. 33:15–16). For Moses, no paradise or Promised Land was worth having without God.

The second passion of a mentor is God's people. He or she will pray, speak, fight, and struggle for others to really get it and grow it. Paul said he was in labor pains until Christ was formed in the believers at Galatia (Gal. 4:19). I've watched Lisa go through labor with our two kids. I've never experienced pain like that. But I've known the labor pain of fighting for others to know God, to see Christ formed in them. Tears; sleepless nights; soul-searching, gut-wrenching prayer; confusion—you name it. If you and I know God, it's because someone labored for us.

LABORING FOR OTHERS

Who has labored for you? For whom are you in labor?

The book of Exodus portrays a beautiful picture of the high priest of Israel. The high priest was to have the names of the sons of Israel engraved on precious stones that were fastened to his shoulders. In addition, he wore a breastplate with twelve precious stones, each representing the sons of Israel. The high priest was to bear the names of God's chosen people upon his shoulders and to "bear the names of the sons of Israel over his heart on the breastpiece of decision" (Exod. 28:9–29). That is the picture of our calling: to bear the names of God's people upon our shoulders and carry them over our hearts into his presence. Whatever our vocation in life may be, first and foremost all believers in Christ are called to be priests (1 Peter 2:5, 9). A priest presents God to people and people to God. We are to fight for others by carrying our spouse, children, church, friends, and enemies before God.

> There is a chamber—a chamber in God himself which none
> can enter but the one, the individual, the particular man.
> Out of which chamber that man has to bring revelation
> and strength for his brethren. This is that for which he was
> made—to reveal the secret things of the Father.
>
> GEORGE MACDONALD, FROM *In Quietness and Confidence* BY DAVID ROPER

Prayer is foundational. Prayer puts us on our knees in humble dependence on the Holy Spirit to move in someone's life. Studying and meditating in the Word of God, depending upon the Spirit of God, and being known within the community of the people of God are also crucial means through which we labor for others. But the discipleship process in a person's life is not complete until the one who gets it and grows it is giving it away to others.

There are many ways through which we can help people grow—Sunday morning sermons, Sunday school classes, small groups, accountability groups, ministry trips, or one-on-one conversations over coffee are all valuable means. In addition to these, my friends and I have discovered two other venues through which we seek to help people "get it and grow it": backpacking trips and "525s." For a complete explanation of these getaways and a sample agenda, you can visit our website.[5]

WHAT WILL KEEP US FAITHFUL TO THE END?

As we relate with family, friends, coworkers, cashiers, and waitresses, God asks us to intentionally and consistently do what doesn't come naturally—we're to live a life of love by helping others get it, grow it, and give it away. We're to develop the strength of character such as humility, gentleness, kindness, patience, and forgiveness that enables us to stay committed to loving people from the heart even when they sin against us or seem unconcerned about our struggles.

Yet the need to be cared for and to rest in the love and protection of someone stronger than you and me is such a deep and legitimate longing of the human heart. Because this longing to have someone care about us is so strong, we feel a natural resistance, if not irritation, at the call to faithfully give to others no matter what. But even if we did give ourselves over to another human being, it wouldn't work because we're all self-centered. We're often preoccupied with our own lives, and we lack the understanding that's needed to fully care for one another.

Here's our struggle: the more we love and serve God by giving to others, the more painfully aware we'll become of our deep desire to have someone take care of us. As we live to help others get it, grow it and give it away, we'll taste joy, but we'll also experience loneliness.

Therefore, we must become men and women who not only know about God but who know him. The path to knowing God always takes us through the desert of loneliness. We'll realize a longing to be loved that no human being can come close to touching fully and consistently. As we continue to pour our lives into others and refuse to demand that others love us, when we gratefully accept the littlest encouragements that people do give us, our souls will feel their deepest loneliness. It is in these desert times, when we refuse to grasp for relief but instead abandon ourselves to God alone, that we will come to know him deeply. Godly character will grow.

Jesus gave us a promise. He said if we will obey him (love God and love others), he and his Father will come to us and disclose themselves to us. They'll make their home in us. And if you've read this far, that's what you want more than anything this world can offer. Stay faithful. The best is yet to come.

IT ALL STARTS HERE!

Since my conversion at age seventeen, I have walked with God for more than forty years. Yet for many of those years, I was blind to how much I treasured things of earth. As I've said earlier in this book, one of the lies I believed was that I *needed* people to give me love and respect by affirming me. I feared people who might not give me love or respect, and I resented them when they didn't. It took a long time for me to clearly see how I was doing this.

For several years God took me into a wilderness where my lie didn't work for me. What I mean by a wilderness is that people didn't love and respect me in the ways I demanded. When I wanted recognition, I got overlooked. When I demanded affirmation, I got criticism and what sometimes felt like mockery.

When I worked hard to impress people, I failed. I was left feeling needy, weak, wounded, angry, resentful, and alone. At times, feelings of shame and failure overwhelmed me. To most people I probably looked fine. I could smile and fake it pretty well. But this battle raged on the inside. This was a dark and self-centered time in my life. This wilderness was one of the dark nights of my soul. And what was worse, I tried to justify my anger and bitterness by focusing on the failures of people who didn't recognize or affirm me. But God didn't rescue me by changing others. Instead, he allowed those struggles to intensify as he patiently worked to help me see the depths of my sin.

As my ugly self-centeredness became clearer, I realized I couldn't change myself. In my helplessness and desperation, I cried out to Jesus for help. Some of his help came to me by way of the paradigm presented in this book. Over the years, Jesus has come to me in countless ways. I've heard his voice. He has spoken tenderly to me. Again and again he has called me his beloved son. I'm learning to hear him speak to me. And his song continues to grow in my heart. He is so patient yet ruthlessly determined to win our hearts' devotion. And I am coming to live in the truth that I am God's dearly loved son who is forgiven and treasured by Jesus. This new song of security in God's love is translating into joyful freedom to confidently give to people. I give with great hope and expectation that God will use me to help others treasure Jesus as he treasures them.

The fear of people no longer has a strangle hold on me. I'm amazed at how God is rescuing me from the lie of needing people to recognize me. But everyday lies pull at me and invite me to forsake God as the center and treasure of my heart. And every day I struggle with the sin of self-centeredness. Yet I am confident of this: God will continue to use my daily struggles to help me grow more deeply in love with Jesus as I am humbled by his patient and steadfast love for me. Change is truly possible. It is possible for you too.

And so dear reader, Lisa and I invite you and urge you to take seriously the things God has stirred in you through the reading of this book. Many Christians are crumbling around us, succumbing to immorality and the pressures and lies our culture bombards us with. The battle is real and intense. It's going to get worse. But we can choose God in the frustrations of life. Every day, all day, God invites us up into the life-giving adventure of making Jesus the treasure of our lives as we keep learning how to gratefully reveal his good heart to our families, friends, churches, and everyone we meet. He invites us to be living sacrifices that live to help others get it, grow it, and give it away.

QUESTIONS FOR SELF-EXAMINATION AND DISCUSSION

1. What are you living for? When you get down to it, what would you, and others who know you, say is your ruling passion in life? Are you happy with that? Why or why not?

2. What do you think and feel when you face the certainty of your death? How does that thought effect your desire to live with divine purpose? What would you want your epitaph on your tombstone to say?

3. Who has been a "Gandalf" in your life? How did that person encourage you to go north? If you've never had a mentor, what's stirred in you by that thought?

4. Have you ever spent time in the wilderness? If so, explain what happened. What did God reveal to you about yourself? What did he forge in you through that experience?

5. Who has labored for you to know God? For whom are you in labor to see Christ formed? Describe how you are in labor for them. If you're not in labor for others, what's holding you back? What will help you take your next step toward investing in someone so they can get it, grow it, and give it away?

NOTES

CHAPTER 1. LIFE IS DIFFICULT

1. M. Scott Peck, *The Road Less Traveled: A New Psychology of Love, Traditional Values, and Spiritual Growth* (New York: Simon and Schuster, 1978), 15.
2. André Malraux, *Anti-memoirs*, trans. Terence Kilmartin (1967; New York: Holt, Rinehart, and Winston, 1968), 1; cited in *The Gift of Therapy* by Irvin D. Yalom (New York: HarperCollins, 2002), 6.
3. Jean Vanier, *Befriending the Stranger* (Grand Rapids: Eerdmans, 2005), 10–12. Used by permission.
4. John Piper and Justin Taylor, eds., *Sex and the Supremacy of Christ* (Wheaton, IL: Crossway, 2005), 37–38.

CHAPTER 2. WILL YOU GO NORTH OR SOUTH?

1. Larry Crabb, *Inside Out* (Colorado Springs: NavPress, 2007), 148.
2. John Piper, *A Hunger for God: Desiring God Through Fasting and Prayer* (Wheaton, IL: Crossway, 1997), 14.
3. C. S. Lewis, *Mere Christianity* (1952, 1980; New York: HarperCollins, 2001), 192.

CHAPTER 3. GROANING

1. Richard J. Foster, *Freedom of Simplicity* (New York: HarperCollins, 1981), 30.
2. Francis A. Schaeffer, *True Spirituality* (Wheaton, IL: Tyndale, 1971), 20.
3. Rick Warren, *The Purpose Driven Life* (Grand Rapids: Zondervan, 2002), 17–18.

4. Donald Miller, *Blue Like Jazz: Nonreligious Thoughts on Christian Spirituality* (Nashville: Thomas Nelson, 2003), 182.

5. Timothy Keller, *The Prodigal God: Recovering the Heart of the Christian Faith* (New York: Dutton, 2008), 91–96.

6. C. S. Lewis, *The Problem of Pain* (New York: Macmillian, 1974), 115.

7. J. R. R. Tolkien, *The Return of the King* (New York: Ballantine, 1977), 283.

8. Philip Yancey, *Disappointment with God: Three Questions No One Asks Aloud* (Grand Rapids: Zondervan, 1988), 245–46.

9. C. S. Lewis, *The Weight of Glory* (New York: HarperCollins, 2001), 36–37.

10. John Eldredge, *Wild at Heart: Discovering the Secret of a Man's Soul* (Nashville: Thomas Nelson, 2001), 62.

11. Ibid., 182.

12. Lewis, *Weight of Glory*, 26.

13. A. W. Tozer, *The Pursuit of God: The Human Thirst for the Divine* (Camp Hill, PA: WingSpread, 2006), 22.

14. Thomas Merton, *The Silent Life* (New York: Noonday, 1957), 14.

15. "Severe mercy" is a term borrowed from Sheldon Vanauken's book, *A Severe Mercy* (San Francisco: Harper & Row, 1987), 211.

CHAPTER 4. GRUMBLING

1. Marty Ahrens, *U.S. Experience with Smoke Alarms and Other Fire Detection Equipment*, National Fire Protection Association, April 2007, http://www.nfpa.org/assets/file//PDF/Reasearch/SmokeAlarmFactSheet.pdf.

2. Gordon MacDonald, *A Resilient Life: You Can Move Ahead No Matter What* (Nashville: Thomas Nelson, 2004), 177–78.

3. Charles H. Elliott and Laura L. Smith, *Overcoming Anxiety for Dummies* (New York: Wiley, 2003), 8.

4. Ibid., 10.

5. Elizabeth Knowles, *Oxford Dictionary of Quotations* (New York: Oxford University Press, 2009), 341.

6. Dan B. Allender and Tremper Longman III, *The Cry of the Soul: How Our Emotions Reveal Our Deepest Questions About God* (Colorado Springs: NavPress, 1994), 197.

7. Cynthia Spell Humbert, *Deceived by Shame, Desired by God* (Colorado Springs: NavPress, 2001), 58.

CHAPTER 5. GRASPING

1. Jean Vanier, *Befriending the Stranger* (Grand Rapids: Eerdmans, 2005), 16–17.
2. David G. Benner, *Surrender to Love: Discovering the Heart of Christian Spirituality* (Downers Grove, IL: IVP, 2003), 17–18.
3. The stuffing and dumping concepts are from Larry Crabb, *The Marriage Builder* (Grand Rapids: Zondervan, 1982), 66–67.
4. Ibid., 32.
5. Shannon B. Rainey, *Anger* (Colorado Springs: NavPress, 1992), 33.
6. John Piper, *Seeing and Savoring Jesus Christ* (Wheaton, IL: Crossway, 2001), 19.
7. Dwight Edwards, *Revolution Within: A Fresh Look at Supernatural Living* (Colorado Springs: WaterBrook, 1982), 26.

CHAPTER 6. GRACE

1. A. W. Tozer, *The Pursuit of God: The Human Thirst for the Divine* (Camp Hill, PA: WingSpread, 2006), 9, 13–14.
2. Blaise Pascal, *Pensées* (New York: Penguin, 1995), 45.
3. Andrew Murray, *Absolute Surrender* (Gainesville, FL: Bridge-Logos, 2005), 70. Emphasis added.
4. Ellen Vaughn, *Radical Gratitude: Discovering Joy Through Everyday Thankfulness* (Grand Rapids: Zondervan, 2005), 69–70.
5. C. J. Mahaney, *Humility: True Greatness* (Colorado Springs: Multnomah, 2005), 20–21.
6. Haddon W. Robinson, *The Christian Salt and Light Company* (Grand Rapids: Discovery House, 1988), 42–43.
7. Larry Crabb, *The Pressure's Off: There's a New Way to Live* (Colorado Springs: WaterBrook, 2002), 222–23.
8. Philip Yancey, *Disappointment with God: Three Questions No One Asks Aloud* (Grand Rapids: Zondervan, 1988), 240.
9. For an excellent discussion on self-talk, see *The Silent Seduction of Self-Talk* by Shelly Beach (Chicago: Moody, 2009).

10. Larry Crabb, *The Safest Place on Earth: Where People Connect and Are Forever Changed* (Nashville: Word, 1999), 5.

11. Dudley J. Delffs, *The Prayer Centered Life: Living in Conversation with the Father* (Colorado Springs: NavPress, 1997), 31–32.

12. Nicholas Wolterstorff, *Lament for a Son* (Grand Rapids: Eerdmans, 1987), 80.

CHAPTER 7. A GREAT GIFT

1. "Opening Credits/'I Feel Wonderful,'" *What About Bob,* DVD, directed by Frank Oz (1991; Burbank, CA: Touchstone Pictures).

2. Henri J. M. Nouwen, *Life of the Beloved: Spiritual Living in a Secular World* (New York: Crossroad, 1999), 27–28.

3. For example, in "Understanding Your Life Theologically: 1 Samuel 23–24" (sermon, Blythefield Hills Church, June 13, 2010), http://www.bhbconline.org.

4. Nouwen, *Life of the Beloved,* 27.

5. John Eldredge, *Fathered by God* (Nashville: Thomas Nelson, 2009), 32.

CHAPTER 8. GRATITUDE

1. Francis A. Schaeffer, *True Spirituality* (Wheaton, IL: Tyndale House, 1971), 11–12.

2. Ellen Vaughn, *Radical Gratitude: Discovering Joy Through Everyday Thankfulness* (Grand Rapids: Zondervan, 2005), 27.

3. For an excellent discussion of the term "wish dream," see Dietrich Bonhoeffer's *Life Together: The Classic Exploration of Faith in Community* (New York: HarperCollins, 1954), 26–28.

4. John Ortberg, Laurie Pederson, Judson Poling, *Grace: An Invitation to a Way of Life* (Grand Rapids: Zondervan, 2000), 16–17.

5. Jonathan Edwards, *Religious Affections* (Uhrichsville, OH: Barbour Publishing, n.d.), 128–34.

6. Richard J. Foster, *Freedom of Simplicity* (New York: HarperCollins, 1981), 9.

7. Mike Mason, *Champagne for the Soul: Celebrating God's Gift of Joy* (Colorado Springs: WaterBrook, 2003), 75.

8. C. S. Lewis, *The Weight of Glory* (New York: HarperCollins, 2001), 30–31.

9. Jonathan Edwards, *The Works of President Edwards,* vol. 3 (New York: Leavitt and Allen, 1851), 11.

10. Vaughn, *Radical Gratitude,* 28.

11. A. W. Tozer, *The Pursuit of God: The Human Thirst for the Divine* (Camp Hill, PA: WingSpread, 2006), 18–20.

12. C. S. Lewis, *The Silver Chair* (New York: Collier, 1976), 21.

13. Dan B. Allender, *How Children Raise Parents: The Art of Listening to Your Family* (Colorado Springs: WaterBrook, 2003), 1–2.

14. Frederick Buechner, *A Room Called Remember* (New York: HarperCollins, 1992), 41–42, 44.

15. David G. Benner, *Surrender to Love: Discovering the Heart of Christian Spirituality* (Downers Grove, IL: IVP, 2003), 76.

CHAPTER 9. GIVING

1. Irvin D. Yalom, *The Gift of Therapy: An Open Letter to a New Generation of Therapists and Their Patients* (New York: Perennial, 2003), 17–18.

2. To increase your understanding and ability to ask good questions, we recommend the books *Encouragement: The Key to Caring* by Larry Crabb and Dan Allender (Grand Rapids: Zondervan, 1990), and *Friendship Counseling* by Kevin Huggins (Colorado Springs: NavPress, 2003).

3. Ken Kolker, "Brick Victim: 'I want them to see what they did,'" *Grand Rapids Press,* March 5, 2003.

4. John Ortberg, *If You Want to Walk on Water, You've Got to Get Out of the Boat* (Grand Rapids: Zondervan, 2001), 79.

5. Henry Cloud, *Changes That Heal: How to Understand Your Past to Ensure a Healthier Future* (Grand Rapids: Zondervan, 2003), 30.

6. Such slavery was quite different than what we're used to today. For an Israelite to sell himself into slavery was similar to being a live-in nanny today.

7. Don Cousins, "It's God's Will That You Become Successful" (sermon, Blythefield Hills Church, Rockford, MI, February 21, 2010).

8. Elisabeth Elliot, *Shadow of the Almighty: The Life and Testament of Jim Elliot* (New York: HarperCollins, 1989), 15.

CHAPTER 10. GETTING IT

1. John Ortberg, *Everybody's Normal till You Get to Know Them* (Grand Rapids: Zondervan, 2003), 82. Emphasis in original.
2. Larry Crabb, *The Safest Place on Earth: Where People Connect and Are Forever Changed* (Nashville: Word, 1999), 22.
3. Gollum's story can be observed throughout the entire *Lord of the Rings* DVD series. But his story is specifically addressed at certain times, one of those being in "A Journey in the Dark," disc 2, *The Fellowship of the Ring*, special extended ed., DVD, directed by Peter Jackson (2001; Burbank, CA: New Line Home Entertainment, 2002).
4. Henry Cloud and John Townsend, *Making Small Groups Work: What Every Small Group Leader Needs to Know* (Grand Rapids: Zondervan, 2003), 56–57.
5. To set the stage for good group interactions, you might read any of the following books: *The Safest Place on Earth* or *Inside Out* by Larry Crabb, *Community That Is Christian* by Julie Gorman, or *Walking the Small Group Tightrope* by Russ Robinson and Bill Donahue.
6. Beyond the outline we present in this chapter, you may want to read Dr. Dan Allender's excellent book on telling life stories entitled, *To Be Told: Know Your Story, Shape Your Future.*

CHAPTER 11. GROWING IT

1. John Piper and Justin Taylor, eds., *Sex and the Supremacy of Christ* (Wheaton, IL: Crossway, 2005), 26.
2. A. W. Tozer, *The Pursuit of God: The Human Thirst for the Divine* (Camp Hill, PA: WingSpread, 2006), 63.
3. I am grateful to my dear friend Dan Lokers for many of the thoughts in this section on connecting with God through the Word of God.
4. Tozer, *The Pursuit of God*, 35.
5. Richard J. Foster, *Celebration of Discipline: The Path to Spiritual Growth*, 25th ann. ed. (New York: HarperCollins, 1998), 15.
6. Fred Bergen, compiler, *Autobiography of George Mueller* (London: J. Nisbet Co., 1906), 152–54, quoted in John Piper, *Desiring God: Meditations of a Christian Hedonist*, 10th ann. exp. ed. (Sisters, OR: Multnomah, 1996), 132–34.

7. Henri Nouwen, "Moving from Solitude to Community," *Leadershipjournal .net*, April 1, 1995, http://www.christianitytoday.com/le/1995/spring/5l280 .html.

8. I encourage the use of Bible dictionaries, Bible commentaries, and word studies to better understand the Bible. *How to Read the Bible for All Its Worth* by Gordon D. Fee and *Cross Talk: Where Life and Scripture Meet* by Michael R. Emlet are good books to help you learn how to study the Bible. The *NLT Study Bible* by Tyndale is also an excellent resource for Bible study and meditation.

9. Piper and Taylor, *Sex and the Supremacy of Christ*, 44.

10. Reading books like *God As He Longs for You to See Him* by Chip Ingram, *The Knowledge of the Holy* by A. W. Tozer, and *Knowing God* by J. I. Packer will help you learn more of the many facets of God's character. *The Practice of the Presence of God* by Brother Lawrence and *A Testament of Devotion* by Thomas R. Kelly give practical help in cultivating a continuous gaze of our soul upon God.

11. These categories come from Louie Konopka, "Son, Servant, Soldier" (sermon, Blythefield Hills Church, Rockford, MI, September 25, 2005).

12. Rowland Croucher and others, "360 Degree Leadership (Bill Hybels)," *John Mark Ministries*, January 5, 2003, http://jmm.aaa.net.au/articles /8448.htm.

Chapter 12. Giving It Away

1. Nicholas Wolterstorff, *Lament for a Son* (Grand Rapids: Eerdmans, 1987), 13.

2. "A Journey in the Dark," disc 2, *The Fellowship of the Ring*, special extended ed., DVD, directed by Peter Jackson (2001; Burbank, CA: New Line Home Entertainment, 2002).

3. Eugene H. Peterson, *Leap Over a Wall: Earthy Spirituality for Everyday Christians* (New York: HarperCollins, 1997), 72.

4. Ibid., 75.

5. Visit our website at www.truenorthministries.net. You can also download three booklets: 1. Leading group discussions. 2. The Truth/Lie Story outlines. 3. A guide for personal reflection on the paradigm of this book. These booklets can be used as the primary content on the trips.

GARY HEIM is pastor of Small Groups and Discipleship at Blythefield Hills Church in Rockford, Michigan; an adjunct professor at Grand Rapids Theological Seminary; and a retreat and seminar speaker. He is a limited licensed psychologist in Michigan, where he had a private counseling practice for over ten years and was a staff counselor for RBC Ministries (Grand Rapids). Gary and Lisa have been married for twenty-five years, and are the proud parents of two college-age children, Brandon and Kailie. Gary enjoys hunting, fly fishing, and backpacking throughout Michigan.

LISA HEIM is a licensed professional counselor in the state of Michigan, where she has had a private practice for the last twenty years, and is an adjunct professor at Grand Rapids Theological Seminary. She holds a Masters degree in Biblical Counseling from Grace Theological Seminary (Winona Lake, IN), where she also served an internship under noted Christian psychologists and authors Dr. Larry Crabb and Dr. Dan B. Allender. In her spare time Lisa enjoys reading, walking, kayaking, home decorating, and gardening.

WWW.TRUENORTHMINISTRIES.NET